Germany between East and West

The future of a divided Germany goes to the heart of East–West relations and European security. No analysis of American or Soviet foreign policy or the future of Western Europe can ignore Germany. This book examines the contemporary role of Germany in international politics, and shows how the 'German question' will continue to affect East–West relations and the politics of the Western alliance in the future. The contributors address such crucial questions as the existence, or otherwise, of a West German 'secret agenda' in its relations with the East; they ask whether the GDR is becoming increasingly distanced from strict Soviet foreign-policy interests; whether anybody, save West Germany, is really interested in changing the central European *status quo*; and where, indeed, the continued West German commitment to eventual unification is actually leading.

Germany between East and West concludes that the nature of the 'German question' has changed, and traces the reasons for this in the politics of both the GDR and West Germany; the latter will, however, retain a special sense of responsibility for peace and security in Europe, and a special practical responsibility for the well-being of the East Germans. The German problem is certainly not dead, but, as this volume shows, it now raises questions far removed from those faced by previous generations.

EDWINA MORETON has been a Harkness Fellow at the Massachusetts Institute of Technology, and a Lecturer in Political Science at the University of Wales, Aberystwyth. She is currently on the editorial staff of *The Economist*. Her previous publications include *East Germany and the Warsaw Alliance* and (as co-author) *Nuclear War and Nuclear Peace*.

Germany between East and West

edited by
EDWINA MORETON

The right of the
University of Cambridge
to print and sell
all manner of books
was granted by
Henry VIII in 1534.
The University has printed
and published continuously
since 1584.

PUBLISHED IN ASSOCIATION WITH
**THE ROYAL INSTITUTE OF
INTERNATIONAL AFFAIRS**

CAMBRIDGE UNIVERSITY PRESS
CAMBRIDGE
NEW YORK   NEW ROCHELLE
MELBOURNE   SYDNEY

Published by the Press Syndicate of the University of Cambridge
The Pitt Building, Trumpington Street, Cambridge CB2 1RP
32 East 57th Street, New York, NY 10022, USA
10 Stamford Road, Oakleigh, Melbourne 3166, Australia

First published 1987
Reprinted 1988 (twice)
First paperback edition 1989

Printed in Great Britain at the University Press, Cambridge

British Library cataloguing in publication data

Germany between East and West.
1. World politics – 1985–1995 2. Germany
– Politics and government – 1945–
I. Moreton, Edwina   I. Royal Institute
of International Affairs
943.087   DD257.2

Library of Congress cataloguing in publication data

Germany between East and West.

'Published in association with the Royal Institute of International Affairs.'
Includes bibliographies.
Contents: The German question in the 1980s/Edwina Moreton – The evolution of the
contemporary German question/Michael Stürmer – The Soviet view/Gerhard Wettig –
[etc.]
1. German reunification (1949–   ) 2. World politics – 1975–1985. 3. World politics –
1985–1995.
I. Moreton, N. Edwina.   II. Royal Institute of International Affairs.
DD257.25.G45   1987   943.087   87–6337

ISBN 0 521 34277 5 hard covers
ISBN 0 521 37891 5 paperback

Contents

Contributors

Jonathan Dean, Union of Concerned Scientists, Washington, DC

Renata Fritsch-Bournazel, Centre d'Etudes et de Recherches Internationales, Fondation Nationale des Sciences Politiques, Paris

William E. Griffith, Massachusetts Institute of Technology, and United States Embassy, Bonn

Michael Kaser, St Antony's College, University of Oxford

Edwina Moreton, *The Economist*, London

Roger Morgan, Department of Political and Social Sciences, European University Institute, Florence

Fred S. Oldenburg, Bundesinstitut für ostwissenschaftliche und internationale Studien, Cologne

Hermann Rudolph, Deutschlandfunk, Cologne

Michael Stürmer, Institut für Geschichte, Friedrich-Alexander Universität, Erlangen-Nuremberg

Gerhard Wettig, Bundesinstitut für ostwissenschaftliche und internationale Studien, Cologne

Acknowledgements

We are indebted to a number of people and organizations for their help in producing this book. The chapters grew from a conference on Germany organized by the Royal Institute of International Affairs in 1986. The conference and subsequent writing was financed by a grant from the Fritz Thyssen Foundation. John Roper both chaired the conference and guided the project throughout. William D. Zuckerman undertook preliminary work for the conference. Pauline Wickham provided valuable editorial advice. Christoph Bluth translated the chapter by Hermann Rudolph. Denise Selleck and Marie Lathia helped prepare the manuscript. But we owe special thanks to all those who contributed their knowledge and insights at the conference, and to the chapter-writers for cheerfully done revisions and not-too-stretched deadlines.

E.M.

I INTRODUCTION

1   The German question in the 1980s

EDWINA MORETON

As West Germany's president, Richard von Weizsäcker, put it recently: 'Experience teaches us that a question does not cease to exist simply because nobody has an answer to it' (*Die Zeit*, 30.ix.83). The question he had in mind is the subject of this book: the question of Germany's future.

Traditionally, in postwar thinking, that question has concerned when and how the division of Germany might be overcome. Reunification has been seen as inevitable in the long term by those who worry that Europe can never be stable while Germans are kept divided – and as an inevitable hazard by those who worry more about how such a reunited Germany would fit among its smaller neighbours in Europe. Yet, looking ahead to the 1990s, the contributions to this book suggest that the issue to worry governments and strategists is no longer that of Germany's reunification as such. Rather like the smile of the Cheshire cat, traces of this issue remain, but its substance has changed. The new question about Germany is threefold: first, what role will West Germany try to play in East–West relations and to what extent can East Germany also be a player; second, how might changes in the security framework in Europe affect the relationship both of East Germany with its allies in the Warsaw Pact and of West Germany with its allies in Nato; and, third, how in the long run will the acceptance of the other state in divided Germany affect the Federal Republic's image of itself and indeed its political credibility? Tracing the threads that lead to this conclusion about the different nature of the contemporary German question is the task of this introductory chapter.

It has become almost a platitude to point out that, as the two German states – the Federal Republic in the West, the German Democratic Republic in the East – reach the end of their fourth decade as separate states, the postwar division of Germany has already endured three times as long as Hitler's supposed Thousand-Year Reich. For many West Europeans, who know and accept West Germany as a normal country, and a full and equal member of the Western alliance, that is already a sufficient

3

practical answer to the question about Germany's future. To those not old enough to remember the division and the years of acute East–West tension over Germany and Berlin that followed, not only is West Germany a normal-looking West European country; its division is normal too. Even many young West Germans increasingly view East Germany as *Ausland* (a foreign country). So why is the 'German question' suddenly back on the political agenda of the 1980s?

One obvious answer is that it is still in Germany, that the European, and indeed the global balance, is decided. A more simple answer is that the Germans themselves have put the question there. As East–West detente elsewhere took a long walk in the Hindu Kush, following the Soviet invasion of Afghanistan in December 1979, West Germany struggled harder than most European countries to keep alive its spirit in Europe. When martial law finally brought an end to the Solidarity challenge in Poland in December 1981, the then West German chancellor, Helmut Schmidt, was visiting his East German counterpart, Erich Honecker, in East Germany. Although West Germans had done their part in sending food parcels, medical supplies and aid to the Poles, the two German leaders seemed determined to insulate their newly evolving political relationship from the deep chill that settled on relations between the superpowers. Although all of Western Europe at the time may have seemed to the Americans irritatingly reluctant to fall in with sanctions on the Soviet Union and the Polish regime, West Germany came in for the most flak.

The reason owes as much to the things West Germany cannot change about its political situation as to those it can: committed by its constitution to work for German reunification, West Germany has been the only power involved in the German question that is not prepared to accept the status quo in Europe. But if West Germany is to resolve the question of partition on its own terms – meaning by encouraging East Germany to overcome the division between the two states and ultimately reunite with West Germany – then it is East Germany's protective power and chief ally, the Soviet Union, that holds the key. Thus, other Europeans may differ with the United States on East–West issues, but only West Germany is so uniquely vulnerable to Soviet pressure and encouragement. That vulnerability, whether future West German governments succumb to it or not, is what makes West Germany's allies nervous from time to time about the future of Germany.

This greater nervousness could be seen during the debate in Europe over the deployment of new American missiles to counter the build-up of Soviet SS–20 missiles aimed at Western Europe. Anti-nuclear movements were active in several West European countries in an attempt to stop deployment, but the greatest worry was again about the West German

4

reaction. In the event, West Germans voted in sufficient numbers in 1983 for the centre–right coalition led by Helmut Kohl to ensure that deployment would go ahead. Under similar circumstances in Britain, once the missile argument had been won, the issue slipped quickly down the political agenda. Although the government's triumph at the ballot box in West Germany in March 1983 was in the circumstances just as resounding, as far as West Germany's allies were concerned, there were still doubts about West Germans' commitment to Nato policy, doubts magnified by the importance of West Germany as Nato's cornerstone on the European mainland. Somehow it seemed that whether the missiles were deployed in Germany or not, West Germany could not win.

West Germany's chief opposition party since 1982, the Social Democrats, also helped perpetuate the issue of Germany's future by voting to oppose deployment of the new Nato missiles in West Germany. That ended the consensus on defence and security policy that had been a cornerstone of West Germany's political stability since the 1950s. The SPD then opened a new phase of party-political Ost- and Deutschlandpolitik with Eastern Europe and the Soviet Union. Since Helmut Kohl's Christian Democrats seemed to have managed to keep up reasonably good relations with East Germany, a policy which the Social Democrats had always seen as their own ever since Willy Brandt's 'new Ostpolitik' of the early 1970s, those Social Democrats closest to Brandt now embarked on Ostpolitik, mark two. Framework agreements in 1985 with the East German communist party, the SED, for a chemical weapons-free zone, were followed by similar talks on a nuclear weapons-free zone. Czechoslovakia and Poland were also to be brought into the scheme. Criticism from the West German government that this amounted to an alternative foreign policy and was a deliberate attempt to undermine the government were shrugged off by the Social Democrats, most of whom seemed happy enough after the depression of their fall from power to have found at least one distinctive policy to pursue.

East Germany has done its bit, too, to keep alive fears about a 'secret agenda' in West Germany's relations with the East. Having at first threatened West Germany with a range of tough responses, including an 'ice age' in German–German relations if deployment went ahead, Honecker eventually settled for a damage-limiting strategy and seemed ready to preserve the special German relationship, despite the missile deployment. Was he acting on his own initiative, to preserve a relationship with West Germany that he too found useful, if only in the hard currency it brought to East Germany? Was he beginning to pull away a little from Soviet apron strings and pursue his own Westpolitik? Or was he simply acting out a role assigned by Moscow to cultivate West Germany and make it harder for any

5

West German government to uphold a similar controversial Nato decision in the future? In other words, was it West Germany that was influencing East Germany to stand up for its own interests, or the other way around?

Where Germany fits

Some Social Democrats in West Germany go so far as to say that West Germany ought to recognize East Germany as a fully sovereign and independent state, although this is disavowed by the party's leadership and would mean contravening the moral foundation of West Germany's Basic Law (*Grundgesetz*). Aside from any emotional tie in West Germany to someday–somehow reunification, such a move would have enormous consequences for the four powers – the United States, the Soviet Union, the United Kingdom and France – who still have responsibilities for 'Germany as a whole', since no peace treaty with Germany was ever signed after the war. And, as we shall see below, it would also have profound consequences for Berlin, which is still formally under four-power administration and whose western part is marooned deep inside East German territory. But would full recognition of East Germany by West Germany answer the question once and for all about Germany's future?

The trouble is that accepting the division of Germany into two separate states does not answer the questions about what role the two Germanies should play in East–West relations, what ought to be the political relationship between them, and how their inevitably 'special' relationship in the heart of Europe will affect the interests of their allies. The German 'question', put in those terms, is bound to remain a sensitive issue in East–West relations. The division of Europe runs through Germany. As not just the military, but also the political and ideological front line in Europe, the division of Germany has been a cornerstone of the postwar political structure in Europe. From a Soviet point of view, and from a Western one, any change in the political loyalties of either part of Germany would radically alter the balance of power, not just in Europe, but around the globe. Indeed, in many respects although East and West have railed against division at various times, it has solved a fundamental nineteenth-century security dilemma for Germany's neighbours in the second half of the twentieth century: what to do about German power in the heart of Europe. Hence the importance that the future of Germany, or the two Germanies, holds for both superpowers, and hence the sensitivity with which both have reacted recently to any signs, imaginary or real, that German–German relations are developing beyond their control.

As Michael Stürmer (Chapter 2) points out in his look back at how the

German question has evolved since World War II, the contemporary German question is very much bound up with the power politics of the age. There is no way to isolate Germany from the ideological and political clash between East and West. Germany's division was not the cause of the East–West split, but it symbolizes it. Thus, Stürmer sees the initial postwar German question in two parts: Who controls Germany? And where do Germans find their identity?

For all practical purposes West Germany seems securely anchored in the Western alliance. The Western powers, although in some respects still controlling powers in Germany, are seen much more these days as guarantee powers, and especially guarantors of the future of West Berlin. East Germany, for its part, has no option but to stick to its alliance, too. So who controls Germany would not seem to be a live issue for the present. Where do Germans find their identity? This would also not seem to be a difficult question to answer, at least for West Germans. Even among those unhappy with the continuing tensions of the East–West division, there seems to be little attraction in the alternative 'identity' in the East. If, as Stürmer insists, the preoccupation with German nationhood has really come to mean concern for human rights, rather than a hankering after particular territory or attraction to a common language, then West Germany is already a nation to which many East Germans aspire. As Hermann Rudolph (Chapter 10) points out in his look at society in divided Germany, the flow of refugees between the two Germanies ever since the war has been exclusively westwards.

Yet West Germans more than any other West Europeans keep the debate about the future open. It came to the surface quite strongly in the wake of the Afghan and Polish crises of the late 1970s and early 1980s, and also during the debate over missile deployments in Western Europe. Evidently some issues affect West Germany more acutely than some of its neighbours. Is it possible then, despite West Germany's apparently secure base in the West, that events will conspire to reformulate the German question in the 1980s and 1990s? If so, this future German question could, depending on what form it took, once again shake the foundations of the European security. Or it could be one less fundamental to European security than the four-power struggle for Germany in the early postwar years, but one that none the less causes concern among West Germany's Western allies and affects West–West relations instead. Richard von Weizsäcker was entirely correct in what at the time was seen as a highly controversial statement about the German question, quoted at the start of this chapter. The pressure for some sort of change is inherent in any unresolved question. So what are the future prospects for change in Germany?

7

The four-power framework

In formal legal terms, the framework of the German question has not changed since the wartime allies fell out over Germany's future in 1945–7. Since the peace treaty envisaged at Potsdam was never signed with Germany after the war, the four powers still retain rights and responsibilities for 'Germany as a whole', despite the creation in 1949 of two separate German states. Berlin is still formally under four-power administration, even though the city has been divided for its German residents since at least the time in 1961 when the East German government built the Berlin wall. For there to be any legal movement towards German reunification, federation, association, or whatever, there would have to be a conspiracy of huge international proportions, in which most or all of the four powers took part. The chances, however, look slim.

The Soviet attitude would be crucial. As mentioned above, the Soviet Union holds the key to a resolution of the German question on West German terms. If Germany's division is to be overcome, whether physically and politically, or somehow socially and culturally, the Soviet Union, as East Germany's protecting power, would have to agree. But there seems little likelihood that the Russians would oblige. There are two schools of thought about Soviet foreign policy in general, and its policy towards Germany in particular. One believes that the Soviet Union is a revisionist power, bent on changing the political map of Europe and, above all, the allegiance of West Germany to the Western alliance. The other school sees the Soviet Union as a status quo power, happy to use Europe's division to its own purposes where it can to undermine the cohesion of the West, but also happy to settle for a divided Europe, in which Germany can no longer pose a challenge to Soviet security. Unfortunately, neither school offers much hope for reunification on West German terms.

In either case, the Soviet Union is bound to find that its most promising point of leverage is West Germany's reluctance formally to accept the status quo in divided Germany. And whether the Soviet Union chooses to pursue its objectives with carrots or sticks, West Germany is bound to be made to feel uncomfortable. Gerhard Wettig (Chapter 3) argues that the Soviet Union is very much working to undermine West German security and its alliance with the United States. Just as the Soviet Union holds the key to reunification, so West Germany is viewed in Moscow as the key to Europe. The long-term goal, therefore, is American withdrawal from Europe, leaving the way open for the region to fall under Soviet political influence. In the short term, what leverage that can be brought to bear will be used to destabilize West Germany and cause dissension in the West. Wettig argues that the Soviet Union has long given up any support for the idea of reunification; on the contrary, it prefers to deal with two Germanies, although would be delighted to see the Western one turn neutral.

In support of this argument is the fact that the Soviet Union, in its dealings with its Germany, still insists on its four-power rights and responsibilities. As Wettig points out, this is both a way of maintaining a legal foothold in all of Germany, and a way of keeping ultimate control of GDR foreign policy. At times this tight rein has caused friction in GDR–Soviet relations. The Soviet Union seems ready to tolerate the development of German–German relations only when it feels in control of the process. On the other hand, if the Soviet Union really is bent on undermining West Germany, why not make some gesture towards reunification of the kind a West German government could not refuse?

But can the Soviet Union offer anything that would tempt West Germany without, in the process, seriously undermining the stability of the regime in East Germany? Just as West Germany forms the bedrock of the Western political and economic alliance, so East Germany has become increasingly important to the Soviet Union, as both ideologically reliable and economically successful, especially since the all-but-collapse of Poland in 1980–1. In the modern world, the Soviet Union should have much less to fear from a reunited Germany than sometimes appears. All the same, the process of achieving reunification would be fraught with risks that the Soviet Union has as yet shown no sign of taking. For the foreseeable future the Soviet Union's revisionist bark may be worse than its bite, at least until it can see a way of achieving its long-term objectives in Western Europe, without putting at risk its control of Eastern Europe.

Whatever its future intentions towards Germany, so long as the German question remains officially open, the Soviet Union will have at times considerable scope for mischief-making in East–West relations. Yet West Germany is today more valuable to the Soviet Union as a potential lever inside Nato than it would be outside. To put the relationship the other way around, when it comes to looking to the Soviet Union to help solve the German question, West Germany's weight in the East in future will be no greater than its weight in the West. As Renata Fritsch-Bournazel (Chapter 5) points out, 'Rapallo' – meaning the option of a secret deal with the Soviet Union behind the backs of the Western powers – is no longer available to West Germany. The distribution of power between the two countries has shifted too far: by throwing itself on Soviet mercy, today's West Germany would simply risk being swallowed up. An appreciation of this limits both West Germany's likely response to future Soviet initiatives in Germany and also the effort the Soviet Union can sensibly put into using its West German lever to good effect.

9

While the German question remains open, the other three powers have as much interest in maintaining the four-power framework around Germany as does the Soviet Union, but for different reasons. Indeed, one of the most remarkable shifts in postwar European politics has been the shift in the role of the three Western powers from that of occupiers to that of guarantors and defenders, both of West Berlin and of West Germany's contention that the German question remains open. Had the four-power framework for Germany not existed at the end of the war, then West Germany would have had to invent it. It is the structure which upholds the unanswered German question. The question has been kept open by West German wish, and allied consent. As William Griffith (Chapter 4) points out, at the time in the 1950s when the alliance between the Western powers and the newly formed West Germany was being crafted, it was perhaps a lucky coincidence that Adenauer's immediate ambitions for Germany happened to fit neatly into the aims of the wider Western alliance. The alliance, and West Germany's part in it, was forged, and could only be forged, as the tension between East and West mounted.

The allies as guarantors and defenders were very much to the fore in the two major Berlin crises, in 1948–9 and 1958–61. Yet, though it forms part of the historical fabric which has strengthened the Western alliance, the second of the two Berlin crises did reveal differences both among the Western allies, and between them and West Germany. In many ways the Ostpolitik of successive West German governments from the 1960s onwards was a reaction to the realization in 1961 that, although the Western allies were prepared to defend the divided status quo in Germany – such as access to Berlin and West Berlin's continued viability as a free city – they were not prepared to be tough in defence of West Germany's maximum demand for a change in the situation in East Germany. Instead, the Western allies have tended to underline the strand of realism in West German thinking that recognizes that national unification of Germany can only come about as a result of the healing of the division of Europe – not in reverse order.

In fact, behind the facade of Western unity erected at intervals in the postwar period to fend off unwelcome challenges from the East, there is moral support in public but no great enthusiasm for what West Germany still says it ultimately wants: German reunification under Western auspices. Of the three Western powers, Britain and France probably have the deepest reservations. As neighbours of Germany in Europe, neither seems keen to advance the day when a reunited Germany would again constitute an economic and political weight at the heart of Europe. (A lack of enthusiasm which finds a deafening echo among Germany's smaller neighbours in the East.) Although, as Michael Kaser (Chapter 9) shows, today the sum of the economic weight of the two separate Germanies is less relatively than it was when Germany was united before the war, the deficit can be accounted for by the retarded growth of East Germany under communist party control. Were the two countries made one and allowed to follow the economic path West Germany has followed since the 1950s, the result could be very different.

When it comes to relations with West Germany itself, both Renata Fritsch-Bournazel and Roger Morgan (Chapter 6) stress the importance of the political reconciliation that has taken place within Western Europe, between the once-victors and the once-vanquished. The Franco-German alliance, sealed in 1963, is one of the great political successes of the postwar world. Yet there are limits to French and British support for West Germany's Ostpolitik. The recent worried reaction in France to West Germany's determination to stick to its German–German policy and detente with the East through thick and thin shows a residual worry about Germany's future. Instead of an overbearing centre of power in Europe, Fritsch-Bournazel points to the dangers of a centre of powerlessness, if West Germany were ever to put national unity ahead of freedom and alliance loyalty and drift towards indecision or, worse, neutralism.

The dangers of that happening may not be rated very high, yet there is one issue where the dangers are more obvious than others: defence. Whether a future conflict in Europe, should it occur, were conventional or nuclear, West Germans know they are sitting on the battlefield. Therefore security and defence policy is bound to take on an extra dimension. But understandable worries about security sometimes seem to produce misunderstandable reactions. During the missile debate of the early 1980s, it was left to a French Socialist president, whose country still remains outside Nato's military structure, to call on West Germany to show loyalty to the United States and the other Nato allies by pressing ahead with the deployment in Germany of new American missiles. It was by no means a coincidence that a readiness to accept a Franco–West German dialogue on defence should have manifested itself at precisely this point too. As Fritsch-Bournazel argues, there may no longer be fear of German militarism, but there could be a fear of creeping West German pacifism that will worry defence planners in the future. As the old Nato undergoes the inevitable stresses and strains of such a mature alliance, it may well be very much a French concern and responsibility to help redesign a structure in which West Germany can feel properly secure. Even so, there are clearly worries in France, especially in the wake of the SPD's defection over the missile issue and the rise of the anti-nuclear Greens, that the nuclear issue and West Germany's role in a nuclear-armed Nato will become at least part of any reformulated German question of the 1990s.

Inevitably, because of its distance from Europe and its very different history, the United States has less reason to be concerned at the future political or economic weight of a reunited Germany. Griffith argues that in fact the United States is the only one of the four powers that could greet such a development with reasonable equanimity. To that extent, American attitudes to Germany might fit easily into the framework of recent American attitudes to Europe as a whole. While political realities have to be accepted, the permanent division of Europe and Soviet control over its Eastern part should not be. The Reagan administration in particular has sounded at times very much like a revisionist power. But, even for the United States, there is change and change. A West Germany that appeared to be slipping its moorings in the Western alliance would not represent acceptable change. Yet more than any other of West Germany's allies, American rhetoric about the impermanence of the division of Europe, and about division being at the heart of conflict, seems to match West German insistence that the German question too should remain open.

That may not be what the United States has intended. As Griffith points out, American suspicion of left-of-centre parties in West Germany dates back to the 1950s and the desire of the SPD then not to foreclose prospects for reunification by too close an integration into the Western alliance. In many ways the potential split between today's SPD and Washington over defence and security could run much deeper. Back in the 1960s, the United States was able to force West Germany to choose America over France as its chief ally. Yet Griffith argues that, in the different mood of the 1980s, the outcome might be different. Should the issue arise again in the future, at the very least any attempt to force such a decision out of West Germany would carry enormous risk. Even under a conservative West German government and a conservative American one, there has been suspicion about the pace and purpose of Ostpolitik. Despite the rhetoric of change, therefore, in practice the United States is as suspicious as its other Western allies of an uncontrolled German–German dynamic.

Hence the odd contrast between America's public attitude to the division of Europe as being unacceptable and its private doubts from time to time about the political reliability of successive West German governments that have insisted on doing something to overcome the – presumably equally unacceptable – division of Germany. As Griffith explains, behind America's support for West Germany's moral stance on reunification is a practical fear that, as Henry Kissinger put it in the early 1970s, Ostpolitik would stabilize East Germany and destabilize West Germany, rather than the other way around. So America, too, is unlikely to initiate any train of events that could result in unacceptable change in the West, rather than the desired change in the East.

The German–German question

Since the four-power framework around Germany seems, for the present, unlikely to change much, might the pressure inherent in the unresolved German question find its escape instead in the development of German–German relations? Ever since these emerged relatively unscathed from the East–West bust-up of the early 1980s, every once in a while a slight shudder of uncertainty has passed down the spine of West Germany's allies – and East Germany's too. On both sides of Europe's divide worries about a possible 'hidden agenda' between the two Germanies have resurfaced.

Looking back over the past fifteen years, there has indeed been a quite dramatic change in the relationship between the two. By comparison with the years when West Germany refused even to recognize the separate existence of an East German state, government to government contacts have flourished; so have the practical daily contacts between the people of the two Germanies even if, again, the contacts are promoted by West Germany and only tolerated by East Germany. But trying to guess where these new contacts might lead is not easy, since on the face of it the objectives of the two states differ considerably.

The biggest shift in West German policy towards the East came in 1969 with the official acceptance of the East German state. Ironically, accepting the political reality of the division of Germany is what has given West German governments since the late 1960s the extra freedom of manoeuvre in their foreign policy, both towards their Western allies and towards the Soviet Union. The refusal before 1969 to acknowledge officially the separate existence of an East German state had ensured that the Soviet Union would put a firm limit on West German relations with the rest of Eastern Europe. As Griffith points out with respect to America's hopes in the 1960s for an arms-control dialogue with the Soviet Union, the continued Cold War in Germany also acted as a brake on East–West relations in general. This left West Germany increasingly out of step with the more pragmatic mood that had developed in the West – a mood of resignation which accepted in practice that Europe would remain divided for the foreseeable future and that, as a consequence, Germany would remain divided too.

West Germany's Social Democrats, who had launched the new Ostpolitik in the late 1960s, had always insisted that they were just as committed as their chief opponents, the Christian Democrats, to the enduring principle of German reunification. But while that remained a practical impossibility they were prepared to accept the status quo in Germany in order, Brandt made clear, to change it. Greater contact between the two Germanies was to serve that purpose. What is more, Brandt's Ostpolitik acknowledged that the key to any real political change in divided Germany lay in Moscow. By improving West German–Soviet relations he hoped to add to the pressure on a reluctant and suspicious East Germany to do at least the minimum necessary to take the brake off a more general East–West detente. On the one hand, therefore, Ostpolitik removed one potential dilemma for future West German governments. No longer would West Germany officially have to choose between maintaining its firm anchorage in Nato and pursuing improved relations with East Germany. Whatever their private reservations, West Germany's allies backed Ostpolitik. On the other hand, the new public role of the Soviet Union in German–German relations opened up a West German flank to criticism that it might someday become too dependent on Moscow for its own good, and that of its allies.

Like his predecessors, both Christian Democrats and Social Democrats, in the 1980s Kohl has been prepared to use the bait of West German trade and credit to encourage the East German regime to allow greater contact between the two Germanies. Alleviating the hardships of division will remain the irreducible element of any West German government's Ostpolitik. However there has been a remarkable change of attitude behind the Christian Democrats' acceptance of Ostpolitik. Fifteen years ago they had vehemently opposed it as tantamount to national treachery; today, though reunification remains their party's goal, this is no longer seen exclusively in 'institutional' form. The phraseology and unspoken assumption may be different from that of the Social Democrats, but the practical effect is the same: to all intents and purposes national reunification is for the hereafter, the real aim is to improve conditions for the East Germans in the here and now.

The second recent change is that Kohl, by force of circumstance as much as anything, is determined to pursue his Ostpolitik despite the Soviet Union if he cannot enlist its help. This switch in West German policy was inevitable, once the Soviet Union decided to punish West Germany politically for having deployed new American missiles.

There are other problems, too, in West German–Soviet relations. Kohl talks of 'German interests' in a way that strikes the Kremlin, always suspicious of a self-confident, conservative West German government, like a bucket of iced water. As the first West German chancellor to have been too young to participate directly in World War II, he represents a coming of age of West German public opinion that many, not just the Russians, find hard to accept. (It has prompted charges of German Gaullism from West Germany's Western allies on occasion, too.) Yet, far from wanting to encourage doubts in West Germany about the country's future in its postwar alliances, Kohl's attempt to remain on good terms with East

14

Germany has been partly designed to head off, not encourage, any neutralist sentiment that might have arisen in the row over missile deployments. The Russians do not have to try very hard, however, to persuade themselves that Kohl is developing his ties with Honecker behind their backs.

While the problem for West Germany has been how to keep the German question officially open, the problem facing the East German regime has been to try to head off any development that undermines its own security and the stability of the GDR. As the smaller and weaker part of Germany, that has more often than not meant fighting West Germany's interpretation of what should be the solution to the German question, or else pretending that the German question no longer exists. The big change in East German–Soviet relations over the German problem came in the 1970s and 1980s, rather than the 1960s. Having for years tried to put a brake on Soviet policy towards West Germany when it threatened to involve East Germany in concessions to West Germany's insistence that the national future of Germany remained an open question, by the late 1970s and early 1980s, East Germany's foot had switched instead to the accelerator. For the first time, it was East Germany that was trying to force the pace of relations with West Germany – or at least move forward farther and faster than the Soviet Union was prepared to. But why?

East Germany's motives are partly economic. Although Kaser shows that German–German trade has if anything grown slightly more slowly than East–West trade as a whole, both he and Wettig make the case that it figures large in East Germany's balance sheets, both as a source of earnings and loans and also as a way of relieving the bottlenecks that bedevil other centrally-planned economies in Comecon. West Germany is East Germany's largest Western trading partner. What is more, trade between the two is carried out on the artificial exchange rate of 1 DM-West to 1 DM-Ost, valuing the East German currency well above its real worth, and well above the price it fetches on the streets of any East German city. The special 'swing credit' available to help finance trade with West Germany also helps, as does East Germany's tariff-free access to the West German market and the huge sums of hard currency that West Germany pays annually in transit fees for access to Berlin, and many other things, including the release of political prisoners from East German jails. And since it is West Germany that is keen to keep the ties between the two Germanies intact, any East German regime is in an excellent position to reap economic rewards, however sour political relations become from time to time. Just as there is an irreducible West German commitment to the well-being of the Germans in East Germany, so that translates into an irreducible material benefit to the GDR government.

15

The new German–German relationship has helped Honecker in other ways too. As Fred Oldenburg (Chapter 8) points out, the more West Germany insists on maintaining contact with the GDR in order to back up its contention that the two German states are part of a single German nation, the more it helps establish the legitimacy of the GDR regime, both in the eyes of its own people and abroad. International recognition and membership of the United Nations has helped, but to East Germany it is still the attitude of West Germany that counts. The much talked of and much postponed visit Honecker has been planning to pay to West Germany for the past several years would now be the ultimate in recognition that an East German leader could expect from any West German government. It would heap irony on irony if this visit were to take place under a conservative West German government.

Both German states, therefore, have an interest in maintaining their contacts, despite the ups and downs of East–West relations. In West Germany's case this has been largely the result of a sort of superiority complex, a feeling of moral responsibility for the Germans in East Germany who cannot decide their own fate democratically. In East Germany, the old inferiority complex of the 1950s and 1960s has given way under Ostpolitik to a new self-confidence that makes the regime more adventurous in its political dealings with the outside world, including West Germany. However, Oldenburg rightly cautions against reading too much into the GDR's new boldness: when the chips are down Moscow can still impose its will. And anyway, there has been no real sign that East Germany and the Soviet Union have disagreed here about ultimate goals, even if there has been the occasional public scrap about means to those ends. All the same, though the motives of the two German states are different, might even this limited convergence of interest some day lead to the development of a common interest in the German–German relationship that could pose dangers for Europe's stability?

The future of Germany

Such worries are inevitably more clearly articulated with respect to West Germany than East Germany, whose closed political system gives little away on such sensitive issues. Also, as the would-be initiator of change in Europe, West Germany perhaps has more of a case to answer. As Morgan argues (Chapter 7), there must be an inherent tension in the fact that Western Europe's strongest economic power and a country that enjoys such high political prestige has been totally unable to resolve the fundamental problem of national division. Golo Mann shared this worry when he wrote of the Germany in the twenty years before 1968 as being

'not an independent centre of energy but . . . a province, or . . . two prov-
inces, one of which became rich without being powerful' (*The History of
Germany since 1789*, Penguin Books, 1974, p.14). Willy Brandt put it more
bluntly and memorably when he once described West Germany as an
'economic giant, but a political dwarf'. Might this increasingly powerful,
but frustrated giant take its future into its own hands?

Morgan concludes that in fact the real push for change in West Germany
comes from a minority and that, rhetoric aside, the Social Democrats will
probably continue to pull towards the centre ground – even on defence
and security issues. Griffith is less sanguine about the outcome of West
Germany's security debate, and to some extent his anxiety about West
Germany's future course is shared by Michael Stürmer, who identifies
what he calls the 'visionary strings' of Ostpolitik. Among these he includes
talk of the so-called Europeanization of Europe (meaning a conscious
assertion of European interests against those of both superpowers, including a decoupling from the United States in some new pursuit of a *Sonderweg*
– special path – for Germany) and also arguments for the kind of domestic
change within West Germany that could bring about a political or social
'convergence' between the Germanies. Failing that, there is also the
possibility that those West Germans who cling to Ostpolitik as an end in
itself might one day conclude that the price for continuing it really does
have to be paid in Moscow. Fears on this score will have been heightened
by the party-political contacts West Germany's Social Democrats have
pursued with East Germany's SED. These appear to be attempting to use
agreements on security issues between the two Germanies to push forward
the stalled detente in Europe. This represents at the very least a complete
reversal of the previous understanding within the Western alliance that
solutions to German security problems can be found only within a wider
European framework.

Yet, looking ahead at least until the 1990s there would seem to be at least
two built-in roadblocks to the pace of change in German–German
relations. The first is East Germany itself. The potential dangers that
Germany-watchers in the West see in West Germany's political frus-
trations over the national question represent real dangers to East
Germany's political stability. The old West German idea of change
through rapprochement (*Wandel durch Annäherung*) has brought about
change more slowly than some in West Germany would wish, but the pull
is there. The problem for East Germany, as Rudolph explains graphically,
is that the pull is almost exclusively in a Western direction – culturally,
materially and above all in human terms. The nostalgia that Rudolph and
others detect in West Germany for a return to the more unsullied
'German' values in the GDR is to many East Germans a luxury to be

17

enjoyed only by an outsider. In East Germany itself, this so called Germanness is considered backwardness to be regretted, not tradition to be hallowed. In Rudolph's eyes, East German society is in reality much more affected by West Germany than vice versa. Put bluntly, even to many 'nationalists' in West Germany, the East Germany of the late 1980s is not an attractive prospect with which to reunify.

The second roadblock to any dramatic change in West Germany's commitment to the Western alliance is West Berlin. Stürmer argues that without the existence of Berlin – its western parts marooned within the GDR and very much a past symbol of the defence of democratic values in postwar Germany – there would be much less impulse for Ostpolitik. In some respects, therefore, the very success of the four-power Berlin agreement of 1971 in promoting the stability and security of West Berlin may itself cause a problem for Berlin in the future if such relative peace and security is taken as an excuse for giving less support to maintaining the separateness of West Berlin. But trying to write Berlin out of the script in Europe is not likely to take the pressure off – quite the contrary. West Berlin's political and economic future may indeed look a little hazier these days in times of peace than it did in the tense days of Stalin's blockade or Khrushchev's ultimatum and the building of the Berlin wall. Yet nobody, except East Germany – which would, if it could, simply swallow the place – has much interest in changing things in Berlin. And while East Germany may not want to co-operate much in ensuring that the city finds a new role for itself in these more peaceable times, it is in no position unilaterally to make changes to Berlin's status and West Berlin's future.

Since even a splitting of the spoils – the absorption of West Berlin into the political structure of West Germany and of East Berlin into East Germany – would mean an end to the four-power framework surrounding the city, none of the four powers seems interested to change things much either. Even in future bad times in East–West relations, or even West German–Soviet relations, Soviet pressure on Berlin in an effort to hasten a solution to the German question on East Germany's terms, or to punish West Germany for some transgression would simply reforge the unity of the Western alliance. And when German–German relations are going well there is no need for West Germany to push for a new formula to solve the Berlin problem either. As, Jonathan Dean (Chapter 11) argues, the situation in and around Berlin reflects the wider state of East–West relations, it is not the obvious place to start pushing towards a solution of the German question.

All this begs the original question: if for the time being West Berlin looks reasonably secure, Germany's allies remain reasonably unrevisionist and the two Germanies have reason to be wary of each other's purposes, what is it about Germany's future that is so worrying? For all the efforts by successive West German governments not to foreclose the idea of reunification in some form, in practical terms reunification is clearly not the real issue. Even among its most vehement upholders in West Germany, there has been a recognition that neither German state can resolve the question unilaterally and, more important, that for reasons to do with the separate development of the two German states, the idea is anyway impractical 'for the foreseeable future'.

That does not mean to say that West Germany's allies should expect it formally to renounce German reunification as a goal; simply that it has increasingly lost force as an issue of practical politics. Even the disturbing threads that several of the book's chapters have identified in West German politics over the past few years do not lead back to the question of German reunification as the main source of the problem, although it could at some point be a complicating factor, given a worry about other issues as well. For the time being, it seems to have been recognized on all sides that, just as it would be folly for West Germany to think it could settle the question of Germany's national future without the backing of its Western allies, so it would be folly on the part of West Germany's backers to object to the human and commercial contacts between the two Germanies. Although these are promoted and financed by West Germany out of concern for common German nationhood, these contacts, if anything, underpin the basic stability of German–German relations.

The real question therefore about Germany's future in the 1980s and 1990s concerns, not the price that West Germany might be tempted to pay for national reunification, but the political role a still divided Germany will play in the wider scheme of East–West relations. The question concerns both Germanies, although East Germany is in a different position since it does not yet have to take notice of signs of unease among public opinion in the GDR about these bigger issues of security and East–West relations. However, on the West German side public opinion has already begun to play a role in the question of West Germany's future security in a divided continent. Here two developments have conspired to raise an important question. The first has been the reawakening in the 1980s of a security debate that had been all but ignored in West Germany since the 1950s. The second is that, unlike in the 1950s when tensions between the two superpowers were simply taken for granted, in the 1980s the debate on security follows a period during which considerable optimism about reducing East–West tensions was rather rudely shattered in the first years of the 1980s for reasons that did not have their origin in Europe but that had profound consequences there. It is also a period when, for reasons of both politics and technology, the nuclear issue has been to the fore. That

19

has given the Soviet Union an opportunity to play on West German nerves about security in Europe in the nuclear age.

The issue is not just one of a lack of progress in arms control agreements (although little, if any, has been made). It is a broader issue of the management of East–West relations across the board. And in many respects the worries that have emerged in West Germany about the stability and reliability of security arrangements in Europe are shared in greater or lesser degree by other Europeans. However because of the special relationship between the two Germanies and because of its continuation despite the chill that settled on West German–Soviet relations, to some extent the lack of progress in superpower negotiations has encouraged 'private' initiatives of the kind that the West German SPD is pursuing with Eastern Europe (and to some extent the British Labour party is pursuing with Moscow on the subject of the renunciation of Britain's independent nuclear deterrent). The trouble is, just as arms control cannot carry the whole burden of East–West relations, it is also clear that Germany cannot either.

Thus the old adage that the division of Germany can only be overcome through a healing of the division of Europe has now been turned around: in the 1980s and 1990s growing worries about security and defence issues among Western publics in general and the West German public in particular mean that a failure to manage properly the issue of security in Europe could well generate new and profound problems for the Western alliance. Because of West Germany's special position as a front line state, the problem could become very specially German. Thus has the nature of the German problem changed. The question is no longer how the German national question itself will affect European politics over the next ten to fifteen years, but how European politics will affect the disposition of the Germanies.

2   The evolution of the contemporary German question

MICHAEL STÜRMER

The German question is one of those perennial problems with a life almost of their own that are never solved but only change appearance. This is what distinguishes it from the nineteenth-century Schleswig-Holstein question, which led to Lord Palmerston's remark that there were three people who knew everything about it: 'The Prince Consort, who is dead. A German scholar, who has gone mad. And I, and I have forgotten.'

Unfortunately, the German question has a tendency not to be forgotten but rather to reappear on the European and global agenda. The reasons date back to the seventeenth century and the rise of the European system, with Germany – no longer a Reich and never to be united under one ruler – in the middle of it. Geography plays a role, since Germany is situated where all the European peninsulas meet and where one power holds the other in check. So does politics, which helped to call the present postwar world system into being and will continue to play its part in the continuing transformation of this system. In 1950 a Foreign Office memorandum stated that Germany had become the pawn which both sides wish to turn into a queen. Thus the contemporary German question seems to have two chief aspects: Who controls Germany? And where do the Germans find their identity?

Germany and the postwar system

No part of the past half-century is lost in the present situation of Central Europe. In 1945, there was no longer a German government, no longer German legislation, no longer a German *Wehrmacht*. The Germans in fact counted for very little. But the German question was still posed, and it was chief among the issues dividing the victors, since neither side was able to impose on the world the Germany of its choice. Thus the perennial German question made itself felt, even though Germany itself was reduced to a geographical term of uncertain dimensions, its future to be determined by the Big Three at their meetings, first at Yalta, and then at Potsdam.

The Cold War was not only fuelled by the German question, it also determined the answers to it that are still with us: in its Central European dimension it can be described as the war of the German succession. The Cold War, of course, raged from China's borders, Vietnam and Korea, through Iran, Greece, to the Balkans and to Prague, Warsaw, Berlin and the demarcation line between the Soviet occupied zone of Germany and the rest of the country. The fate of Germany brought the Cold War to one of its chilliest episodes. And it was itself partly determined by the geographical and political freeze that the Cold War imposed on the map of Europe after 1945.

The new world system after 1945 had little or nothing to do with the old one that had been eclipsed when, in George F. Kennan's words, the great seminal catastrophe of our century began. After 1945 global politics were bipolarized, Europe was divided, and the conflict betwen the super-powers hung on the nuclear balance. In the words of Raymond Aron: 'Paix impossible, guerre improbable.'

The bipolarization of world politics was expressed in two conflicting ideologies: on the one hand, the Wilsonian promise to make the world safe for democracy; on the other, the Leninist threat to make the world safe for communism. The division of Europe implied not only the virtual dis-appearance of Germany as a power, but also the end of a European system deserving the name. It had gone down in the Thirty Years War of the twentieth century. Hitler's was indeed, in retrospect, the last bid for world pre-dominance; it was, however, beyond the limits of time, of ethics, of civilization, and contrary to everything the Europeans could and would support. When the Reich collapsed, Central Europe was reduced to the thin line separating the forward armoured columns of the Russians, the Americans and the British, and to the four-power status of the former German capital, the soon-to-be-divided city of Berlin. It took Germany's West European neighbours some time to realize that, with the centre of Europe transformed to rubble and misery, their own power was also diminished and they were reduced to dependence on the United States.

Nuclearization of the conflict between the American superpower and Soviet expansionism could, through the nature of the nuclear system, no longer be acted out in classical military form. 'La guerre de Troy n'aura pas lieu': not because Greeks and Trojans became more enlightened, but because deterrence triumphed over war, defence over aggression. War in the European theatre was suspended in 1948, and it has been that way ever since. From this the Cold War ensued, as the twin child of fear and reason. After a little over a decade the era of concerted conflict-management followed, often referred to as detente.

In Central Europe, the war of the German succession acquired the name of the Cold War. At the same time, the Cold War offered the Germans, more particularly those in the West, the opportunity to change their role from object to subject. Double containment became the formula under which the West Germans, within less than a decade, were readmitted into the power game. Double containment meant both containment of the Soviet Union, which could not be held back without German territory and manpower, and containment of Germany, of the German question and of the hidden potential in it. This was made easier by the total defeat of Germany, the bipolar structure of postwar politics, the widespread fear of a third war, and the extended reach of the Pax Americana.

Whatever allied wartime planners had been plotting for the future of Germany, they must have been surprised at how different Central Europe looked only ten years after the unconditional surrender of the *Wehrmacht*. Germany was divided, but in a rather different way from that envisaged by the European Advisory Committee. The partition of Germany had become the great divide of the victors of World War II. Moreover, the Western powers had been drawn not only into the control position that they had wanted, but also into a guarantee role that they had not wanted, least of all the United States. At Yalta, President Roosevelt, in a conversation with Stalin, had indicated that within two years United States troops would have left the European continent. Stalin understood that access to Western Europe and to the shores of the Atlantic would thus be gained by the heirs of Catherine the Great. That is why he changed from advocating German partition at Yalta to supporting German unity at Potsdam. Still in 1948, when Stalin's man at the Berlin Control Council left the conference room for good, he complained bitterly that the Americans had not honoured what the Russians had taken as a promise that they would be able to dominate Europe.

By being amputated and partitioned, Germany paid the price, not only of losing World War II, but of discord among the victors. At the same time, it was this discord which offered a chance to the vanquished. While Dr Kurt Schumacher, the man of sorrows at the helm of Germany's postwar Social Democratic Party, wanted to reunite a Socialist Reich and lead it into an anti-communist Western system, Adenauer understood that for the time being and perhaps for a long time, no Reich was feasible, whether socialist or bourgeois. The only opportunity left to Germany was

23

to play the Western game, to be the most European nation among the Europeans, and to translate Germany's geostrategic position into political negotiating power.

It is both enlightening and revealing to re-read Adenauer's letters from the immediate postwar period. 'Asien steht an der Elbe' (Asia has reached the Elbe), was his analysis in the summer of the vanquished, after 8 May 1945. The future agreements between the victors concerning Germany as a whole were, in Adenauer's eyes, not worth the paper they were written on. Adenauer used the Iron Curtain metaphor four months after Yalta and one month before Potsdam. What it meant was very clear: ideas for the joint management of Germany, for peace and for the world at large were an illusion which was destined to evaporate very soon.

Whatever Adenauer's inner feelings were about the shattered ruins of Bismarck's Reich – some historians accused him of using the power conflict to administer the *coup de grâce* to the nation-state – Adenauer understood the utter isolation of Germany and the Germans through his particular brand of extreme realism. He also grasped that the only asset in German hands was the old geopolitical role of the land between the Meuse and the Elbe, the potential of 50 million Germans on the Western side of the German catastrophe, the fear of Stalin in London and Paris, and the role that the United States would have to assume, however reluctantly, sooner or later to give reality to the Pax Americana which had been at the heart of American involvement in Europe since 1941. Adenauer read the political, strategic and geographic situation in 1945 realistically and what he hit upon was a concept not for the renaissance of a German nation-state – although this remained Schumacher's vision and is still that of many of his followers today – but of Europe united under American economic leadership, military protection and political guidance, with the Western parts of Germany acting as a European bridgehead while also being part of a West European security framework.

This *Rest-Deutschland* – the future Federal Republic – was, in Adenauer's eyes, not only a refuge and bulwark but also the bargaining chip that the Germans could use in a deal with the Western powers, who sooner or later would have to understand that without Germany they were lost. In 1945, Adenauer's vision was that of a lonely old man who had inherited from Weimar times a great name and gone uncorrupted through the trials and tribulations since 1933. In 1948, Adenauer's vision was the view of the most important CDU leader in West Germany. And between the Berlin blockade and the Korean war it also came to be shared by the man in the White House. In his memoirs Harry S. Truman remarked that without West Germany the defence of Western Europe would be nothing but a rearguard action on the shores of the Atlantic Ocean.

Thus the German *Länder* emerged, then the bizonal structure and finally, in 1949, the Federal Republic of Germany. By the conditions of its creation, this new German entity was not a state in search of a foreign policy, but a foreign policy in search of a state. Legitimacy came through the pathetic vote for the Western zones expressed by a stream of more than 14 million refugees and expellees, of whom about 12 million reached their goal. In 1948, 38 million people had been living in what is now the Federal Republic of Germany. Twelve years and a national catastrophe later, the population had grown to over 50 million, and it now stands at about 60 million.

Why did this Second Republic, having started under much worse auspices than the First Republic, not follow the disastrous path of Weimar? The Weimar Republic had emerged almost at the beginning of those political upheavals and social revolutions that marked Germany's path through the twentieth century. The Federal Republic emerged at the end of our Thirty Years War. Moral and physical breakdown sealed the past, and Stalin's grim shadow helped to reconcile the West Germans to their present. The Grundgesetz, the Basic Law that governs in lieu of a constitution, used what legal devices it could to build a dam against the return of Hitler and the putsch tactics of communist takeovers that had been so successfully employed not long before in Budapest, Warsaw and Prague. However, the Western occupying powers still controlled political and economic life. World events soon forced them to move from occupation to alliance, while still retaining a safeguard of last resort through their presence in Berlin – a presence that every Bonn government has appreciated and cultivated, and will continue to do so.

As there was no longer anything worthy, at least politically, of the name of Central Europe, West Germany's Western orientation came about almost as a matter of course. There was simply nothing there that the idea of a Central European identity could be built upon. There was only the dividing line. The Germans' Western orientation was sealed by the Basic Law and its attempt to reawaken Germany's older republican traditions and to blend them with federalism, the welfare state and the rule of law. On paper, the arrangement looked less perfectly democratic than the Weimar constitution. But in practice this constitution has proved to be a stable framework for a stable democratic system that, in spite of many shrill voices, has always emphasized consensus more than strife. The idea of nationhood was not given up or replaced by European integration, but it was carefully blended into a vision of Europe. This new nationhood was not based on territory or language but on human rights and the right to the pursuit of happiness. In addition, the idea of national unification was set into a framework of a united Europe. This is written into the preamble of the Basic Law, a more complex document than recent critics give it credit for, since it is both national and European.

The next important thing, perhaps – after national catastrophe, the Cold War, the promise of freedom, and the hope of national reunification through European unity and Soviet weakness – was the fact that, with generous aid from the United States, the Second German Republic was much more prosperous than the first one had ever been. Prosperity helped the Germans to find democracy attractive and natural. This started with the Marshall Plan and the currency reform in 1948, it continued with social market economy – capitalism with a heart – and the Europe of the Six, and it culminated, just over a decade after unconditional surrender, in an industrial leadership role for West Germany in Western Europe. At the same time, the major West European powers were reduced in size, as the stardust of empire was brushed from their feet while the independent nuclear deterrent became a rather pricey and much coveted symbol of their sovereignty. The Federal Republic, growing in prosperity, grew also in political status, somewhat ironically, as a result of General de Gaulle's decision to pull France out of the integrated military structure of Nato. Thus West Germany became the key partner of the United States in Europe – a role that was, and still is, both attractive and onerous.

Detente and the currents of Ostpolitik

At the beginning of the 1960s, and as a result of the same historical currents, the very foundations of West Germany had been shaken by the second Berlin crisis. It had brought the world close to the brink of uncontrolled disaster. It ended up postponed like a chess game, but the impact on Germany and on the rest of the world was tremendous. For the West German political establishment there were two lessons to be learned from the building of the Berlin Wall in 1961. The first was that in the era of nuclear parity United States superpower had reached its limits, that sooner or later the Cold War would change its nature, and that, somehow, West Germany would have to define for itself a new role in the changing framework of the East–West conflict. The second lesson was closely related to the first: that the period of 'transition' to a unified Germany envisaged by the Federal Republic's founding fathers could outlast the century, and that East Germany had established itself as the other state in a divided Germany. Partition was to last long, and the Soviet Union would not do any deals over the heads of the East German communists, the SED.

26

After the Cuban missile crisis in 1962, and under the impact of detente, it slowly sank home that sooner rather than later the government in Bonn would have to come to terms with the superpower status of the Soviet Union, the permanence of the Oder–Neisse border with Poland, and the existence of the other state in Germany. It was this mixture of factors which changed attitudes as much as any political assumptions about Germany's postwar role. Adenauer's Westpolitik now offered the basis from which a very tentative Ostpolitik could develop. There was much fear in Western Europe that somehow the American involvement in Vietnam would increase tensions with the Soviet Union in Europe, or that American withdrawal could be paid for politically in West European currency. Nato's 1967 Harmel report on detente and deterrence answered these anxieties. On West German insistence, it also identified the partition of Germany as the real source of tension in Europe. Soon, however, the hot line and the 1963 test-ban treaty seemed to open up new approaches to international problems. Meanwhile the West Germans were politely but insistently asked by successive American presidents what their contribution would be. In the mid-1960s some of the dogmas of the past were beginning to be looked upon as rather burdensome, and the West German initiative for a general European system of renunciation of force included, after some hesitation, East Germany, although the state was supposed not to exist. However its not-being-there made it increasingly difficult for the Bonn government to offer advice to the Western powers on how to deal with the question of Berlin, its access routes and its future viability. Within West Germany the Free Democrats were looking for ways to play an opposition role *vis-à-vis* the overwhelming weight of the grand coalition, and it found it in Deutschlandpolitik. There was both push and pull from outside too: the pull came from Paris and Washington to jump on the detente train, and the push came from the problem of Berlin, for which there could be no solution until the Federal Republic redefined its own role *vis-à-vis* Moscow, Warsaw and East Germany.

Thus, the new Ostpolitik was not really so new, in that twenty years of Westpolitik had left some room for manoeuvre towards the East, and in that the policy helped to defuse the dangerous situation of the Western sectors of Berlin. This came about through the sequence of treaties from Moscow and Warsaw in 1970, the Four-Power Agreement on Berlin, the Basic Treaty of 1972 between the Federal Republic and East Germany – and subsequent follow-up agreements including most recently the draft agreement on cultural exchanges.

Ostpolitik, however, *was* new in that it wrapped old pragmatism into a new philosophy described in very ambiguous terms as 'Wandel durch Annäherung' – change through rapprochement. There were visionary

27

strings attached to Ostpolitik. One was the idea of a future 'European-ization of Europe', with uncertain borders and an uncertain internal structure. It was reflected up to a point in the Helsinki process: but the ensuing discord about the meaning of Helsinki between East and West and even within the West was a mark of the initial differences. The second string attached to Ostpolitik was that there should be a degree of domestic change, as Willy Brandt once put it, sufficient to allow some convergence between the different social systems of East and West; just how much, was not revealed. It came to nothing and served only to set off new political and ideological conflict within Germany. The third string concerned the national implications of Ostpolitik – and especially the temptation to offer Moscow a price for progress in German–German relations that might, at a later stage, also include the Western orientation of the Federal Republic. Henry Kissinger found this, among all the illusions accompanying the policies of the previous fifteen years, the most dangerous, and he directed a timely warning towards Bonn in 1972: 'The Brandt–Scheel government has initiated a process which, if it fails, endangers its political survival and, if it succeeds, could win a momentum that would unhinge the political stability of Germany.' Kissinger also underlined that no West German government would have the power to conduct its Ostpolitik on a purely national basis. Without the military umbrella of the alliance, it would endanger not only Berlin, but also the very existence of the Federal Republic. Its security would continue to depend on unswerving support from its allies, especially the United States: 'Ostpolitik can only succeed if supported by the alliance. Otherwise the Federal Republic would be unable to motivate the Soviet Union to genuine compromise.'[1] At the time, this warning must have sounded premature. Events since have underlined its relevance.

The future agenda

Although Kissinger has since left the stage, every Bonn government, whatever its intentions, would be well advised to make his analysis the yardstick by which to measure the range and role of Deutschlandpolitik. No German government can ever throw more weight into the scales of the East than it has into those of the West. This has been a particularly painful insight since the mid-1970s, when detente fell on hard times in Africa, Afghanistan and Poland.

Was it possible, or advisable, to divide detente? The answer to that question has remained uncertain and has divided not so much detente but the West. Could Germany, East and West, remain an island of detente in a sea of troubles? The answer was ambiguous: it separated German Social

Democrats from French Socialists after the imposition of martial law in Poland in 1981, and it sent the spectre of Rapallo limping through the editorial pages of influential French and American journals. Both the Schmidt and the Kohl governments have argued that Deutschlandpolitik could and should serve as a regional arena where detente could continue, and that it reassured the Germans, East and West, that new Nato missile deployments would not be the end of the world. In fact, the difference between Kohl and Schmidt was much smaller than that between Schmidt and his predecessor government. It was Schmidt, not Kohl, who first ended the inherent ambiguities of Deutschlandpolitik that had so characterized the era of Willy Brandt and his adviser, Egon Bahr.

The postwar system will endure as the framework of the present and the foreseeable future. The German question is very much a part of this system. It covers the partition of Germany and inner-German relations, the status of Berlin, West Germany's European and transatlantic ties and the uneasy relationship between East Germany and the Soviet Union. All these elements are suspended from the framework like parts of a mobile in an exhibition of modern art. No elements of this real-life mobile can be set in motion without all the other parts moving as well. The points from which the structure is suspended are two, Washington and Moscow, and their relationship dominates the activity of the political mobile of Central Europe.

History being, of course, not a work of art, will not leave the structure unchanged. Within the framework of the first postwar decade all the parts – European partition, the bipolar world and nuclear strategy – have undergone change and will continue to do so. But in which direction will change go? And what chance is there to influence it?

Conventional wisdom has it that the aim of Deutschlandpolitik is to overcome some of the more inhumane aspects of German and European partition, and that it serves *den Menschen* (the people) – although this term is truly untranslatable in its innocence. Of course this is only part of the truth. Deutschlandpolitik, to a large and perhaps dominant extent, is an attempt to safeguard the viability of Berlin, while the three allies look after the beleaguered city's security. Without the precarious situation of Berlin in the middle of Soviet-controlled East Germany, there would be much less impulse for Deutschlandpolitik, and global antagonism would reign supreme. Remaining four-power responsibilities for Germany would have long fallen into disuse. German partition would look even worse than it does today, and the superpowers would find it difficult to define another place which would serve both as warning system of trouble ahead and as an arena where military conflicts can be translated into legal language. Deutschlandpolitik also serves to keep the face of the nations of

29

East Central Europe turned in a westward direction. It projects the image of the West onto the East. Thus it is to a large extent business on behalf of the West as a whole. Deutschlandpolitik, fundamentally, is not about changing the map of Europe, and it is not about reunification. It is conflict management in the troubled heart of Europe, and its purpose is really a future European peace order rather than a quick political fix.

Deutschlandpolitik is intimately tied to the ebb and flow of East–West relations. It can flourish only if the climate between the American eagle and the Russian bear is not too cold. That is why the Germans have tried – by clinging desperately to the terminology, the appearance and the left-overs of detente – to keep some channels of communications open. That is why the Kohl government has tried to remind the German public of its contribution to the Geneva summit meeting between Reagan and Gorbachev in November 1985 – a contribution that was rather complex, comprising not only toughness in the Euro-missile affair, and firmness in support for SDI, but also a constant willingness to play, towards East Germany, the salesman and even the financier of many good things the East Germans need in order to keep their own social contract of stability through prosperity alive. The role of honest broker between East and West is of course a temptation far beyond the means of the government in Bonn, although not beyond the ambitions of some of the players on the West German stage. By the same token, enhanced East–West conflict has invariably put pressure on Deutschlandpolitik, while making it all the more valuable as an element of stability in an unstable world.

Since the mid-1950s West German ties to the West have undergone some change for the better, some for the worse. German–American relations will never again be the honeymoon of the first postwar decade and of the formative Adenauer years. They have become what Ambassador Richard Burt recently called 'a mature relationship' – which seems to be a diplomatic way of saying that the fire of love has been replaced by mutual interest on a solid basis of shared assumptions, beliefs and interests. Inside West Germany once again, as throughout the 1950s, not only policies, but also the very assumptions on which they rest, have become controversial. This applies not only to discussion about the Soviet threat in general and the appropriate response to it, but also to the Nato dual-track decision of 1979 and the German involvement in SDI.

New unrest is an expression of the old familiar boredom with civiliz-ation; a quest for identity reveals uncertainties about Germany's place in the history and political geography of democratic Europe; and there is panic to escape the bipolar nuclear system. All this not only influences the Greens and the pacifists, but also rocks parts of the Social Democratic Party. It extends far beyond the bounds of Deutschlandpolitik, but the perennial German question once again ensures that new departures in Germany itself are bound to have profound and unsettling global implications. At present, the problem that troubles most of the observers of the German scene is not what is actually happening in Deutschlandpolitik, but the worry that a Federal Republic in the future might throw its very existence into some future deal with the Soviet Union which would not only destroy the Central European balance, but also mark the end of the postwar system. The war of the German succession would thus find a totalitarian end.

By contrast, the GDR seems to be a rock of bloc solidarity. From time to time *Pravda* warns against national ambitions and softness in dealing with the West, and some of these warnings are clearly directed at East Berlin. Closer inspection, however, shows that it is not only currents from the West that affect East Germany. The regime there has also been trying to profit from the malaise which hit Comecon in the wake of the second oil shock in the late 1970s and from the Polish crisis in the early 1980s. East Berlin is clearly trying to widen its freedom of manoeuvre to safeguard the economic benefits of its special relationship with West Germany, to bolster its own prestige and precedence, and at the same time to press for acceptance by West Germany of the four Gera demands (see Chapter 8, p.113), originally intended in 1980 to forestall further dialogue. Ever since 1961, the SED has had to look for a *modus vivendi* with the fragmentary nation under its control. It has bought stability by increasing the standard of living, and thus making itself dependent to no small degree on Western supplies, since Eastern ones are not always forthcoming. This is understood, and so far accepted in Moscow. One of the reasons is, of course, the reassuring presence of 380,000 Russian troops in the GDR. Thus the interesting questions about the GDR are *not* about its ultimate security, nor even its participation in military planning, since very little has changed over the years in this dimension. But there has been a change of climate, influenced bit by bit and very carefully from the West. And there is a general tendency for East Central Europe to try to regain some historical identity and some space for political manoeuvre while retaining, for the respective communist regimes in power there, the ultimate Soviet guarantee of regime security. The SED has been able to establish itself within the Eastern system as a key factor and a centre of power.

The bilateral relationship between Bonn and East Berlin is of course far from independent of outside influence. In the West, it is dependent on the confidence and support that the Federal Republic finds among its allies and partners. In the East it is dependent on what lessons the men in the Kremlin want to teach the West Germans, how far they trust their brothers in East Berlin, and to what extent they profit from the relationship.

To sum up, the key elements of the postwar system are still operative: the partition of Germany and Europe and the virtual non-existence of a European system; the bipolar structure of the global conflict; and the nuclear discipline imposed on the chief antagonists. But all the factors have changed and continue to do so. European history and geography being what it is, West Germany has a key role to play and therefore attracts an inflated measure of attention from onlookers from East and West. In fact, the German stage offers, to the outside world, a bewildering multitude of scenes: economic bliss and breakdown of consensus in security matters; Deutschlandpolitik still running its steady and moderate course, while nightmares recur of a special German path (*Sonderweg*) to instability and disaster.

Prophesying would be simpler if it were not about the future. The Foreign Office memorandum on the German question written in 1950 and mentioned at the start of this chapter does not sound so obsolete today. It was an attempt to list the disadvantages and indeed dangers of any permanent division of Germany that might result from Russian policy. These were:

(a) 'The absence of a four-power solution, though it is primarily indicative of the present world-wide struggle between communism and Western civilisation, has also become in itself one of the major factors in the tension between the Russian and the Western powers.

(b) 'In a divided Germany without a peace treaty, the appeal of German unity can be used to inflame German nationalism.

(c) 'In the contest between the great powers, Germany has become a pawn which both sides wish to turn into a queen . . .

(d) 'So long as Germany remains divided, the situation of the Western Powers in Berlin will remain precarious and, in the event of renewed Russian pressure there, the risk of war may again arise.

(e) 'The longer the Russians maintain their grip on the Eastern Zone the harder it will be ever to bring that Zone within the German Federal Republic.'

Notes

1   Kurt Birrenbach, *Meine Sondermissionen* (Düsseldorf: 1984) pp.326–7.

II THE FOUR POWERS AND GERMANY

3   The Soviet view

GERHARD WETTIG

Ever since World War II, Soviet leaders have seen Germany as crucial to their policy towards Western Europe. Stalin was convinced that 'the existence of a peace-loving democratic Germany beside a peace-loving Soviet Union excludes the possibility of further wars in Europe, puts an end to bloodshed in Europe and makes impossible the enslavement of European countries by the world imperialists'.[1] Soviet control over Germany would make the United States presence on the European continent untenable, and thus assure the USSR's domination on its side of the Atlantic. Conversely, a Germany firmly tied to the West was bound to be a roadblock to decisive Soviet influence in Western Europe. This analysis has shaped the Kremlin's attitudes and actions towards Germany throughout the postwar period.

To be sure, the ways and means of handling the Germans have changed greatly. Stalin felt that the Germans' drive for reunification was the historical force which the Soviet Union could successfully exploit against the United States and its allies. That part of Germany which the Kremlin controlled was to provide the political glacis from which all of the country could be won over sooner or later, by appealing to this desire for reunification.[2] This 'German unity' line was downplayed after the uprising in East Berlin of 17 June 1953 had revealed the extent to which communism was resisted even by those Germans who were exposed to Soviet control. From then on, Soviet advocacy of German reunification was little more than a tactical propaganda device. The all-German slogans were dropped completely when, in 1966, the West German Social Democrats finally decided to take the East German communists at their word and offer a direct party-to-party dialogue with the SED.[3]

Evidently, the change of approach did not reflect a willingness on the part of the Kremlin to renounce its aim of control and communization in exchange for neutrality, whilst counting on being able to dominate Germany in the future. As far as can be judged, the Soviet leadership has never really considered giving up East Germany in return for some

35

Western concession on Germany's status.[4] The GDR was viewed in Moscow not as a pawn or a bargaining chip but as a power position that could be used for further political advance.

What has changed over time is the Soviet leaders' perception of how useful the continued issue of German reunification can be in the pursuit of their goals. Whereas Stalin felt that the German desire to live in a single state was both a powerful force that would prevail in the long run and a beneficial trend that lent itself to exploitation by the Soviet Union, his successors were more impressed by the anti-Soviet potential in German nationalism and German unity. They have acted on the assumption that the only hope of establishing firm and lasting control over Germany is to keep it divided. Their best hope would be for a communist East Germany plus a neutralized, increasingly dependent Federal Republic. West Germany would then cease to be either a barrier to the Soviet Union's political advance into Western Europe or a potential challenge to the stability of East Germany.

This Soviet determination not to give rise to the slightest hope for German unity became obvious during the missile deployment debate of 1980–3. Soviet propaganda tried hard to provide the West German public with an incentive for opposing the deployment of American missiles in the country. All kinds of expectations, both positive and negative, were raised – but Moscow remained conspicuously silent on anything which related to the prospect of German unity or even political rapprochement. Obviously, the Kremlin feels that East Germany's relative domestic stability and the East German leadership's reliance on Soviet backing could be jeopardized if inter-German relations were to enter a more dynamic phase.

The Soviet leaders regard caution as the better part of wisdom. Keeping firm control over what they have is preferable to the brightest hopes for big but uncertain gain in the future. That has been the Soviet attitude to East Germany. Stalin professed his belief that founding a separate German state in his sphere of influence was tantamount to erecting 'the corner-stone for a united and peace-loving Germany'.[5] His successors also opted for German partition. The leverage which control over the GDR provides is exploited in order to influence the Federal Republic's behaviour. The stronger East Germany is as a Soviet stronghold, the more chance it has to influence the West Germans.[6]

West Germany's Ostpolitik gave the Kremlin greater opportunity to bring East German leverage to bear on the Federal Republic. The Four-Power Berlin Agreement of 1971 ratified more than a decade's development which had shifted West Berlin's former exclusive reliance on Western protection to partial cooperation with the Soviet Union and notably East Germany. Dependence on East German goodwill was thereby enhanced, and East Berlin was quick to make use of this financially but also politically. West German emphasis on the need for more personal contact and communication between the two parts of the divided country provided the SED leaders with ample leverage *vis-à-vis* Bonn. Soviet officials, to be sure, were often far from enthusiastic about the emerging cooperative aspects of inter-German relations. At times these seem to have revived deep-seated suspicions that 'their' Germans might seek emancipation and draw closer to their Western countrymen. But so long as the Soviet Union remained confident that it could cope with the new situation, the Kremlin was not insensitive to the opportunities which Ostpolitik presented *vis-à-vis* the Federal Republic.

Making use of East Germany is one element of Soviet policy. Another one is to look for legal justification for the Soviet claim to a *droit de regard* in Central Europe. Any development which might result in change is strictly controlled. It is for this reason that the Soviet Union still insists on four-power residual rights in Germany, since these provide a basis for Western non-recognition of the GDR's claims to sovereignty over the Berlin access routes.[7] The Soviet interpretation of West Berlin's status as a four-power territory with the exclusion of the eastern part of the city, is designed to give the Soviet Union a maximum say.

It is significant that the Soviet Union stubbornly insists that its forces in the GDR are stationed there on grounds of 1945 rights in 'Germany':[8] i.e. not on the basis of voluntary agreement with East German approval. The Kremlin's willingness to stick to its occupation rights *vis-à-vis* its East German ally is a deep-rooted, if little publicized, point of contention between the two. Soviet rejection of the four-power rights claimed by the West concern the responsibilities only of the three Western powers and leave Soviet claims in respect of the Germans unaffected.

The Soviet assessment of West Germany's importance

When the Federal Republic joined Nato in 1955, Soviet leaders felt that they had lost a major political battle in Europe. However, they did not give up hope that the defeat they had suffered could be reversed. They almost immediately invited Adenauer to Moscow, established diplomatic relations with West Germany and for some time showed a friendly attitude towards Bonn. Only when this brought no return did Khrushchev finally resort to hostile action in Berlin. This pattern, using alternately the carrot and the stick in order to weaken West Germany's ties to Nato, has been repeated ever since.

The role of the Federal Republic became even more crucial in Soviet eyes, when de Gaulle announced France's withdrawal from the military organization of Nato in 1966. As seen from Moscow, France was in the process of leaving the Western alliance altogether and other member countries were likely to follow suit. It was necessary to make West Germany turn away from Nato as well. If that could be done, the breakdown of the alliance and American withdrawal from Europe would be inevitable.[9]

Even when Soviet leaders realized that France was only withdrawing from the military structure of the alliance, they still saw the Federal Republic's attitude as decisive for Nato. Ever since, they have seen West Germany as indispensable for Western Europe's defence, since no other member-country is able to provide either the necessary territory or manpower. If Bonn should ever opt out, Nato would lose its military viability and hence its capability to deter the Soviet Union in the European theatre.[10] Also, political attitudes in the Federal Republic are seen as setting trends in West European alliance politics.[11]

There are additional factors which make West Germany important for Moscow. The country carries considerable weight in the European Community, which could scarcely survive without the economic contribution and the stabilizing function of the Federal Republic. Accordingly, both Western efforts to increase West European integration (a process that the Kremlin has so far attempted to impede) and Soviet attempts to stimulate West European high-technology exports (which Washington sees as contributing to Soviet military power) depend for their success largely on Bonn's cooperation.

The Kremlin has pursued both maximum and minimum goals, depending on which seemed feasible at any given point. Whenever the political situation in Europe is stable, the best the Soviet leaders can hope for is to promote Bonn's 'independence' from Washington and to strengthen West Germany's commitment to economic and technological cooperation between East and West. When American–Soviet relations become strained and West European public opinion shows signs of disquiet, the Soviet leaders can hope for something better. They appeal to West European governments, notably to Bonn, to assert their interest in detente, in opposition to the United States, and to exercise corresponding pressure for 'moderation' in Washington. At the same time, they try to convince West European publics that they should support the Soviet Union's 'peace-loving' policies. This was the game they played with Chancellor Schmidt's government in the early 1980s. Contrary to their expectations, however, what followed was not a takeover by leftist Social Democrats and the peace movement, but the Federal Republic's return to more conservative government. In 1983, the peace protesters proved themselves incapable of fulfilling the expectations which had encouraged the Kremlin to stall the Geneva INF negotiations eighteen months earlier: deployment of American missiles went ahead unhindered and, consequently, West Germany's ties to Nato were not put in jeopardy.

Whatever the short- and medium-term goal at any given moment, over the long term the aim is to eliminate the United States presence from Western Europe and disrupt Nato cohesion. Occasionally, leading Soviet functionaries have been quite frank about that. In an interview in *Der Spiegel*, Zagladin responded when asked whether he recommended neutrality to the West Europeans: 'That would be unrealistic in the short run. But we have always advocated a dissolution of the blocs and we still think of that as a long-term goal today.'[12] It goes without saying that a 'dissolution of the blocs' would mean an American withdrawal back across the Atlantic and would deprive the West Europeans of their framework for military cooperation. On the Eastern side, little would change: that is, Soviet dominance over all of Europe would be established. In the long term, then, Soviet leaders strive for the Federal Republic's withdrawal from Nato and exploit any available means towards that end. Their political doctrine, however, warns them against being 'unrealistic', i.e. encourages them to go for what seems attainable at a given moment. The final step can be taken only when all preceding steps have been taken. In practice, therefore, in the short term, more modest goals often have to be pursued.

If it seems impossible to get West Germany to break away from Nato for the time being, one has to look for a more realistic goal. So the Kremlin appeals to the Federal Republic to exercise restraint over what is portrayed as a maximalist and threatening American stance. If Bonn follows such advice, Moscow can gain in either of two ways: either Washington's effort *vis-à-vis* the Soviet Union is seriously impeded, or there is serious dissension between the two most important Nato members – or both. Whatever weakens allied cohesion in the West is seen as another step towards the more distant goal of promoting an 'independent', if disunited, Western Europe outside the Atlantic framework.

Confusingly, the Soviet Union is a status quo power when it comes to frontiers in Europe, but a revisionist power in a power-political sense. The problem becomes more complex when one looks at the German question. Soviet leaders are not inclined to export communism to West Germany by means of national expansion on the part of East Germany. On the contrary, they would seem to prefer not to have German unification for the foreseeable future, even under the auspices of East German communism. The reason is power politics: a unified German state would be too big politically and therefore to be distrusted – so it is much better to have, on the one hand, a client state which is dependent on Soviet protection and, on the other, a second state which may some day be incorporated into the Soviet sphere of influence as a non-communist, if leftist, state.

The assumption that the Kremlin seeks hegemony over all of Europe is consistent with the evidence provided by Soviet policy-making. During the INF controversy, Moscow's efforts had been directed, not towards reaching some balance of interests with the West German government and its Western allies, but at fostering domestic opposition to challenge the successive Atlanticist governments in Bonn (first Schmidt and then Kohl), so as to topple them if possible. Such behaviour is consistent with Soviet political doctrine. Shifting the correlation of forces in favour of 'socialism' is the first duty of foreign policy.

The Soviet Union's systematic military build-up since the mid-1960s has to be viewed in this context: Soviet leaders have expressed their conviction that more than anything else military power assures their country's voice will be heeded throughout the world. More specifically, Soviet spokesmen have made clear that the principle of military parity should be implemented in such a way that each of the two world powers would control its geostrategic sphere of influence. By this interpretation, the Soviet Union is entitled to unlimited power in Eurasia and elsewhere in the Old World, while the United States is restricted to North America.[13]

Patterns of political action

Soviet leaders are aware that West German governments are generally reluctant to play the game as envisaged. Thus, appropriate incentives have to be provided. It is in this context that the second level of Soviet foreign policy comes into play. As commentators in Moscow have explained over and over again, the Soviet Union conducts a peculiar kind of 'honest and open diplomacy'. In contrast to Western governments, the Soviet leadership directs its proposals and initiatives 'not only to one address but to two addresses': i.e. both to the governments and to the peoples. The expressly stated purpose is to promote the Kremlin's goals 'simultaneously from above and from below'.[14]

For a long period of time, Soviet leaders had little opportunity to exert pressure from below, even if Western governments made foreign policy choices which met with disapproval in Moscow. In the second half of the 1960s a sustained effort was made to change this. The Soviet Union's campaign against West Germany, under slogans of 'European security', created some external pressure but failed to affect the Federal Republic's domestic politics to any significant degree. After the Final Act of the

Helsinki process on Security and Cooperation in Europe (CSCE) had been signed in August 1975, the Kremlin prepared a massive propaganda campaign throughout Western Europe, aimed at furthering Soviet goals under the new CSCE heading. The effort, however, did not really get off the ground, in part because of the manifest unwillingness of the biggest West European communist parties to support the venture.

It was only the campaign against the 'neutron bomb' in 1977–8 which gave Soviet propagandists the feeling that they had finally got through to a larger audience in Western Europe, notably in West Germany. What is more, President Carter's subsequent decisions to forgo production and deployment of the weapon created the impression in Moscow that Soviet propaganda pressure had paid off and inflicted a defeat on United States 'imperialism'.[15] It is this perception which strongly encouraged the Kremlin to repeat the strategy in December 1979 when Nato sought to confront the Soviet Union with the alternative of cutting its own SS–20 missile arsenal or accepting Western counterarmament. The Soviet leaders saw no reason to do either, since they had the capacity to break the Western governments' resolve by fostering and organizing massive counteraction 'from below'.

The main target of the Kremlin's effort[16] was the Federal Republic, since West German deployment or non-deployment was viewed as crucial to Nato's ability to implement the December 1979 decision. The Soviet propagandists and their 'allies' in Western societies did what they could, not only to intensify opposition to deployment, but also to channel protest and opposition in an exclusively anti-Nato and anti-American direction.[17] At the same time, Soviet leaders delayed official talks on the INF issue (although in public they were pressing for such talks). When finally negotiations were under way in Geneva, they decided in summer 1982 not to accept any deal at the negotiating table, in the belief that the 'peace forces' in Western Europe, particularly in the Federal Republic, would succeed in preventing Nato's deployment.[18] The ploy failed. But the Kremlin leaders did not feel their effort had been totally wasted. They concluded instead that the ground had been prepared for another campaign in Western Europe against the United States and Nato, this time aimed at eroding any support for President Reagan's Strategic Defence Initiative (SDI).[19]

Soviet attempts to mobilize the West German public against the policies of their government under the auspices of 'peace and disarmament' represent action at the societal level 'from below'. The East German role in Soviet foreign policy towards the Federal Republic is also considerable at this level, particularly through the SED *Westabteilung*'s (Western department) control over, and support of, the West German Communist Party (DKP) and West German front organizations. East Germany has an important role to play, too, in action 'from above': that is, it has the capacity to grant or deny favour to the West Germans with regard to West Berlin's access routes and to contacts between the two Germanies. In this way Moscow can use the GDR to exert leverage in government-to-government relations.

Thus, whenever the Kremlin felt it was worthwhile to demonstrate good relations with the Federal Republic (usually to draw attention to, and exploit, rising tensions in the relationship with the United States), East Germany was given considerable leeway in developing cooperation with Bonn (e.g. immediately following the Soviet invasion of Afghanistan and after the decision to deploy new Nato missiles in Europe). Conversely, whenever the West German government was on the verge of taking a decision which Moscow disliked, it received strong, if unspecified, warnings that this could jeopardize the benefits derived from East Germany. The only part of the East German–West German relationship not to be threatened in this way is economic relations. The Kremlin has a strong interest in keeping these going irrespective of political circumstances, and therefore takes the attitude that economics should be decoupled from East–West politics. The way of showing pleasure or displeasure to Bonn is the degree of visibility and warmth in the political relationship, a relationship which, in the period of detente, is viewed as important to the West German government at home.

Warnings that East Germany may be obliged to take political retaliation have been given in public with a view to fostering West German public opposition to the policies pursued by the government. However, the amount of pressure the Kremlin can exert through its East German ally should not be overrated. There are several inherent constraints which limit the use of such threats for propaganda purposes. After all, the Soviet Union and its allies must be portrayed as non-threatening countries if their policies of 'peace and disarmament' are to seem to serve the West's best interests and hence to deserve the Western public's support. Seemingly arbitrary threats do not fit into that picture. If West Germans were to see East Germany as being nasty simply for the sake of punishing their government, this could produce counterreaction and lead to greater identification with the government and against East Germany and the Soviet Union. For that reason, both Moscow and East Berlin were careful not to confront the Federal Republic with an 'ice age' in inter-German relations as some people feared (and Honecker at first appeared to threaten) following the West German decision to deploy new American Pershing and cruise missiles.

Intricacies of the inter-German relationship

It would be wrong to assume that Soviet leaders look at East Germany's dealings with Bonn solely from the viewpoint of how to influence the Federal Republic's policies toward the United States and Nato. To be sure, West Germany's Westpolitik looms very large in their minds. Nonetheless, other foreign policy interests have to be taken into account as well, notably East Germany's stake in the economic benefits of inter-German relations and the Soviet Union's own economic needs. As far as East German policy is concerned, the extent of Soviet tolerance varies proportionately to the degree that the Kremlin feels it can control inter-German developments. That has been clearly borne out by the complicated picture which emerged in 1984.

After deployment of American missiles had begun in the Federal Republic and in other West European countries, the Soviet leadership decided that it was wise to try to strengthen what common bonds there were with the West Germans rather than to antagonize them. Clearly, it was important to promote as much economic cooperation as possible at a time when the Soviet Union had little chance of receiving credits and technology from either the United States or Japan. Soviet policy-makers also sought to separate the Federal Republic from the United States, at least to some extent. Thus the West Germans felt themselves treated as the 'good guys', who were in the Soviet Union's good graces. The underlying theme was: 'We have such an excellent bilateral relationship, why should we fall out with one another just for the sake of the Americans? Be less subservient to Washington!'

These political manoeuvres, however, did not work. Instead the Federal government realized its domestic opportunity. It pointed out that, contrary to the Soviet Union's previous dire warnings, there was no imminent danger of war. Relations with the East had not worsened, but improved. Thus Soviet policies were exploited to disprove the sombre warnings which Soviet alarmist propaganda had been directing at the West German public. Those leaders in the Kremlin who felt that this friendly approach to West Germany was in any case detrimental to the Soviet Union's interests finally managed to convince their colleagues that Bonn's misuse of Soviet favours had become intolerable. In April 1984, the decision was taken to punish the Federal Republic politically for its anti-Soviet obstinacy. Relations chilled dramatically. Anti-West German hostility – accusing West Germans of reviving 'revanchism' – began to dominate Soviet public statements.

At this point, a problem began to emerge between Moscow and East Berlin. During the previous months, the East German leadership had been all too happy to see the Soviet Union pursue a lenient policy towards Bonn, since this enabled East Germany to pursue its policy of 'damage limitation' in German–German relations, a policy which promised to bring economic rewards for East Germany. In other words, it was hoped that the INF controversy would have as little negative spillover as possible so as to secure maximum economic and financial benefit from West Germany for the East Germans. The East German regime was reluctant to renounce such favourable prospects when the Kremlin decided to turn against Bonn. It also sought to make itself more popular with the East Germans by having Secretary-General Honecker solemnly accepted as a welcome guest in the Federal Republic.

One group, the most influential group in the Soviet Politburo, understood the East German situation and accepted that Honecker should continue his policies. As late as the second half of July 1984, a Soviet spokesman publicly assured the SED leaders in East Berlin that their policy was fully in accord with Soviet interests.[20] There was, to be sure, another group in the Soviet Politburo which sharply disagreed with this opinion and which had been putting pressure on the East Germans since the spring to curtail contacts with Bonn. Honecker, however, felt he could afford not to oblige, since he had the continued support of the most influential Kremlin leaders behind him. After a long period of fruitless effort, the Soviet opponents of his course felt that their only hope of pressing their cause in East Berlin was to revert to thinly veiled anti-East Germany polemics in those Soviet newspapers which were under their influence.[21]

There were sound economic reasons for the bulk of the Soviet leadership to allow East Germany to deviate from the Soviet Union's hard-line policy towards Bonn. The Soviet Union itself badly needed West Germany's economic cooperation. Soviet leaders have always been inclined in such circumstances to separate economic interests from political differences. They continued to follow that line during 1984. The difference this time was that for the first time in relations with Bonn, East Germany was the one pushing for continued political cooperation, while the Soviet Union dragged its feet. But the GDR had a special interest in good relations, which required them to do official business with Bonn. What the GDR expected to gain thereby, notably a DM 1 billion loan, was also bound to benefit the Soviet Union indirectly.

Moreover, Honecker and his Politburo colleagues demonstrated to the Kremlin that they badly needed whatever economic help might be available to them. Since the second half of the 1970s, the Soviet Union had reduced its deliveries of energy and raw materials to East Germany, which had therefore been forced to import increasing amounts of oil and other primary products. Much of the hard currency to finance these imports could only be had from West Germany. It could also be argued that while

East Germany was getting less and less in the way of raw materials from the Soviet Union, it was simultaneously being asked to contribute more and more assistance to needy members of the socialist community. Undeniably, the East German leaders had to make sure that their people's level of consumption could be maintained, so as not to damage the country's social and political stability – and that was clearly also in Moscow's interest. Under such circumstances, the Kremlin would have had a problem justifying a decision to veto East Berlin's policies towards Bonn.

Significantly enough, the opponents of closer German–German relations within the Politburo went public only after the GDR had finally secured its credit. They, too, seem to have somehow felt that the Soviet Union should not be too harsh with its East German ally when vital economic interests were at stake. Once those interests had been satisfied, however, Honecker was seen to be too reliant on further West German cooperation. Why should he be allowed to visit the Federal Republic and thereby show his acceptance of the very West German government that the Soviet Union rejected? It was only gradually that such argument came to be accepted by the rest of the Kremlin leadership. Presumably, the Soviet decision to resume political contacts with the United States has finally tipped the scales: once the two superpowers were talking again, the smaller countries would do better to shut up. It was in late August 1984 that Honecker learnt of Moscow's decision not to allow his visit to Bonn to go ahead. He immediately complied with what the Kremlin had decided.[22]

A new policy line towards the Federal Republic

Since September 1984, the policies of the Soviet Union and East Germany *vis-à-vis* the Federal Republic have essentially coincided. East Germany had followed the Soviet example in giving higher priority to relations with other Western countries. Political business with Bonn is being done with as little public show as possible, and official level contact is avoided whenever possible. At the same time, meetings of Soviet, East German and East European leaders with Social Democratic politicians from the Federal Republic are marked by ostentatious cordiality on the Eastern side and receive unusual attention in the East European press, as Willy Brandt's visit to East Berlin and Johannes Rau's stay in Moscow in autumn 1985 demonstrated. The SED leaders have even gone so far as to create the impression that some humanitarian concessions which had previously been 'sold' to the West German government, had in fact been granted to Brandt so as to give him the credit for them with the West German public.[23]

The Soviet and East German purpose is obviously to add credibility to

45

the SPD's claim that a 'second phase of Ostpolitik' is both necessary and likely to produce good results, and that the present government's policies lack commitment to the cause of peace and detente. It is in this spirit that the SED has cooperated with the West German Social Democrats in wording a draft agreement on a chemical weapons-free zone in Central Europe.[24] The aim is to demonstrate to the public both that CDU/CSU and FDP do not really care for negotiating arms limitation, and that arrangements to that end are easily achievable with a modicum of Western goodwill. A similar agreement on confidence-building measures has been drafted by the SPD and representatives of the British Communist party.[25] Similar ventures are being prepared by commissions which the West German Social Democrats have set up with the Soviet Communist party and other communist parties in Eastern Europe.

From the Soviet perspective (one which certainly is not shared by the West German SPD), the effort to work out positions on security with a big Western 'workers' party' serves the purpose of promoting and intensifying the 'struggle for peace and disarmament' which has to be waged against the United States and Nato in Western Europe, particularly in the Federal Republic. The attempt to convert public opinion to opposition to SDI is only one side of the coin. The other is to establish the appearance of commonality with Social Democratic forces wherever possible, so as to channel the arms control commitment of the West European, notably the West German, political left in an anti-American and anti-Nato direction.

The fact that Soviet leaders prefer West Germany's Social Democrats to the present conservative–liberal government led by Helmut Kohl, and that they also sought to enhance the Social Democrats' chances for the 1987 federal election, does not imply a final decision in favour of the SPD. They have always been willing to respect political realities, irrespective of whether they like them or not. For this reason, they have been careful not to make their preference for the SPD more obvious than is necessary and not to burn their bridges to the CDU/CSU and FDP. The Kremlin will manage to adapt itself to the political circumstances again should it become clear that the Social Democrats have no chance of returning to power in Bonn for the time being.

Notes

1 Congratulatory telegram of Stalin to the leaders of the GDR of 13 October 1949, in: *Dokumente zur Deutschlandpolitik der Sowjetunion*, vol. 1 (Berlin (East): Rütten and Löning 1957), p.238.
2 See Stalin's instructions to an SED delegation in July 1947 as reported by Erich W. Gniffke, *Jahre mit Ulbricht* (Cologne: Wissenschaft und Politik 1966), pp.250–1.
3 See Gerhard Wettig, *Community and Conflict in the Socialist Camp. The Soviet Union, East*

Germany, and the German Problem 1965–1972, translated by Edwina Moreton and Hannes Adomeit (London: Hurst 1975), pp.20–47.

4 For case studies and sources see e.g. Hermann Graml, 'Die Legende von der verpassten Gelegenheit', *Vierteljahreshefte für Zeitgeschichte*, vol. 29 (1981), pp.304–41; Gerhard Wettig, 'Die sowjetische Deutschland-Note vom 10. März 1952', *Deutschland Archiv*, vol. 15 (1982), pp.130–48; Peter März, *Die Bundesrepublik zwischen Westintegration und Stalin–Noten* (Frankfurt/Main–Bern: Verlag Peter Lang 1982), pp.127–70; Hermann-Josef Rupieper, 'Die sowjetischen Deutschland-Noten 1952', *Vierteljahresheft für Zeitgeschichte*, vol. 3/1985, pp.547–57; Rolf Steininger, 'Eine Chance zur Wiedervereinigung? Die Stalin-Note vom 10. März 1952, *Darstellung und Dokumentation auf der Grundlage unveröffentlichter britischer und amerikanischer Akten* (Bonn: Verlag Neue Gesellschaft 1985); Gerhard Wettig, 'Die sowjetischen Deutschland-Noten 1952', *Vierteljahreshefte für Zeitgeschichte*, vol. 3/1985, pp.547–57; Rolf Steininger, 'Eine Chance zur Wiedervereinigung? Die Stalin-Note vom 10. März 1952, *Darstellung und Dokumentation auf der Grundlage unveröffentlichter*

5 Congratulatory telegram (see note 1).

6 See V. Khvostov, 'Istoricheskoe znachenie Germanskoi Demokraticheskoi Respubliki', *Mezhdunarodnaia zhizn'*, 12/1966, pp.90–6; Iu. Kotov, 'GDR – vazhnyi faktor mira v Europe', *Mezhdunarodnaia zhizn'*, 3/1967, pp.70–6; V. Khostov, 'Mezhdunarodnoe znachenie GDR', *Mezhdunarodnaia zhizn'*, 7/1969, pp.11–17.

7 See Gerhard Wettig, *Community and Conflict in the Socialist Camp*, pp.64–70, 104–8; N. Edwina Moreton, *East Germany and the Warsaw Alliance. The Politics of Détente*, (Boulder/Colorado: Westview 1978), pp.115–22, 182–90.

8 For the recent Soviet–East German controversy see B.D.B., Soviet Forces in the GDR, Radio Free Europe Research, RAD Background Report/83, 21 August 1985, pp.1–3.

9 See 'Opasnye tendentsii', *Novoe vremia*, 6/1967, p.4: V. Kriukov, 'Germanskii vopros i sovremennost', *Mezhdunarodnaia zhizn'*, 2/1967, p.19. For Soviet attempts to encourage or push Bonn out of Nato, see Gerhard Wettig, *Community and Conflict in the Soviet Camp*, pp.20–47.

10 See Trond Gilberg, 'The Soviets and the Noncommunist Left', in: *Soviet Policy toward Western Europe*, ed. by Herbert J. Ellison, (Seattle-London: University of Washington Press 1983), pp.154–5.

11 For example, in the early 1980s, the Federal Republic's willingness to deploy or not to deploy American INF missiles was seen to be decisive (cf. V. Shaposhnikov, 'O nekotorykh problemakh sovremennogo dvizheniia', *Mirovaia ekonomika i mezhdunarodnye otnosheniia*, 12/1981, p.23).

12 Der Spiegel, 8 June 1981, p.119.

13 See Aleksei Arbatov, *Voenno-strategicheskii paritet i politika SShA* (Moscow: Izd. pol. lit). 1984. The author argues that 'parity obtains when the Americans and the Soviet Union confine themselves to their respective geostrategic spheres, i.e. to North America and Eurasia respectively. Any American capability in Europe is considered an illegitimate bid for 'superiority'. On the other hand, whatever measure of military power the Soviet Union may choose to have in Europe it cannot per se be viewed as a 'superior' force which constitutes a threat to the other side. The Soviet claim has been echoed by pro-Soviet 'peace forces' in West Germany (see statement by Gerhard Stuby in Norman Paech/Gerhard Study, eds., *Juristen gegen Kriegsgefahr in Europa* (Cologne: Presserverlag Theurer 1983, pp.122–3).

14 Vl. Kuznetsov, 'Mir i demokratiia', *Novoe vremia*, 13/1983, p.5.

15 See Stevens D. Symms and Edward D. Snow Jr, 'Soviet Propaganda and the Neutron Bomb Decision', in: *Political Communication and Persuasion*, vol. 1, no. 3 (1981), pp.257–68. For Moscow's assessment of the anti-ERW campaign see V. Nekrasov, 'Volia miroliubivoi obshchestvennosti', *Kommunist*, 6/1980, pp.108–9, 113.

16 The basic guidelines for the 'ideological struggle' to be waged in West European countries had been worked out by the International Department of the Central Committee Secretariat in the aftermath of the 1969 international communist conference: Mezhdunarodnoe kommunisticheskoe dvizhenie. Ocherk strategii i taktiki, pod obshchi redaktsiei V.V. Zagladina (Moscow: Izd. pol. lit. 1970). For details of the Soviet concept underlying the Soviet Union's involvement in the anti-deployment campaign see Gerhard Wettig, 'The West European Peace Movement in Moscow's Longer View', *Stragetic Review*, Spring 1984, pp.44–54.

47

17 One of those cases in which Soviet covert manipulation has indeed been crucial, is the 1980 initiative of the 'Krefeld Appeal' (cf. *inter alia* the documents in: *Beiträge zur Konfliktforschung*, 2/1981, pp.118–49, and in: Gottfried Linn, *Die Kampagne gegen die Nato-Nachrüstung. Zur Rolle der DKP*, Bonn: Hohwacht 1983; and the information contained in: Drucksache 9/466, 22 May 1981, Deutscher Bundestag, pp.1–2).

18 See Gerhard Wettig, 'Pitfalls of Journalistic Reporting on Arms Control', to be published in: *Aussenpolitik*. German Foreign Affairs Review, 2/1986. It is largely irrelevant that the CPSU International Department (which, to be sure, successfully suggested a number of anti-INF mass demonstrations at instances of Soviet liking) was never really in control of most West German peace protest groups. What matters instead, is Soviet expectation (which may have failed by a narrow margin only) that the protesters' resistence would eventually prevent American missile deployment in the Federal Republic.

19 Statement by Grigori Lokschin at the IIF symposium of 13/14 April 1985, *Wissenschaft und Frieden*, 1–2/1985, pp.18–29.

20 Interview with Aleksandr Bovin, in: *Berliner Zeitung*, 19 July 1984.

21 See the respective articles printed in translated version in: *East Berlin and Moscow: the Documentation of a Dispute*, compiled and introduced by Ronald D. Asmus, RFE Occasional Papers, Nr. 1, Radio Free Europe, Munich, 1985, pp.46–9, 53–4, 57–8.

22 The analysis of Soviet–East German relations is largely based on a detailed earlier study of the author's (see Gerhard Wettig, 'The Present Soviet View of Trends in Germany', in: *The Future of Soviet Policy Toward Western Europe*, R–3254–FF/Nato, Santa Monica/Cal.: The Rand Corporation, September 1985, pp. 66–97).

23 For details of the underlying inter-German agreement see interview by Federal Minister Heinrich Windelen in: *Informationen*, ed. by the Ministry for Intra-German Relations, 20/1985, p.18.

24 See texts of the draft agreement and the two-part communiqué in: *Neues Deutschland*, 20 June 1985.

25 Sicherheitspartnerschaft anerkennt Recht auf eigenen politischen Weg. Gemeinsame Erklärung von PVAP and SPD', *Vorwärts*, 30 November 1985.

4 The American view

WILLIAM E. GRIFFITH*

The basic change in American policy towards Germany, from punishment to cooperation, occurred in 1946–7, primarily as a result of two factors: a turn towards conservatism in the United States and the simultaneous replacement of the wartime alliance with the Soviet Union by rising hostility between Moscow and Washington. There has not yet been any basic change with respect to American policy towards East Germany, but this policy has evolved in the past three years, as the result of the American perception of limited foreign policy differences between Moscow and East Berlin and also in order to bring it more into accord with the policy of the Federal Republic.

American policy towards West Germany

Since 1949, when it was founded, the United States has increasingly been involved with the Federal Republic because of its rising strategic and economic importance and its essential role in Washington's continuing global competition with Moscow. What is more, the United States remains the principal guarantor of the freedom and security of West Berlin, a vital interest of the Federal Republic but one which Bonn, alone or even with its European allies, cannot defend. Moreover, it remains the view of the Federal Republic, as well as that of the other major European members of Nato, that West Germany itself cannot be defended except by the American nuclear guarantee and the massive ground troop presence of the United States in Europe and especially in the Federal Republic. By contrast, until the past three years, Washington saw its relations with East Berlin as relations with a satellite of Moscow. East Berlin usually took a harder line toward the United States, at least with respect to West Berlin, than Moscow itself did. In any case, Washington saw relations with East Germany as a vital interest of the Federal Republic and was therefore guided by Bonn's policy toward East Berlin, except on issues involving the American role in West Berlin.

49

Much has been written about German–American relations up to the end of the 1970s.[1] In addition, it has been conclusively demonstrated[2] that Stalin, not Truman, was primarily responsible for beginning the Cold War. Moreover, it is wrong to think that in the American perception the Cold War began about Germany. Rather, it began about Iranian Azerbaijan and Korea, and even before out of distrust about Soviet policy in Poland. However, by 1947 Washington perceived that Stalin was willingly allowing the wartime alliance to founder, primarily over the German question, where his maximum objectives, formulated during World War II, were the communization of all of Germany or at least of East Germany.[3] The first Berlin crisis and the Korean War ended four-power comity and control in Germany, and the resultant American initiatives were primarily responsible for the creation of the Federal Republic.

Germany was so defeated, exhausted, and war-weary, and Great Britain and France so weak, that in its three western zones the American policy of establishing a democratic, capitalist, federal West Germany prevailed. It did so all the more because Russian communism was, and still is, discredited in the minds of almost all Germans by historic enmity, economic and religious hostility, Nazi anti-Bolshevik propaganda, and the rape and pillage that the Red Army brought to Germany in its train, and because Konrad Adenauer dominated the first period of the Federal Republic.

Adenauer's policies were formed by his Carolingian heritage, his distaste for Prussia and its militarism, his conviction that Franco-German reconciliation must be a major aim of German foreign policy, and his cold, realistic view that German reunification was not in the cards because Moscow would only allow it if it were communist-controlled (and perhaps not even then.) The danger of German nationalism, he was convinced, could only be contained by submerging Germany in West European unity under Franco-German guidance, with West Germany becoming equal to France within this context. He was also convinced that West German security could only be preserved by the United States. With the exception of this last point, his ideas in 1945 were in large part influenced by those which he had developed in 1919–23.[4]

American anti-Germanism had been short-lived after 1918. American loans to the Weimar Republic were greater by far than those of any other country. The same phenomenon occurred rapidly after 1945, encouraged by the intensification of American anti-Soviet public sentiment and government policy. Adenauer's conviction that European unity was absolutely necessary agreed with the convictions not only of Monnet, Schuman, and de Gasperi, but also of their American friends and supporters, who dominated Washington's thinking in the 1950s. For them it seemed the only way to avoid another Franco-German war and also to avoid Germany becoming nationalist or neutralist and, even more, the only way to prevent Western Europe from falling under Soviet influence. (The American government, along with most Americans and West Europeans, initially thought the Korean War to be only a prelude to a Soviet attack on Western Europe.)

Thus Adenauer and Truman, Eisenhower, Acheson, and John Foster Dulles were natural ideological and Realpolitik allies. The higher the tension with the Soviet Union, the more firm their alliance became. A revealing example of this occurred in 1952, when Stalin offered Adenauer a united, neutral Germany with an army of 100,000. The Western powers, including the United States, opposed it. So did Adenauer, who was convinced that if he did not rapidly reject it he would lose what he had carefully cultivated, the confidence of the West. He was also convinced that Stalin was only trying to block the projected European Defence Community.

What Washington then, and later, did not fully understand was that Adenauer's support of Franco-German reconciliation and West European unity, like that of Monnet, Schuman, and de Gasperi, was not only a defense against the Soviet Union and a means to avoid another European war. His long-range objective was for a united Europe to achieve political equality with the United States and thus make Nato an alliance of two equals, rather than one dominated by the United States. Adenauer also knew that West Germany alone, given the distrust in which it was held in Western Europe, could only achieve this aim, as well as contain inevitably reviving German nationalism, within the framework of a European union. (When Chancellor Kohl declares that he is the 'grandson of Adenauer', he has this same policy in mind.)

Because this policy, both under Adenauer, and now under Kohl, fits into America's support of European unity, and because it would make Western Euorpe stronger *vis-à-vis* the Soviet Union, keep West Germany in Nato and the EC, and thus prevent it from going nationalist, neutral, or pro-Soviet, it is unlikely to be strongly or effectively resisted by the United States.

Meanwhile, for Washington the priority of the West German Social Democratic party (SPD) for German reunification over West German membership in Nato and the EEC rapidly overshadowed the fact that the SPD leader Kurt Schumacher, not Adenauer or the Western allies, had in West Berlin in 1946 first confronted the Soviets and foiled the Soviet-sponsored German communist attempt to merge with the SPD. Moreover, General Clay vetoed a nationalization of industry law in the SPD-ruled state of Hesse, thus further increasing distrust between the American government and the SPD. These years of American differences with the SPD make more understandable the later American concern about the SPD's Ostpolitik.

In the mid-1950s American relations with Adenauer worsened, although not decisively, as a result of his reaction to the 1955 Geneva summit meeting and declining American priority for German reunification as compared to the rising American priority for arms control negotiations with the Soviet Union. Adenauer feared that German reunification, and West Germany itself, would be subordinated in American policy to priority for arms control and other agreements with the Soviet Union. Such policies were contrary to West German interests and were made by Washington without adequate consultation and consideration of West European and specifically West German interests. Adenauer feared what he saw as the naivete of all but a very few Americans – Foster Dulles, Acheson, Clay, and McCloy. His nightmare was an American 'return to Potsdam', some form of four-power control reimposed on the Federal Republic, or at least a situation in which West Germany would not be equal in a European federation with the other European states. In sum, Adenauer feared what General de Gaulle feared: *le double hégémonie* over Europe by Moscow and Washington.

Adenauer's fears of Washington were greatly increased when Eisenhower gave way to John F. Kennedy. Because the Kennedy administration became committed to priority for detente with the Soviet Union over West German wishes, Kennedy saw Adenauer as an overly rigid relic of the Cold War. American policy most sharply diverged from Adenauer's when in 1961, during the second Berlin crisis, Kennedy proposed to the Soviet Union an 'International Access Authority' for Berlin, with equal Western, Soviet, and neutral participation. Adenauer used de Gaulle, with the latter's full knowledge, to veto any such concession, although in this case the Russians vetoed it as well. After his victory in the Cuban crisis, Kennedy intensified his detente policy, thus further increasing Adenauer's suspicions of him.

Even so, the dominant school in West German foreign policy remained 'Atlanticist'. This was strikingly demonstrated when Adenauer negotiated with de Gaulle a Franco-German treaty which seemed to the Atlanticists to tilt Bonn away from Washington toward Paris. The treaty was finally ratified by the Bundestag but with a pro-Nato preamble which in de Gaulle's view deprived it of its real content. This episode demonstrated that the West German need for an American security guarantee, plus the distrust of many Protestant and Social Democratic West Germans for Gaullist France, meant that American pressure to choose between Paris and Washington could sometimes aid the majority in Bonn to tilt toward the latter. Nevertheless, the treaty did eventually help to bring the Federal

Republic and France closer together, something which in principle and generally in practice the United States did not oppose.

Whether Washington should have, or still should, push Bonn to make such a choice, and whether it still could succeed in doing so, is another matter. Because Franco-American relations have improved after the departure of General de Gaulle from French politics, Washington now has much less reason to try to do so. Moreover, Bonn is stronger and more likely to resist any attempt to force it to make such a choice. Indeed, the United States has now neither the need nor the reason to try to do so, and it would fail if it tried. Fortunately it has not recently tried to do so.

Soon after these events Adenauer's advanced age so weakened his power position that he was forced to retire as chancellor. Distrust by many West German conservatives for such 'liberal' American leaders as Kennedy has continued until the present day. Adenauer's replacement, the politically ineffective Ludwig Erhard, gave priority to restoring close relations with Washington, and President Johnson did the same because the Berlin crisis had subsided after Kennedy's victory in the 1962 Cuban crisis. Adenauer and Strauss on the right and the SPD on the left opposed a primarily American (rather than French) orientation in Bonn's foreign policy.

In 1969 a great change occurred in Soviet–West German relations. On the one hand, the Russians felt that they had reconsolidated their hold over Eastern Europe, and the United States seemed tied down in an endless war in Vietnam. American policy in Vietnam was arousing major opposition not only in Western Europe but within the United States as well, so Moscow could afford detente with Bonn and a weakened Washington. Moreover, because the Russians feared that they might be on the brink of a war with China, they needed detente with the West European states. Washington under Johnson and Nixon wanted detente with the Soviet Union in order to achieve an honourable ending to the Vietnam War and because the Democratic party and much of the Republican party believed that arms control agreements with the Soviet Union should be given priority. In West Germany, although the replacement of the CDU in power by an SPD–FDP coalition had primarily domestic causes, it did mean that the SPD could put its own Ostpolitik into practice.

The SPD's Ostpolitik provided for detente first with the Soviet Union, then with Poland, and finally with East Germany, in order to preserve 'the substance of the German nation', as Willy Brandt, the new SPD chancellor, put it. Its aim was eventually to help bring about 'change through rapprochement' (*Wandel durch Annäherung*) within East Germany. The SPD favored this policy not only because it would, the party believed, bring detente and therefore a peace settlement in Europe and in Germany closer, but also because after the building of the Berlin Wall in 1961 reunification seemed impossible. Bonn should therefore help preserve an all-German sense of nationhood and bring about 'human improvements' (*menschliche Erleichterungen*) in East Germany.

For the United States, however, East Germany, unlike West Berlin, had low priority. The same was even more true for the other West European states, especially France, for whom Brandt's Ostpolitik smacked of nationalism and neutralism. Nixon's national security adviser, Henry Kissinger, initially had grave reservations about Brandt's Ostpolitik, which he feared would stabilize East Germany and destabilize West Germany. He had distrusted the SPD in the postwar period. However, he realistically did not try to stop the new policy.[5]

Brandt's treaties with Moscow and Eastern Europe were completed and ratified by 1973. Only two years later, Soviet and Cuban involvement in Angola began unravelling Soviet–American detente. This was accentuated by Russian involvement in Ethiopia in 1978. Detente collapsed when the Soviets invaded Afghanistan in December 1979. Angola occurred at a time when detente and Ostpolitik in Europe seemed to Brandt and his successor Schmidt to be successful. From the viewpoint not only of the SPD–FDP coalition, but increasingly from that of the majority of the CDU/CSU as well, it brought greatly increased travel from the Federal Republic and West Berlin to East Germany, increased West German trade with the East, and furthered detente in Europe, notably by the CSCE process. What it did not do was to decrease repression in East Germany.

But from the American view, detente had failed to restrain the Soviet Union's military buildup and expansion of influence in the third world. Many Americans came to feel that the Federal Republic, like the rest of Western Europe, wanted to remain an island of detente in a world in which the Soviet Union was becoming increasingly strong and expansionist. There was seen to be a danger that West Europeans would make unilateral concessions to the Soviet Union, thereby falling prey to 'self-Finlandization'.

All this was a part of what by 1987 seemed to be a sea-change in American domestic policy and, at least during the first Reagan administration, in foreign policy as well. Its causes were primarily domestic. Thirty years ago, two-thirds of Americans thought of themselves as liberal and only one-third as conservatives. By now the proportion is roughly the reverse.

This change had several causes: an increasing impatience with what conservatives saw as 'big government' and excesses of the welfare state, reverse discrimination, and bohemian moral behaviour; a major revival of Protestant fundamentalism, the fourth in American history; and a rise of nationalism which replaced both the turning inward and neo-isolationism

54

that had briefly dominated American foreign policy immediately after the loss of the Vietnam War, and also the internationalism which had characterized the American east coast establishment and most of the political class since World War I. This resulted in priority for containing Soviet expansion in the third world and for an American defence build-up.[6]

By the end of the first Reagan administration two other trends had recurred. The first was a shift of economic and political power within the United States away from the traditionally pro-European northeast toward the 'sunbelt', and an increasing interest in, and economic ties and competition with, the rapidly developing Pacific rim states: Japan, South Korea, Taiwan, Hong Kong, and Singapore. The second was an increasing congressional concern that American defence expenditures in Europe were too high and that the Europeans (and the Japanese) should assume more of the common defence burden, thereby allowing some American troops to be withdrawn from Europe. This trend was by 1987 far from dominant, but increasing public and congressional, as well as West European, pressure to cut the massive American deficit will probably make the issue of defence cuts in general and American troop strength in Europe, and especially in the Federal Republic, more important in the future.

In West Germany public opinion was also changing, but not entirely in the same direction. As elsewhere in Western Europe (with the exception of Spain) it had moved toward conservatism. But conservative in West Germany is something quite different from conservative in the United States. It does not involve anything like Reagan's cutting back on the welfare state or the abandonment of detente or Ostpolitik. On the contrary, Kohl has intensified the SPD's Ostpolitik and scored significant successes thereby, notably with East Germany. He has been aided by the increasing perception in West Germany, much greater than in the United States, that East Germany and Hungary have recently shown significant, albeit limited, differences in foreign policy with the Soviet Union.

Moreover, although German reunification is seen in both German states as not in the cards for the foreseeable future, a common sense of, and pride in, German identity has revived in both.[7] In addition, the image of the United States has been significantly, albeit not decisively, tarnished in West Germany, and to a lesser extent in East Germany as well, by the Vietnam War, crime, drugs, and President Reagan's initial policies concerning the Soviet Union, which many Germans thought too confrontational. In Europe the improved American image as a result of the 1985 Geneva summit meeting was at least temporarily tarnished by the American air attack on Libya, American's refusal to sign the 1986 Bern CSCE communiqué, and its announcement of non-compliance with the SALT II treaty.

The CDU/CSU's Ostpolitik did not create the kind of American distrust which the SPD's Ostpolitik did, because CDU/CSU and Republican ideologies and policies were otherwise similar, and because Kohl seemed to be reviving the West German economy and improving relations with France, the United States, and even with East Germany. The improvement of relations between Bonn and Washington also resulted from the good personal relations between Kohl and Reagan, in contrast to the personal distrust between Carter and Schmidt (one more example of the importance of personalities in international relations). One might have thought that the Democrat Carter and the Social Democrat Schmidt would have got along very well, as Kennedy and Brandt had. But the contrary was the case, because Schmidt made no secret of his contempt for Carter, and because Carter vacillated long not only on the neutron bomb issue but more generally between Secretary of State Cyrus Vance's priority for arms control agreements with the Soviet Union and his national security adviser Zbigniew Brzezinski's increasing disillusionment with detente and concern about the Soviet military buildup and what he saw as dangerous Soviet expansionism in the third world. Carter came down on Brzezinski's side immediately after, and as a result of, the December 1979 Soviet invasion of Afghanistan, and Vance resigned shortly thereafter; developments which further increased Schmidt's distrust of American policy and Carter's irritation with Schmidt.[8]

Thus in the final phase of the Carter administration and during the first Reagan administration, the American and West German roles were reversed: Washington became more hostile to the Soviet Union than Kennedy had been, and Schmidt, and later, and to a lesser extent, Kohl became less so than Adenauer had been.

In 1977 Schmidt had first proposed deployment of new intermediate-range American missiles in Europe to counter the build-up of Soviet SS–20 missiles. After initial scepticism Carter had embraced his argument. By 1979, however, under increasing pressure from within the SPD, Schmidt insisted that simultaneously the United States must negotiate with the Soviet Union to end all INF deployment, Western or Soviet, in Europe. The Schmidt government fell, because the FDP withdrew from it, primarily on domestic economic issues. But it was unlikely that he could have maintained SPD support for INF deployment and therefore would have fallen on that issue eventually. After he fell the SPD turned against INF deployment so strongly that only sixteen congress delegates (including Schmidt himself) voted against an anti-INF party congress resolution.

Thus for the first time since 1960, when the SPD, under Herbert Wehner's influence, had for electoral reasons abandoned its opposition to Nato, the EEC, and American nuclear weapons on the soil of the Federal

Republic, the SPD again turned against American and Nato foreign policies. Although it did not challenge Bonn's membership in Nato and the European Community (EC), in other respects its challenge to Nato and American foreign policy was even greater.

Historically anti-militarism has always been strong in the SPD. It had become firmly committed to detente with the Soviet Union, especially in Europe; it was proud of its Ostpolitik successes; and it was strongly opposed to what it saw as Reagan's dangerously confrontational policy *vis-à-vis* the Soviet Union. These policy changes were the result of a major, new phenomenon in West German political sociology: the rise of a new left wing in the SPD, composed of educated, radical young professionals who had begun the 'long march through the institutions' after the New Left failed in the 1960s and who staffed the West German peace movement. They advocated the 'Europeanization of Europe', a policy adopted by the SPD leadership after Schmidt's fall. This policy proposed that Western and Eastern Europe should both remain within their respective alliances but that each should strive for more autonomy from its own superpower and that both should form a 'security partnership' in Europe to deepen detente there.

The policy in fact was more critical of American than of Soviet foreign policy, although favorable to neither. It was strongly opposed to INF (and SDI) deployment. By 1986 it had led to the establishment of working groups between the SPD and the CPSU and the East European ruling communist parties. The SPD leadership argued that the necessary absolute priority for peace and arms control required that, since Kohl would not, they must themselves pursue what they called 'the second phase of Ostpolitik', which featured party-to-party contacts with the SED and the Soviet and other East European communist parties. The purpose was to draw up, in advance of the SPD returning to power and in the hope of influencing the Bonn government's policies, a series of agreements on such issues as nuclear and chemical weapons-free zones.

There were signs that some of the proponents of this policy were reviving the traditional German disdain for mass culture in general and American mass culture in particular. In addition, some of them, realizing the irresistibility of the revolution of high technology, advocated coping with it in such a way that Europe would not fall under the technological domination of the United States and Japan, and that high technology would not so negatively effect social groups disadvantaged by it. The SPD would appeal to the new technocrats of high technology (the 'yuppies') it produced. The Greens went even farther than the SPD left in their ecological, pacifist, and neutralist opposition to current American foreign policy, but they did not share the latter's interest in cultivating the new technocrats.[9]

Once INF deployment occurred, the West German peace movement rapidly declined. By 1986 Reagan's SDI project was strongly opposed by the SPD, and the FDP was far from enthusiastic. However, in early 1986 an agreement was concluded between Bonn and Washington for German firms' participation in SDI. The SPD's nomination as its chancellor-candidate of Johannes Rau, the recently victorious Minister–President of the largest West German state, Rhineland-Westphalia, who was strongly pro-Nato and opposed much less of American foreign policy,[10] seemed likely to moderate the SPD's opposition to Nato policies, at least until after the January 1987 Bundestag elections.

The narrow victory of the CDU (and FDP) in the mid-June 1986 state elections in Lower Saxony and the quashing of charges against Kohl with respect to illegal party funding made observers see his chances of reelection in January 1987 seem fairly promising. However, even though Rau tried to modify it, the party's opposition to so much of current American foreign policy is potentially damaging to German-American relations. It was hardly surprising that this opposition was viewed unfavourably in Washington, and even more so in Paris.

American policy towards East Germany

The recent improvement of American relations with East Germany was the result, on the American side, of the perception, as had previously been the case with Yugoslavia, Romania, and Hungary, that there were significant differences between Soviet and East German foreign policy, centring on East German relations with West Germany. In the case of East Germany, however, there was an additional reason: the traditional American desire to have a policy with East Germany parallel to the Federal Republic's. Since this subject has been analyzed in detail elsewhere,[11] it need only be summarized briefly here.

Since at least 1980 a debate among experts has been going on in Moscow and in East Berlin about the proper policy to follow toward West Germany, with some experts in both capitals being for a more hostile policy and others for a less hostile one. In late 1983, despite strong SPD opposition, the West German Bundestag voted for INF deployment, which then began. Moscow, which had all along been trying to use the INF issue to split Bonn from Washington, not only broke off the INF Geneva negotiations but also tried to get its East European allies to limit their political and economic relations with West Germany. East Germany and Hungary resisted this, primarily because they wanted to continue to import technology and get credits from West Germany in order to remain competitive in exports to hard currency countries and thereby maintain their consumerist policies. Erich Honecker, the East German leader, who had in the 1970s followed strongly anti-Washington and anti-Bonn policies, immediately after INF deployment declared that he did not 'enjoy' Soviet counter-INF deployment and that both East and West Germany have a 'community of responsibility' to prevent war ever again breaking out on German soil. Articles written in Hungary, some reprinted in East Germany, implicitly criticized excessive Soviet pressure while reasserting Hungary's intention to remain firmly within the Warsaw Pact and CMEA (the Soviet-dominated trading block).

After he had received massive West German credits and had increased emigration and travel to West Germany in return, in September 1984 Soviet pressure forced Honecker to 'postpone' his scheduled visit to Bonn. But thereafter his economic relations with West Germany did not suffer and political ones suffered only briefly. The debate was still continuing in Moscow at the end of 1985 and Hungary resumed its criticism of excessive Soviet domination. As of the beginning of 1986 Gorbachev had reinforced economic solidarity within CMEA, over considerable East German and Hungarian opposition, but he was still allowing the debate to continue. However, it seemed that he would not allow Honecker to make his 'postponed' visit to West Germany in 1986.

In January 1984 the then Assistant Secretary of State for European Affairs, Richard Burt, visited East Berlin, Budapest, and Sofia. This visit was indicative of an improvement in relations between Washington and East Berlin. Progress was slow, for issues of claims and Jewish reparations were (and are) still pending. Nevertheless, the climate between Washington and East Berlin improved significantly. The major significance of these developments, however, was in their effect on America's relations with West Germany, and even more on West German policy toward East Germany.

The Soviet–American–West German–East German quadrangle

These developments in Soviet–East German (and Soviet–Hungarian) relations, which were widely covered in the West German media but very little in the American media, took place in an atmosphere of a consensus in the Federal Republic about Ostpolitik, but one in which the SPD and the CDU/CSU differed strongly about what the latter called the SPD's 'alternative foreign policy'. In the United States, by contrast, public opinion polls showed by 1984 that a substantial majority of Americans gave priority to arms control negotiations, while retaining their strong distrust of the Soviet Union. The pressure for reducing the federal deficit plus declining public support for massive defence increases had led to zero real growth in 1985–6 American defence expenditures.

On the other hand, there were some continuing defence and security issues on which Washington and Bonn would continue to have to work. Potentially the most important was the possible effect of American efforts to cut their budget deficit, notably through the Gramm–Rudman act, on the level of American troop presence in Europe, and especially in the Federal Republic. In early 1986 it was impossible to foresee clearly the prospects in this respect, but one had to wonder whether American budget cuts could leave the American troop presence in Europe intact.

By early 1986 conservative Germans were expressing concern lest the United States accept a 'zero–zero' INF compromise with the Soviet Union, leaving Europe defenceless against Soviet conventional superiority. It seemed that one of the principal bones of INF contention with Moscow would be the latter's demand that the British and French nuclear forces be frozen and the United States be forbidden to transfer nuclear weapons to them (e.g., the Trident weapons system to Great Britain.) President Reagan declared that he would not accept this demand, but Gorbachev seemed likely to continue to use it to try to split the United States from Great Britain and France and both of these countries from Germany. However, the closeness of Franco-German relations made this latter outcome unlikely.

Conclusion

On balance prospects for American–West German relations look optimistic, for both countries are recovering economically, personal relations between Reagan and Kohl are good, and the issues between the two seem susceptible to compromise. Indeed, they are primarily economic rather than political or strategic, and insofar as the American federal deficit is reduced and the price of oil remains low or goes lower, with favourable economic results world-wide, compromise should be easier.

It also seems likely that American relations with East Germany will continue gradually to improve. Also Gorbachev's apparent interest in activating Soviet policy in Western Europe, which should probably help improve Soviet–West German relations, can hardly be carried out if the Soviet Union continues to crack down on East Berlin and Budapest.

Contrary to fears in Moscow, Paris, and some American nongovernmental circles, West Germany is going neither nationalist nor neutralist, and neither is East Germany. Each hopes to acquire more influence within its own alliance and thereby more autonomy from its own superpower, but neither intends to leave its alliance. Bonn has much better chances of achieving this than has East Berlin. Each fully realizes that only by remaining in its own alliance can it hope to get more autonomy while retaining security.

However, the differences between West and East Germany, and between American relations with both, remain more important than the similarities. West Germany knows that it can only gain more influence within a united Western Europe. Polls showed that the majority of its citizens remained pro-American and pro-Nato. The revolution in high technology, *the* major development of our times, is moving economic, and therefore political power in West Germany from north to south, just as it has been moving in the United States from east to southwest. As in the United States the German south is conservative, and it is also pro-French and pro-American.

There remain the issues of German reunification and West German Ostpolitik, about which there are likely to continue to be differences, at least in emphasis, between Washington and Bonn, and far more between Washington and East Berlin. It is often said that there is no country other than the Federal Republic which really wants the reunification of Germany, since this would mean either that Germany would once again dominate Europe or that it would be neutralized and then fall under Soviet hegemony.

There is one other country, the United States, which has little to lose and much to gain from the reunification of Germany, insofar as it were to occur within the broader context of the reunification of Europe and not as a result of some West German, or even all-German, initiative opposed by the other European states. Why is this so? In the first place, the Soviet Union has become, and is likely to remain, so strong, while Germany – even a reunited Germany – would remain relatively so weak and so bound by European unity that it would not dominate Europe. Secondly, the reunification of Germany would inevitably change the balance of power in Europe to the disadvantage of the Soviet Union and to the advantage of the United States.

But these are essentially theoretical arguments. There is no serious possibility of them becoming part of international politics in the foreseeable future. The Soviet leadership never, not even in 1952, intended to allow the reunification of Germany; there is no sign that it will do so in the future; and in the nuclear age it cannot be forced to do so. The division of Germany remains one of Moscow's greatest gains from World War II, because it means the permanent diminution of German power in Europe and the world.

This should not, and does not, mean that the United States has any reason to abandon its post-1945 advocacy of the reunification of Germany, within the context of the reunification of Europe. To do so would strike at the foundations of the Washington–Bonn alliance and of Bonn's integration into Nato. After all, the French government, which is in reality anything but enthusiastic about it, advocates the reunification of

Germany, because it realizes that it cannot otherwise maintain Franco–German reconciliation and thereby help to prevent the rise of German nationalism and neutralism. What interest can the United States have to do otherwise? The pull of common history and cultures, of common security interests, and of decades of alliance and close personal associations are very likely to insure the maintenance of the close alliance between Washington and Bonn – a consummation devoutly to be wished.

Notes

*The views presented in this paper are the author's own. They should not be attributed to the American Government or to the American Embassy in Bonn, where he was from September 1985 until January 1987 Minister–Counselor for Cultural Affairs, on leave from the Massachusetts Institute of Technology, where he is Ford Professor of Political Science.

1 Roger Morgan, *The United States and West Germany 1945–1973* (London: Oxford, 1974) and Hans W. Gatzke, *Germany and the United States. A 'Special Relationship'?* (Cambridge, Mass: Harvard, 1980). For historical background, see Manfred Jonas, *The United States and Germany. A Diplomatic History* (Ithaca, New York: Cornell, 1984). For Soviet policy toward West Germany, see Harry Gelman, ed., *The Future of Soviet Policy toward Western Europe* (Santa Monica, Cal. RAND R–3254–FF/Nato, Sept. 1985), especially the chapters by John Van Oudenaren and Gerhard Wettig; and Roland Smith, *Soviet Policy Towards West Germany*, IISS Adelphi Paper no. 203, Winter 1985.

2 Vojtech Mastny, *Russia Enters the Cold War* (New York: Columbia, 1979.)

3 Alexander Fischer, *Sowjetische Deutschlandpolitik im Zweiten Weltkrieg 1941–45* (Stuttgart: Deutsche Verlagsanstalt, 1976.)

4 William E. Griffith, *The Ostpolitik of the Federal Republic of Germany* (Cambridge, Mass: MIT, 1978). Two recent works, Henning Köhler, *Adenauer und die Rheinische Republik* (Opladen: Westdeutscher Verlag, 1986) and Rolf Steininger, *Eine vertane Chance. Die Stalin-Note vom 10.März 1952 und die Wiedervereinigung* (Bonn: Dietz, 1985), seem to me largely polemical in nature and do not change my conclusions. A new history of Ostpolitik has just been published by one of its ideological authors: Peter Bender, *Neue Ostpolitik. Vom Mauerbau bis zum Moskauer Vertrag* (Munich: dtv, 1986.)

5 Henry Kissinger, *White House Years* (Boston: Little Brown, 1979) and *Years of Upheaval* (Boston: Little Brown, 1982.)

6 Daniel Yankelovich amd John Doble, 'The Public Mood: Nuclear Weapons and the USSR', *Foreign Affairs*, Fall 1984 and the various studies on the same subject by the Chicago Council on Foreign Relations. See also Thomas L. Hughes, 'The Twilight of Internationalism', *Foreign Policy*, Winter 1985–6.

7 Richard Löwenthal, 'The German Question Transformed', and Walther Leisler Kiep, 'The New Deutschlandpolitik', *Foreign Affairs*, Winter 1984–5.

8 Zbigniew Brzezinski, *Power and Principle* (New York: Farrar Straus and Giroux, 1982) and Cyrus Vance, *Hard Choices: Four Critical Years in Managing American Foreign Policy* (New York: Simon and Schuster, 1983.)

9 Peter Bender, *Das Ende des ideologischen Zeitalters* (Berlin: Severin and Siedler, 1981); Peter Glotz, *Manifest für eine neue europäische Linke* (Berlin: Siedler, 1985); Heidemarie Wieczorek-Zeul, 'Prozess der Integration nur in Reformschritten', *Vorwärts*, July 20, 1985; Horst Ehmke, 'Überlegungen zur Selbstbehauptung Europas. Ein Diskussionspapier', *Politik Aktuelle. Informationen der SPD*, no. 1, Jan. 1984, modified and adopted by the SPD as 'Konzept für die Selbstbehauptung Europas', 11 Apr., 1985. For analysis, see Erich Hauser, 'Die Entdeckung Europas durch die SPD', *Frankfurter Rundschau*. I am also much indebted to an unpublished paper by Prof. Lily Gardner Feldman of Tufts University. For a recent critical American study of the intellectual origins of the peace move-

ment and peace research, see Jeffrey Herf, 'War, Peace, and the Intellectuals: The West German Peace Movement', *International Security*, Spring 1986.

10 See the speech by Rau at Aalen, 16 Dec., 1985 in *SPD Intern*, no. 17, 17 Dec., 1985.
11 Ronald D. Asmus, 'The Dialectics of Detente and Discord: The Moscow–East Berlin–Bonn Triangle', *Orbis*, Winter 1985; William E. Griffith, 'Super-Power Problems in Europe: A Comparative Assessment', ibid., Winter 1986.

5   The French view

RENATA FRITSCH-BOURNAZEL

A poll sponsored by the French weekly *Figaro Magazine* in 1983[1] showed that 48 per cent of French people over the age of eighteen considered West Germany to be France's best ally; Belgium was in second place, followed by the United States. Germans, responding to the same question, placed the United States first (77 per cent) but 53 per cent cited France followed by Britain. What has been called 'Das Bündnis im Bündnis',[2] or the alliance within the alliance, has, during the past two decades, become a cornerstone of foreign policy for both governments. There are, however, many complex obstacles, real or imagined, to the Franco-German relationship. According to Brigitte Sauzay of the French Foreign Ministry, who regularly interprets for M. Mitterrand and M. Kohl, the relationship between France and West Germany is nothing more than a *mariage de raison*, or a marriage of convenience, which still has not been consummated.[3]

To be sure, Paris and Bonn actively press for the development of their alliance. Their common interest is to create a European voice that can be heard and to subordinate bilateral differences to that idea, although their approach to the most important foreign policy issues is far from identical. France and West Germany do not share the same outlook regarding East–West relations, as Bonn remains more open than Paris to the expansion of ties with East Germany, Eastern Europe and the Soviet Union. In the security field, France is still driven by a deep and highly popular commitment to national independence, whereas West Germany assures her defence through her membership in the Western Alliance. Yet, despite the disappointments and shortcomings that come from occasional clashes of interest, French and West German political leaders see no realistic alternative to upholding the Paris–Bonn axis as the most dynamic element of the European Community.

With no other country did France attempt to achieve such a close relationship, although for a time during the Fourth Republic it appeared that Britain rather than Germany was France's most favoured ally. Perhaps the greatest achievement of the diplomacy of France and Germany in the postwar period was to overcome the age-old hatred between two countries that had, as the French never tired of repeating, provoked three major wars between them in less than a hundred years. The initiative for this reconciliation had to come from the French, and in the period of the occupation of Germany and the early years of the Bonn Republic, the French did in fact create bonds that were not merely economic and political but also personal.

By the mid-1950s bonds of understanding that had been created on an individual level had begun at least to dilute the venom left by the German occupation of France. At the same time, an institutional framework had been created in which the French and Germans could work together. Yet it would be unrealistic to think that, even after the reconciliation of the 1950s, some residue of distrust did not remain, especially at times where there seemed any possibility of West Germany disengaging herself from her Western ties should the prospects for reunification dramatically improve.

Even though Germany has been divided now for more than forty years, the 'German question' remains at the heart of East–West relations in Europe. Renewed interest in the long-term future of France's closest ally has been sparked in recent years by intensified political and economic activity between the Federal Republic of Germany and the German Democratic Republic. Although there is no imminent solution to either the division of Europe or of Germany, the fact of Germany's division is an important consideration for French policy.

Yalta and Potsdam revisited

The fortieth anniversary of Yalta stimulated a variety of commentaries on French attitudes toward the current division of Europe. On the one hand, once any Soviet–American negotiations begin, commentators are quick to invoke the shadow of a 'new Yalta'. On the other, although diplomats refer almost automatically to the Potsdam agreements whenever the German problem is discussed, such references evoke nothing like the same emotional response. Indeed, the vast majority of Frenchmen would be hard put to say who was at the Potsdam conference in 1945 and what was decided there.

Perhaps the most unfortunate and flagrant insult to de Gaulle's pride was the refusal of Roosevelt and Stalin to invite him to the Yalta conference in February 1945, where only Churchill's strong advocacy won for France the right to a zone of occupation in Germany and thus a future position of equality in the diplomatic negotiations on Germany. Even more surprising, given the fact of French participation in the occupation of Germany, was

President Truman's assumption that the French ought not to be invited to the Potsdam conference in July. It was hardly surprising that de Gaulle should have threatened after Potsdam to block the implementation in Germany of any decisions with which he did not agree.

At that time, the principal aim of French diplomacy was to avoid the repetition of what had happened after Versailles. In a famous memorandum of November 1918, Marshal Foch had declared that if the Rhine were not made into the western military frontier of the German people, Germany would still have every opportunity of repeating the events of 1914, by invading Belgium, Luxembourg and France, and by reaching the North Sea and threatening England. The British and Americans had refused to listen to him, and his prediction had come true. De Gaulle was determined to act in such a way that, on this occasion, the Rhineland would be detached from the German state and permanently occupied by French troops. In addition, firm in the belief that the Prussian or Nazi warlords could never have implemented their sinister plans without the wealth of the Ruhr, he advocated the internationalization of that region.

In the summer of 1945, however, it was obvious that the Big Three were no longer inclined to dismember Germany. They had already renounced the idea of 'pastoralizing' and 'de-industrializing' the country, to which Roosevelt and Churchill had agreed at Quebec in November 1944 on the basis of the Morgenthau Plan. Instead, the process which was soon to lead the victors to court the vanquished, and to seek their support – first political, then economic, and finally military – had already begun.

While official policy on Germany as pursued by the Fourth Republic initially considered concrete guarantees the only means of 'preventing Germany once and for all from regaining its potential for attack',[4] there were those who warned against repeating the 'mistakes of the Versailles Treaty'. A remarkable memorandum by the Etat-major général de la Défense nationale stated as early as July 1945 that in view of her military and economic weakness France must pursue foreign policy as *l'art du possible* and not make exaggerated demands. Above all, she was co-responsible for her neighbour's destiny and German readiness to accept 'new ideas of peace' from the West following the collapse of National Socialism. A rigid security concept comparable to that of Marshal Foch was a virtual invitation to break loose from the whole system. Instead of depriving the Germans of all hope, ways must be opened to enable them to develop freely, just as France 'must be constantly present to encourage this development'.[5]

Certain principles contained in this memorandum call to mind the idealistic aspirations of the Resistance leaders towards a reconciliation with Germany in the framework of a European political entity dedicated to democracy and social justice. Changing the Germans by means of rapprochement and the promise of equal treatment in future were two important steps towards a policy concept aimed at guaranteeing France's security with, rather than from, Germany. Four months after returning from Dachau, Joseph Rovan coined the term '*l'Allemagne de nos mérites*', or 'the Germany we deserve'.[6] His views centred on two basic principles: the awareness of a shared responsibility for the prospects of democracy in Germany and the conviction that both nations could only jointly master their destiny in the postwar world.

At the official level the reconciliation concept was not able to prevail until the new circumstances created by the Cold War and internal economic constraints forced French diplomacy to accept Anglo-American plans to proceed with the orderly reconstruction of the German economy. Moreover, particularly in 1947–8, the French perceived the contradiction between, on the one hand, their negative policy in relations with France's Western allies and, on the other, their developing fear of an internal Communist take-over and of the relentless expansion of Eastern European communism westward. The main immediate threat was no longer perceived as German, but as Russian. Spelt out in practical terms, that meant a radical reorientation of French policy towards Germany. If it were no longer possible or even desirable to dismember Germany into smaller state units or to ensure international tutelage of her economy, then it became imperative to secure a normalization of relations with Germany at the same time as channelling her daunting potential towards peaceful and cooperative enterprises.

In January 1948, when the gap between the Soviet and Western zones was growing wider every day, the political adviser to the French military government in Berlin defined the change in objectives as follows:

The Germany we envisage must be a peacetime Germany . . . Instead of being a plaything in the hands of other powers, she must feel that her own interests and future have been taken into account. What we can offer the Germans in the present situation is effective and active participation in the reconstruction of a Europe we envisage as a structured and harmonious formation.[7]

Two and a half years later this vision of the future was to become reality. The proposal launched by the French Foreign Minister, Robert Schuman, on 9 May 1950 was based on the idea that France could only go on controlling German power if France herself accepted being controlled. The main advantage of reciprocal control was the future birth of a new political unit that would make the notion of control obsolete.

This policy underwent a decisive slowdown a few weeks after having been launched. The Korean War engendered new fears in Europe, and above all led the United States to insist on German participation in European defence. A mere five years after the end of World War II, this prospect was likely to, and did, arouse the worst fears of German militarism in Western Europe and above all in France. That is why Jean Monnet, probably the most imaginative expert of the Fourth Republic, transposed his integrationist model of the 'Schuman plan' to fit the requirements of a European Defence Community for which a treaty was duly signed in May 1952. But the prospect of a European army which would bring French and German soldiers side-by-side, had a profoundly divisive effect on French public opinion and eventually contributed significantly to the demise of European unification as an attainable goal.

The psychologically premature formula of the European army had not been devised to gain time, but to transform a bad thing, German rearmament, into a good one – a further step on the road to a united Europe – while at the same time removing all freedom of action from the reconstituted German forces. To use a phrase much in vogue in those days, it was in essence a matter of 'arming the Germans without arming Germany'. The rejection of the European Defence Community (EDC) treaty by the French National Assembly on 30 August 1954, did not prevent German rearmament within the twin framework of a Western European Union (which was legally binding but without real political importance) and the Atlantic Treaty (based on an alliance without any strict military obligations). The latter took away by its organization all genuine autonomy from German military power for the benefit of a supreme command directly subordinated to the President of the United States.

The Cold War virtually destroyed all that remained of the Potsdam agreements, leading to the rearmament of the Federal Republic, rapidly followed by that of the GDR. Indeed, if there are any perfectly clear and categorical clauses in the 1945 agreements, they are those which provide, with no time limit, for 'the complete disarmament and demilitarization of Germany and the elimination or control of all Germany industry that could be used for military production', and which state that 'all German land, naval and air forces . . . shall be completely and finally abolished'. France has shown herself the least eager of all the Western Powers to accept German rearmament, although her motives in the matter stem less, perhaps, from loyalty to texts for which she was not responsible than from fear for the future.

She was not very keen to see the defeated enemy of yesterday become the major continental power once more, due to the exigencies of the Cold War and America's need for men and wealth to sustain it. 'There is not only a problem of containing Russia', Robert Schuman was fond of saying, 'there is also a problem of containing Germany'. This was the reason why he wished to induce the Federal Republic to merge into a greater European unity, where her dynamics would be employed exclusively upon peaceful works.

Nevertheless, in spite, or perhaps because, of the depth of the alienation between the two countries, imaginative efforts were undertaken to bridge the gap. De Gaulle himself, as early as 1955, only one year after having rejected the European Defence Community, proclaimed the necessity of a reconciliation of the two peoples on both sides of the Rhine: 'Whatever we may feel and no matter how hard it may be, from now on France and Germany are bound to walk hand in hand, like one alexandrine with the other'.[8] The common effort of creating the EEC and Euratom in 1957 enabled them to cooperate in the formation of organizations in which their national sovereignty would be abrogated to some degree but in which the presence of other members would calm the tensions that might arise from a completely bilateral agreement.

Remnants of inequality in the Franco-German partnership

Satisfied though one may be with what has been accomplished, as shown by the amazing newspaper headline 'France–Allemagne über alles'[9] in connection with the twentieth anniversary of the Elysée Treaty (on 20 January 1983), even today a certain asymmetry characterizes the Franco-German tandem. As a former occupying power, France stands in a special relationship of a quite specific nature to the Federal Republic. The close involvement of the two superpowers in European affairs, to be sure, has modified the Franco-German relationship as much as the defeat of Hitler, but the maintenance of Allied rights and responsibilities has perpetuated France's special status as one of the four major powers 'more equal than the others'. The four-power role has been, throughout the period since World War II, one of the instruments of French foreign policy, for the preservation of the country's influence abroad.

The disappearance of the occupation regime has decisively changed the pattern of relations between Germany and the two predominant powers of Western Europe, France and Great Britain, but the latter still enjoy the vestiges of the superior status they obtained in 1945. Four-power control over Berlin, even though it has ceased to exist de facto, is the most tangible manifestation of France's legal position as a victor in World War II, a position for which General de Gaulle had struggled so hard.

'The real sovereignty of Berlin was awarded to the victors of World War II',[10] de Gaulle once stressed in a revealing talk with the American journal-

69

ist Sulzberger. Ten years after de Gaulle's departure from power, President Giscard d'Estaing's visit to the former capital of the Reich made clear that the French position with regard to the Berlin question had not fundamentally altered. Unlike British and American heads of state whose visits to West Berlin have always been arranged as part of a state visit to the Federal Republic, the French President chose to fly directly to Berlin from his own country. This sharp reminder of France's status as an occupying power was best summarized in the President's speech at the Berlin State Library: 'Our rights represent your freedom. Our rights represent your security.'[11] Forty years after the end of World War II, President Mitterrand decided, however, to take into account the West German bid for more equality in the Franco-German relationship. On 10 October 1985 in a symbolic gesture, Chancellor Kohl was invited to join President Mitterrand during a stopover at the Bonn–Cologne airport and, for the first time, a French and a West German statesman arrived in Berlin simultaneously.

The French attitude to the present and future role of Berlin is clearly influenced by the double concern of holding on to the legal responsibilities secured in Berlin and of resisting moves by another power that might dilute France's privileged right to participate as one of the Big Four in any decision about the German question. In the 1950s and the 1960s the Soviet Union tended to view Berlin as a convenient lever for pressure against the West. In the 1980s, the deliberate raising of tensions in Berlin has become counterproductive to Soviet efforts in other areas which the Soviet Union considers more important. The Four-Power Agreement of September 1971 has brought fifteen years of relative stability, but it is still in the Berlin context that Soviet leverage for influence in and over the Federal Republic is rooted, as well as the Soviet claim to equality with the United States in Europe. For the Fifth Republic, the Berlin Agreement presented an opportunity to secure France's war-won rights and responsibilities on a more solid foundation and to maintain her claim to preserve a valuable *droit de regard* in relation to any future development of the German question.

Moreover, in another respect, France (and Great Britain as well) has considerable advantages over the Federal Republic. France survived World War II as a great power with freedom of action more or less unlimited by international obligations. In the community of nations she finds understanding for the fact that she reserves nuclear armament for herself, a status symbol and form of insurance against unpredictable international change. West Germany has rearmed, but, barred from possessing nuclear weapons, it depends entirely for its security on the American deterrent. Most discriminations have been lifted but the main one remains, namely the ban on nuclear weapons.

'Germany is a frying pan on a stove whose controls are in the hands of others', to paraphrase Stanley Hoffmann's evaluation of Europe's strategic position.[12] The dilemma imposed on the Federal Republic by geography and by the partition of the continent – having the largest stake in the maintenance of an effective nuclear deterrent in Europe, yet fearing most the application of that deterrent – has affected West German views on American discussions of limited nuclear options and nuclear war fighting. The recent debate on Nato's INF program was but the latest manifestation of the permanent German fear of becoming a battlefield once again. On the other hand France's relative immunity from the anti-nuclear protest movement of the early 1980s goes beyond the fact that Nato's medium-ranged missiles were never intended for French soil. It stems from the commonly held belief that France's autonomous deterrent makes the national territory a 'sanctuary'.[13]

In the 1960s, the Federal Republic resented Gaullist France's decision to leave Nato and to pursue a strategy that treated West Germany mainly as a 'glacis' for French protection on which French nuclear artillery would fall, but not as a partner in forward defence. Today one could argue that the decision of 1966 is one of the reasons why France appears liberated from a certain number of complexes and fears concerning her security. Being outside the military structures of Nato, France had to feel responsible for her own security, whereas countries that must rely on others for their own security may have greater difficulties preserving a national military responsibility or identity. The confidence, which reigns throughout the *hexagon* with regard to its nuclear deterrent, may seem naive, foolishly chauvinistic, or simply reckless. It may provoke irritating reactions in Europe and in the the United States, but no one can deny that this confidence exists, or refuse to take it into consideration.

France is not a model for other Nato countries. Either they are too weak or – in the case of West Germany – the political costs of a quest for autonomy are too high, both at home and abroad. Yet, some French observers tend to believe that the nuclear issue might very well become the German problem of the 1980s. According to Gabriel Robin, diplomatic adviser to President Pompidou and President Giscard d'Estaing and former Director of Political Affairs at the Quai d'Orsay, it is inevitable that, at some point, the German problem, unless otherwise dealt with, will turn into a nuclear one and affect the Franco-German partnership in a negative way.

Inequality is more acceptable when one shares it with others; it is frustrating when this is not the case. The Germans had long expected that France and Great Britain would not be able to sustain the burden of nuclear armament, but they have confounded German opinion . . . Nuclear weapons appear to be the single stumbling

71

block; they account for the dependence in the field of security; they symbolize inequality; they have made Germany's division dangerous.[14]

It was long a Gaullist trauma that the Federal Republic, the main ally of the United States in Europe, might emerge as the hegemonial power of the continent and reduce France to a peripheral role. This worry led to the 1963 Franco-German treaty, which was conceived as a counterweight to the political, economic and military ties between Bonn and Washington. The treaty nearly failed to get off the ground when the Bundestag passed the treaty as a tribute to Adenauer, but stripped it of its substance by adding a preamble that reaffirmed West Germany's reliance upon the Atlantic Alliance as the central pillar of its foreign policy. De Gaulle shrugged off his disappointment: 'Treaties are like maidens and roses. They each have their day.'[15]

At the end of 1963, in fact, very few would have predicted the treaty's exceptional longevity. Now, with France noting that political currents in West Germany aim at emancipation from or even a parting of the ways with the United States, an entirely different worry has come to the fore. There are fears that the Federal Republic might, by virtue of an ongoing weakening of her ties with the United States, lose her balance and France be too weak to offset the danger of Bonn's decoupling from the United States. Shortly before he died, the philosopher and publicist Raymond Aron outlined this widespread feeling:

The French today are no longer afraid of German militarism but of German pacifism, which is an extremely remarkable reversal of attitudes. But French people who give thought to political matters realize that nowadays the German pillar of the Alliance has become vulnerable and grown unsteady, and the Atlantic Alliance is based mainly on relations between Bonn and Washington.[16]

The emergence of a centre of powerlessness in the heart of Europe would be just as serious a threat to the security of France and peace in Europe, as in days gone by a German centre of power was in the middle of the continent. Many Frenchmen tend to respond to what they see as an alarming resurgence of 'national neutralism' among neighbouring Germans by showing greater enthusiasm for integration and aiming at forms of European defence on which a consensus might be reached. Sceptics may agree with Pierre Messmer, General de Gaulle's Defence Minister, who said back in 1960 that the topic of European defence was first and foremost 'a fine-sounding flourish that makes a fine conclusion to a speech'. French insistence on maintaining nuclear autonomy clearly sets limits to the Franco-German 'community of destiny' conjured by political leaders, although non-nuclear initiatives such as the '*Force d'action rapide*', or Rapid Deployment Force, testify to a fresh readiness to further expand the 'alliance within the alliance'.

Competing roles and conflicting priorities

The principal French motive in 1969 for lifting the veto on British adhesion to the EEC had been the notion that Britain's weight joined to France would be useful in keeping Germany from becoming too strong inside the EEC. Pompidou, responsible for lifting the veto, believed the Germans were on their way to becoming so crushingly predominant economically that they would come to dominate Europe politically as well. The Pompidou vision of a Paris–London axis had all of the balance-of-power motivations of earlier French policy in this century, i.e. building a Franco-British counterweight to German power.

But the Europe of the 1970s was different from that of the 1930s. The pressing priority was not creating a counterweight to German power, but to Soviet power. On the other hand, the development of an independent Ostpolitik, challenging French leadership as the Soviet Union's most active *interlocuteur* in Western Europe, threatened in French eyes to upset the whole European balance. In an apparently paradoxical way, Chancellor Brandt's overture to the East, which de Gaulle had been recommending for years, diminished France's influence in Europe and reactivated traditional French fears that Bonn was at best a fickle partner, ready to be seduced by a 'new Rapallo'.[17]

De Gaulle believed that European and German reunification could succeed only if Russians and Germans composed their differences in accord with the Western countries, not against them as had been the case in 1922, when the two 'pariahs' of the Versailles system joined forces. He also felt that France was best placed to move this concept gradually forward, as she was tied to Bonn by the Elysée Treaty of 1963 and was progressively improving her relations with Moscow. For France to use mediation and, to a certain degree, arbitration to settle Soviet–German differences seemed to be the best guarantee of her long-run security objectives and global aspirations. This concept envisioned the emergence of a Europe stretching from the Atlantic to the Urals drawn together by history, culture and national interests, with West Germany realizing her foreign policy goals, including reunification.

This policy towards the East owes part of its persistent popularity to certain ambiguities. It had been approved by the French Communist Party already during the lifetime of General de Gaulle, and it was even said during the 1965 presidential elections that the Kremlin, also, 'voted for de Gaulle'. But between the man who often dreamed of a 'Europe from the Atlantic to the Urals', and those who would prefer to see it extend from 'the Urals to the Atlantic', a convergence of views inevitably has its limits.

De Gaulle's reactivation of the traditional affinities between the two halves of Europe brought home to the Germans in the Federal Republic that they were historically out of phase, and helped to strengthen forces of change within the political parties. By presenting specific proposals for dealing with the German problem in a European framework, France gave further momentum to the West German debate on foreign policy priorities and carried the issue into the realm of alternative strategies. In 1959, General de Gaulle was the first Western statesman to recognize the Oder–Neisse line as the final frontier of a unified Germany. In 1965, he alone advocated a recognition of the postwar borders, together with West German permanent participation in European integration, as a precondition for movement towards German unity.

The Czechoslovak crisis in 1968 checked the French rapprochement with the East that had reached its most exalted state during de Gaulle's visit to the Soviet Union in 1966. After the Soviet-led intervention of August 1968, the more static model of the European security system was reconfirmed, at least for the time being. On the other hand, the failure of the Prague spring, as well as Gaullist policies, hastened the day when the Federal Republic would begin moving eastward on her own, without France as a broker or mediator, much less as arbiter. The desire for more independent German policies, at first only an undercurrent, soon came to the surface, appearing initially as a particular German brand of Gaullism.

France had little choice but to back West Germany's efforts to improve her relations with Eastern Europe. However, in the whole complex of issues involved in Brandt's Ostpolitik, France's major interest has been to ensure that any arrangement does not infringe on rights that belong to the four powers. Even though Bonn's Ostpolitik of the 1970s followed, rather than preceded, other dynamic Western approaches to the East, in France the fear was that Bonn might turn its interest toward Eastern Europe in a new version of earlier nineteenth- and twentieth-century *Schaukelpolitik* that kept Germany swinging back and forth in alliance between East and West. A free-wheeling powerful Germany trying to manoeuvre between the two blocs, seeking to exploit the country's unique geographical position in the heart of Europe for its national goals, and reversing Adenauer's postwar policy of alliance with the West clearly would pose a challenge to the European balance of power. Except for the fear of a German finger on the nuclear trigger, no other political issue in the Franco-German partnership weighs so heavily psychologically as the Federal Republic's attitude toward the East.

'We all know that the Germans, whenever they join forces with the Russians, are soon afterwards on the outskirts of Paris,' the French High Commissioner, André François-Poncet, once said with reference to the 'precedent' set by Rapallo and the Hitler–Stalin Pact.[18] In the run-up to the

1984 European Parliament elections, his son, former Foreign Minister, Jean François-Poncet, called for a 'leap forward' on the ground that France can only counter the long-term spectre of 'national neutralism' by means of stronger commitment to European unity and interlinking of her security with that of the German neighbour.[19] Both statements are based on suspicions that Bonn's decision in favour of throwing in their lot with the West might one day be cancelled by a new generation of Germans who seek a way out of the German dilemma in a *renversement des alliances*. On the quiet, many French people feel the Federal Republic might betray and destroy the European edifice built after World War II, and do so for a Soviet mess of potage that gives it deceptive hope of reunification.

At the time of Brezhnev's 1981 visit to Bonn, Chancellor Schmidt, who rightly rejected the notion of 'mediator' as an incorrect description of Bonn's role in East–West relations, looked for a conceptual expression that would not be associated with the idea of equidistance between the two blocks. When he chose the term 'Dolmetscher', or interpreter, he nevertheless became the victim of historical images equating 'interpreter' with Rapallo or with a new brand of traditional German 'see-saw policy' between East and West. As a result, a number of French observers considered even the terminology as evidence that Bonn was moving away from the West. Ostpolitik, it was argued, had effects far beyond those intended: unable to manage the forces they have unleashed, the Germans have in fact become prisoners of the East, and the Western Alliance is merely a 'reinsurance treaty'[20].

In many ways the European framework provided France with an elegant and immensely fruitful solution to her century-old dilemma: how to contain Germany without having to depend on a fragile system of alliances. It must not be forgotten, however, that the supporters of European policies in France have always been in one or other of two camps: those who seriously meant equal rights for the Germans and were prepared to allow the Federal Republic every option, including that of reunification; and those who saw in integration a means of institutionalizing France's political superiority, of controlling the Federal Republic and of cementing the division of Germany. Fear of a reunited German colossus in the heart of Europe is no longer debated any too frequently in France today, but it would be wrong to assume that it has vanished entirely from the collective consciousness.

Le Monde took the 1979 European Parliament election campaign as an opportunity for asking leading French politicians how they felt about German reunification. Representatives of the Giscardian majority such as Simone Veil felt a united Europe would contain West Germany, whereas an isolated Federal Republic might seek salvation in neutrality or even a bid to enforce reunification. Opposition leader François Mitterrand, as he then was, frankly said that reunification was neither desirable nor possible in terms of the European balance of power, France's security and the preservation of peace. The Prime Minister, Raymond Barre, took refuge behind the statement that the problem did not arise and was unlikely to do so in the foreseeable future.[21]

This was perhaps still true at the end of the 1970s, but today a majority of French people consider the German question to be back at centre stage, making it essential for Bonn's closest ally in Europe to reconsider Germany's unsolved national problem. 'If we are to establish a lasting relationship with the Germans,' concludes Henri Froment-Meurice, former French Ambassador to the Soviet Union and to the Federal Republic, in a recent book on the future of Europe, 'we must bear in mind the dimension of German unity. Any policy aimed at or even conveying the impression of preventing the Germans from one day regaining their lost unity will in the long term be doomed to failure'.[22]

Interestingly enough, a majority of Frenchmen – who probably never were as nervous about Germany as the elite – were matter-of-factly telling opinion pollsters in 1985[23] that today the reunification of Germany would be 'legitimate' (59 per cent), compared with less than a third who regard such an event as 'a major political risk for Europe' (28 per cent) or for the 'French economy' (27 per cent). This change of mood is in tune with the shift in President Mitterrand's public attitudes in recent years. During the 1984 visit to the United States, he had indeed revised his pre-election attitude on German unity, moving far towards making his commitment to Franco-German solidarity more credible. In a television interview in Atlanta, he said that 'the German longing for reunification did not present any risk for the centre of Europe and the world'.[24]

It would certainly be premature to conclude that no French politician or intellectual would agree anymore with François Mauriac's famous assessment of the German question which has long been considered as revealing the 'true' feelings of the French people: 'I love Germany so much that I rejoice at the idea that today there are two of them.' It is difficult to deny that in the minds of some French people, there still is a desire to keep Germany in a sort of secondary position in Europe, implying the maintenance of the division and of a certain indirect control over Bonn's foreign policy, alliances, and military power.

A new search for identity

In recent years, the French have been concerned that the temptation of closer ties with East Germany was pulling the Federal Republic away from her Western moorings. It is probably true that the Germans, a people fragmented for long stretches of their history, have always brooded over the question of their identity more than other peoples have. But this has rarely been as true as it is in the 1980s, and French observers begin to warn that the West Germans are in danger of becoming obsessed with the idea of a special relationship with the East Germans. A conference on relations between the two Germanies conducted by the Aspen Institute of Berlin in May 1984 made clear that traditional French suspicions about a 'two-faced' Germany, tempted to deal with the East while looking steadily to the West, are shared by others. But the perspective differs from capital to capital.

The view from Paris is the most straightforward. The success of the Paris–Bonn 'couple' has lain in the conscious and deliberate reconciliation of conflicting interests, not in any intrinsic convergence of views and politics. For the Franco-German relationship, therefore, East Germany is the constant shadow in the background, the alternative partner as well as the lure the Soviet Union is using in the hope of drawing Bonn away from its anchorage in the West. Most French politicians would likely agree with the traditional West German view of a special responsibility towards the other part of Germany and are sympathetic in particular to the goal of removing barriers to contacts between the German people. But there are limits to French support for Bonn's Deutschlandpolitik. Although welcoming West German contributions to more stable contacts at the frontlines of the Cold War, there is some concern in France that the effort to deepen and broaden German–German ties could develop a dynamic of its own which might lead the Federal Republic to shield its 'special relationship' with East Germany while the Soviet Union uses the pull of inter-German ties to try to influence West German politics. Particularly since the advent of detente in the late 1960s, the Soviets have held out the possibilities of improvements in German–German contacts as an ever-present 'carrot', while the prospect of reducing existing contacts has served as Moscow's 'stick'. However, Soviet actions so far suggest, as Edwina Moreton has observed, that the idea of a reunified and powerful Germany in the heart of Europe is no more welcome a prospect in the 1980s and 1990s than it was in the 1950s. The German problem remains unsolved and for the foreseeable future insoluble because 'West Germany lacks the leverage to solve it and because the Soviet Union lacks the political will.'[25]

This 'lack of leverage' is precisely one of the reasons why it has gradually become part of French conventional wisdom that the Federal Republic is chafing at established Western ties and that neutralism is on the rise in West Germany. Former Foreign Minister Michel Jobert put it bluntly: 'If I were German I would have grasped a long time ago that I had to act like a submarine, moving forward when possible and never ever surfacing – of course this adds up to a certain neutralist behavior.'[26] From a similar perspective, the deployment of Euromissiles on the soil of both German states, instead of bringing to an end the quest for reunification, as the Socialist Party's former Secretary for International Affairs, Jacques Huntzinger, hoped it would,[27] might have given it a new twist. In a recent evaluation of Franco-German security cooperation, the former Director of Political Affairs at the Quai d'Orsay, Ambassador François Puaux, concluded that in 1983 one could observe 'surprising fraternizations and the objective complicity between the two Germanies aiming at a certain freedom of action *vis-à-vis* the superpowers and at asserting their national interest'.[28]

France is mainly concerned about the German mini-detente of the 1980s because of the questions that a rapprochement between East and West Germany could pose for Bonn's commitment to the Western world. Indeed, as seen from Paris, West Germany's attitude is increasingly schizophrenic, torn between loyalty to the West and the need not to alienate the East. In the wake of the Afghanistan crisis, Fritz Stern observed that 'geography, history and deep-rooted economic realities combine to make Germans conceive of themselves as constituting simultaneously a barrier and a bridge to the East'.[29] Forty years after the end of World War II, Ostpolitik has built up its own momentum. To most West Germans, some kind of detente with East Germany and the Soviet Union has ceased to be an option and has become a national necessity. But its successful pursuit depends on continued Western integration.

In recent years, French diplomacy has chosen to take into account this double loyalty by intensifying her own relations with East Germany. Prior to the 1970s, France had scrupulously avoided recognition of the East German regime, in order not to alienate her West German ally. During the 1950s and the 1960s, the communist-led association 'France–RDA' was the only pressure group arguing for diplomatic relations between the two countries. At the time of Brandt's Ostpolitik, France waited until February 1973 before recognizing East Germany and it took one more year to exchange Ambassadors between Paris and East Berlin. Since the mid-1970s, relations have been developing mainly in the economic and cultural fields, the most spectacular result being the signing of a cultural agreement in 1980 that included the opening of 'cultural centres' in each other's capitals.

Since the end of the 1970s, political relations have also been upgraded. In October 1979, French Foreign Minister Jean François-Poncet visited East Berlin. About six years later, Prime Minister Laurent Fabius was the first of the three Allied heads of government to visit East Berlin. However, an incident which occurred during the visit showed that East Germany did not hesitate to embarrass her guest when it came to status symbols. The presence of Defence Minister General Hoffmann in uniform at the official dinner of June 10, 1985 was a deliberate violation of the demilitarized status of Berlin, and Mitterrand's gesture toward Chancellor Kohl, during his visit to West Berlin four months later, has been interpreted as a sort of compensation for Honecker's diplomatic *faux pas*.

Looking ahead

More than forty years after the end of World War II, the unresolved German question remains on history's list of unfinished business. It is clear that the desire to maintain contacts between the two Germanies will remain a fundamental aspect of West German domestic and foreign policy for the rest of this century, irrespective of which party is in power. This West German policy will sometimes be of concern to France; yet the three Western allies have been officially committed to German reunification since the Federal Republic entered Nato and the WEU in 1955.

One might indeed question the extent to which the French in practice support the goal of 'reunification,' in the sense of a process leading to a unitary national state of close to 80 million people in the heart of Europe, but one has to admit that France has never disputed the right of the German people to self-determination. The traditional Gaullist theme of 'going beyond Yalta' through the progress of democracy and communication in communist Europe has been picked up by President Mitterrand in recent years. The West Germans, on the other hand, have backed away from insisting on the priority of the solution of the German problem in terms of state reunification and focus instead on the living conditions of the East Germans and gradual liberalization of the communist regimes in Eastern Europe.

The Germans in the Federal Republic expect their political system to concern itself intensively with improving East–West relations; at the same time, the public is by no means so unrealistic as to force its political leaders into dangerous policies bordering on appeasement. The national consensus has shifted away from achieving the immediate goal of reunification to a deeply felt wish to normalize over the long run those conditions in the heart of Europe that today are anything but normal. The overwhelming majority of the West Germans has no desire to leave the Western alliance, but some inclination to stay out of superpower conflicts that might get them involved against their wishes or interests. It is remarkable that Mitterrand, unlike de Gaulle, has done nothing to encourage greater

German independence from the Western Alliance. For the first time in the history of the Fifth Republic, the President of France has, in effect, asked West Germany to be a reliable and strong ally of the United States. In his speech to the Bundestag, in January 1983, François Mitterrand explicitly warned of the danger of Western Europe decoupling from the United States, and urged the West German to carry out the Nato decision of December 1979 to deploy Pershing II and land-based cruise missiles. The French stand on the Nato decision, however, brought to the forefront the dilemma of reconciling the desire to anchor West Germany in the West with the refusal of integration and insistence on military autonomy.

Mitterrand's speech in Bonn may have been designed to influence the course of internal German politics, but it has had profound repercussions on external perceptions of French strategic priorities. The problem for France is that a policy of close identification with the Atlantic Alliance inevitably puts the independence of the French nuclear arsenal into question – at least in the eyes of the Kremlin. Mitterrand's predecessor had kept his support for the December 1979 decision private partly to avoid this contradiction. On the other hand, there is a growing awareness in all major political parties that France could not remain aloof in a crisis situation in Europe, if only for geographic reasons. The possibility of a West European defence effort organized around Paris and Bonn might very well be a way to stem the erosion of West German loyalty to Nato, by demonstrating that military security is a legitimate European as well as transatlantic concern.

Almost twenty years after the Franco-German treaty of 1963, Mitterrand's 1982 decision to revive the dormant military cooperation provisions of the treaty was a further proof of the French intention to become more directly involved in the defence of Western Germany, as well as an admission of the impossibility of hiding behind a nuclear Maginot Line. This does not mean that, even in a remote future, French strategic forces could be substituted for the American nuclear umbrella. Even modernized, France's nuclear force would not be credible for such a role, and such a commitment given in advance would violate French military autonomy. It means simply that in an age of nuclear parity, deterrence in Europe requires combining the residual risk of a conflict becoming nuclear with conventional forces strong enough to deny a quick victory to the Soviets.

The French President has in fact gone beyond Franco-German military cooperation, and proposed a *relance* of Western Europe. The most innovative suggestions here concern accepting majority rule in the European Community in non-vital matters and drafting a treaty of political cooperation based on the so-called Spinelli draft of a treaty for political union endorsed in February 1984 by the European Parliament. Mitterrand's initiative corresponds to a general conviction in France that the European Community's institutional and financial paralysis cannot go on, but it is also aimed at giving to the Federal Republic a new mission in Western Europe.

Good relations with Bonn have been the keystone of Mitterrand's European policy, as with that of his predecessors back to 1958, if not 1950. The choice France makes between the pursuit of one or the other policy option is based as much on a reading of the German situation as of Soviet and American policies. The major danger inherent in this approach is a misreading of West German priorities and concerns. The French may discover that their anxiety about West Germany is excessive as far as security and East–West issues are concerned, but that there is a real danger of increasing parochialism in this country. In recent years, a cluster of domestic issues – unemployment, social injustice and environment – have become the principle popular concerns, whereas international issues emerging during the Euromissile crisis – nuclear weapons and the threat of war – continue to command the attention of only a minority. It might very well be, as Alfred Grosser observed in a comment on the meaning of 'solidarity with Germany' that the lack of a long-term vision for the future will become a more serious problem to deal with than the imaginary danger of German 'national neutralism'.[30]

Notes

1 *Figaro Magazine*, 9 July 1982.
2 Robert Picht, ed., *Das Bündnis im Bündnis. Deutsch-französische Beziehungen im internationalen Spannungsfeld*. (Berlin: Severin and Siedler, 1983).
3 Brigitte Sauzay, *Le Vertige allemand. Essai*. (Paris: Olivier Orban, 1985), p. 255.
4 AMRE (Archives du Ministère des Relations Extérieures), Y–54–1, Aide-mémoire Alphand, 8 September 1945.
5 AMRE, Y–54–1, Memorandum on German policy, 31 July 1945.
6 Joseph Rovan, 'L'Allemagne de nos mérites', *Esprit* 11, 1945, pp. 529–40.
7 AMRE, Y–54–1, Note by Jacques Tarbé de Saint-Hardouin, 20 January 1948.
8 In a letter to Joseph Rovan, quoted by the latter in 'Réflexions sur la crise allemande', *Politique étrangère*, no. 1, 1983, p. 39.
9 *Quotidien de Paris*, 20 January 1983.
10 Cited in Edward A. Kolodziej, *French International Policy Under De Gaulle and Pompidou: The Politics of Grandeur*. (Ithaca, London: Cornell University Press, 1974), p. 162.
11 *Le Monde*, 30 October 1979.
12 Stanley Hoffmann, 'NATO and Nuclear Weapons: Reasons and Unreason'. *Foreign Affairs*, Winter 1981/2, p. 343.
13 On the ambiguity of French public images in the security field see Renata Fritsch-Bournazel: 'France: Attachment to a Nonbinding Relationship', in Gregory Flynn, Hans Rattinger ed., *The Public and Atlantic Defense*. (Totowa N J, London; Rowman and Allanheld, 1985), pp. 69–100.

14 Gabriel Robin, 'The German Problem Revisited', *Atlantic Quarterly*, Autumn 1983, p. 196.

15 *Le Monde*, 3 July 1963.

16 Raymond Aron, '1918–1933–1948–1963. Réflexions autour de quelques dates–clés'. *Documents*, no 4, 1982, p. 34.

17 On the role of the 'Rapallo myth' in French political attitudes toward Germany see Renata Fritsch-Bournazel, 'Rapallo et son image en France'. *Documents*, no. 2, 1982, pp. 3–12.

18 Cited in Luigi Barzini: *Auf die Deutschen kommt es an. Die unzuverlässigen Europäer*. (Hamburg, Albrecht Knaus, 1983), p. 93.

19 Jean François-Poncet, 'Certitudes et incertitudes allemandes', *Le Monde*, 10 November 1983.

20 Joseph Rovan, 'Bonn: vers une autre politique extérieure?' in *Après la détente. Un dossier de la revue 'politique internationale'*. (Paris: Hachette 1982), p. 241. For a less gloomy perspective see Alfred Grosser, 'La RFA, la France et les super-grands', *ibid.*, pp. 193–204.

21 See Henri Ménudier, 'Deutschfeindlichkeit im französischen Wahlkampf zum Europäischen Parlament' in his book on *Das Deutschlandbild der Franzosen in den 70er Jahren*. (Bonn: Europa Union Verlag, 1981), pp. 218–34.

22 Henri Froment-Meurice, *Une puissance nommée Europe*. (Paris: Julliard, 1984), p. 176.

23 Sondage IFOP pour Le Monde et RTL. *Le Monde*, 28 June 1985. This shift in attitudes occurred in the early 1980s and has been rather consistent since then, as shown in similar polls by *Le Nouvel Observateur* (10 February 1984) and *Géopolitique* (Winter 1984/5).

24 TV interview of 25 March 1984, quoted from *Die Welt*, 26 March 1984.

25 Edwina Moreton, 'The German Factor' in Edwina Moreton, Gerald Segal ed., *Soviet Strategy Toward Western Europe*. (London: George Allen and Unwin, 1984), p. 135.

26 In an unpublished interview 8 August 1984 with Andreas Wilkens: *La politique française à l'égard de l'Union soviétique pendant la Présidence de Georges Pompidou (1969–1974)*. Paris: Institut d'Etudes Politiques, 1984 (Mémoire pour le DEA en Sciences Politiques sous la direction du professeur Alfred Grosser).

27 Huntzinger's statement that 'the deployment of Pershing II blocks any solution of the German problem for the next twenty years' has been abundantly used by the SPD as a proof of French duplicity in the context of President Mitterrand's speech to the Bundestag in January 1983. See Egon Bahr, 'Deutschland und die Atomwaffen' in *Mut zur Einheit. Fetschrift für Johann Baptist Gradl*. (Cologne: Verlag Wissenschaft und Politik, 1984), p. 43.

28 François Puaux, 'La France, l'Allemagne et l'atome: discorde improbable, accord impossible', *Défense nationale*, December 1985, p. 18.

29 Fritz Stern, 'Germany in a Semi-Gaullist Europe', *Foreign Affairs*, Spring 1980, p. 881.

30 Alfred Grosser, 'La Solidarite avec l'Allemagne. Il faut cohabiter avec les atouts et les faiblesses de l'autre', *Le Monde*, 15 March 1986.

6   The British view

ROGER MORGAN

Introduction

British views of the 'German problem' derive partly from the position of the United Kingdom as a member of the Western alliance (together with the United States, France and the Federal Republic); partly from Britain's legal position as a victor in World War II (together with the United States, the Soviet Union, and France); and partly from its membership of the European Community. This combination of relationships, especially the status of World War II victor, also gives Britain a share of the direct responsibility for Berlin. This point, in particular, is worth examining in some detail for the light it sheds on British policy towards Germany in general.

The British position with regard to Berlin is based firmly on Britain's legal status as one of the four powers exercising four-power control over the whole of Berlin by virtue of the agreements of 12 September and 14 November 1944. Even though this four-power control over Berlin has, of course, ceased to exist *de facto*, the British view (like that of the United States and France) is that it remains valid *de jure*, and that this situation was not affected by the practical arrangements following from the Four-Power Berlin Agreement of September 1971. The connection between the legal rights of the Western allies and their political relationship to their West German allies (including West Berliners) was summarized by President Giscard d'Estaing during his visit to West Berlin in October 1979, when he used the formula 'the rights of the allies represent the liberty of the Berliners'. This statement of France's legal rights in Berlin, though sharply formulated, applies in essence to the views of Britain and indeed of all three of the Western allies, namely, that Berlin's special status must be preserved.

There are several reasons for Britain's strong insistence on its interpretation of the legal status of all of Berlin. First, the United Kingdom, like the United States and France, maintains its legal rights in Berlin, and its military and other responsibilities there, because of Britain's relationship with the Federal Republic, and the wish and need of Germans and Berliners that the British presence should be maintained: to depart from this position would, in effect, allow 2 million Berliners to be absorbed into East Germany. Furthermore, any renunciation of British (or other Western) rights and responsibilities could strengthen the Soviet view that four-power responsibility as a whole should be ended, and this would leave Berlin more exposed to the uncertainties of intra-German relations and East–West relations in general.

But there are also other political considerations. Any such renunciation would reduce British influence in seeking a long-term solution to the German question (perhaps reunification), and would perhaps also reduce Britain's influence in the short run over the evolution of relations between its ally, the Federal Republic, and the German Democratic Republic. What is more, the co-responsibility of Britain for the status and security of Berlin helps to consolidate its ties with the United States, France and West Germany. The regular consultations of the four foreign ministers on Berlin problems provide a convenient forum for the discussion of other Alliance issues as well. (The six-monthly meetings at foreign minister level should not be confused with the more technical meetings of the so-called 'Bonn Group', in which the four countries are represented at official level.) And, lastly, West Berlin is (presumably) valuable to Britain, as to the other Western powers, for intelligence-gathering purposes.

These factors, to which others could be added, explain Britain's insistence on its rights and responsibilities in Berlin. This view has had several consequences, including the insistence of the occupying powers since 1949 that 'Land Berlin' is not part of the Federal Republic, and their maintenance of special procedures for the application in West Berlin of federal legislation and regulations.

As this sketch of the British attitude to Berlin indicates, there is a combination of calculations on Britain's part: solidarity with Bonn, concern to exercise some control over the German situation in the short run, and concern to play a part in promoting a long-term solution of the German problem in conformity with the overall stability of Europe. This mix of calculations influences the British approach to the 'German question' in general. Although the legal differences between London and Bonn on the status of West Berlin are well known, they do not affect their fundamental identity of views on the main issues which face them.

The current British debate

The first point to note about British views of the current debate on the 'German' question is that the issue has aroused much less public comment in Britain than in many of Germany's other partners and neighbours. This is made clear, for instance, by a recent study of foreign comment on the German question.[1] Among the numerous statements from France, the United States, Poland and elsewhere reported in this comprehensive study, there are very few from Great Britain, and none at all from responsible British politicians. This may be partly explained by the fact that the authors have based their study essentially on material that had appeared in the public media, thus missing occasional statements by British ministers. But even so, it is remarkable that representatives of the British press and mass media should have given so little attention to a theme which has so greatly preoccupied their colleagues – in France and the United States, for instance – throughout the first half of the 1980s.

The few British comments which were brought to light by the media study were couched in very general terms. One British observer summarized the German question as consisting of two parts: first, the question how far the Federal Republic could still be regarded as a reliable member of the Western alliance (with reference to the renewed demand for reunification, and to the slogan of 'Rapallo'); and, second, the question how far Western-style liberal democracy was still secure in Germany (with reference to the peace movement, anti-Americanism, the 'Greens', and a more socialistically oriented 'neutralist nationalism'). Another statement, from a British journalist, reported that there was concern in Britain about the 'unreliability' of the 'German spirit' ('deutsche Seele'), and that many people in Britian shared Winston Churchill's impression that 'the Germans either throw themselves at your feet, or at your throat'.

The absence of a continuous, well-informed discussion in Britain about developments in Germany has several reasons. As suggested above, the British media do not report fully or frequently on German affairs (nor, indeed, on those of continental Europe in general); the political elite of the country, in so far as it is concerned with West European affairs at all, has been preoccupied by the question of Britain's role as a member of the European Community; British foreign policy commentators tend to give considerable attention to their country's relationships outside Europe (with the United States, with Africa, with UNESCO and the UNO in general, and with the Commonwealth); and a practical conception of Britain's role in European affairs, including a relationship with the states of Central and Eastern Europe, is developing only very slowly.

In contrast, the diagnosis of the German question, and conceptions about how to answer it, are quite clearly formulated among the group of professionals responsible for British policy on these matters. It may indeed be true that, at a general level, the British reaction to the whole heated German debate about the German question is to say: 'If you Germans want to go on with this exciting rhetoric about the openness of the German question, then please tell us what you intend to do about it.'

At another and more durable level, the British reaction is to say: 'Since the reality of Germany's situation will not change – and, as you Germans say yourselves, you know it – then why not face facts by toning down the rhetoric?' Spelling out this idea more clearly, the better-informed British observers might say: 'Since the only hope of Germany's reunification lies in a new European situation where East and West are reconciled, so that a unified Germany is no threat to either, it is a pity that the Germans insist so strongly on their own national right of self-determination, rather than concentrating on working for the broader concept of a European peace order.' This, the argument goes, would be the only situation in which their right of self-determination, like that of the Poles and Czechs and many others, has any hope of being put into practice. British policy would now in practice (as opposed to legal theory) welcome a clear West German acceptance of the present Eastern frontier of Germany, as a contribution to creating this peaceful order in Europe.

To express it more concretely, the prevailing view of the German problem in Britain – among those who think about these matters at all – is that the only solution to Germany's division lies in overcoming the division of Europe (of which the division of Germany is only a part), and that such a process can come only from a gradual reconciliation between the Western powers (especially the United States) and the Soviet Union. German reunification as an ideal is morally right and also politically the best basis for a stable peace in Europe, so the British would say; but a German reunification that was not based upon a general reconciliation between the two Cold War alliance blocs (and based instead, for instance, on the attempt to create a unified and neutralized German state between them, by removing the Federal Republic from Nato and East Germany from the Warsaw Pact) would be certainly destabilizing for Europe and potentially catastrophic for peace.

To examine more closely the structure of this dominant view of the problem – the view that the German problem must be seen as essentially an aspect of the power relationship between the Soviet Union and the West – we have to look back at the decisive years immediately after the end of World War II: the fundamental views recorded by the British policy-makers of that time are certainly influential, *mutatis mutandis*, on their successors of today.

From World War to Cold War

From the time when the division of the German Reich into allied zones of occupation was worked out in the wartime discussions of 1943–4, through the Yalta and Potsdam agreements of 1945 and the creation of the Anglo-American 'Bizone' in 1948, to the establishment of the Federal Republic in 1949, British policy towards the German question evolved in a relatively straight line. In the wartime period after Hitler's attack on Russia in 1941, Churchill hoped to maintain a long-term alliance with Stalin (though he was much less hopeful of this than Roosevelt), and this hope led to a strongly punitive policy towards Germany: the Reich should be disarmed, curbed in its economic strength, and deprived of some of its territory (for instance, by the splitting-off of Saxony, Bavaria, the Palatinate and Württemberg, which – so Churchill proposed at Teheran in 1943 – should be attached to a new Danubian Federation to be based on Austria and Hungary). At a later stage, in 1945–6, when the difficulties of working with the Soviet Union in occupied Germany became clear, British policy shifted towards the idea of building up the Western part of Germany as an ally *against* the Soviet Union. Finally, with the worsening of the Cold War between East and West in 1947–8 (particularly after the Soviet blockade of West Berlin which started in spring 1948), this line of policy went further with the currency reform, the merging of the British and American zones into the Bizone, the creation of the Federal Republic in 1949 and – after the Korean War of 1950–2 – British agreement to the rearmament of West Germany as a member of Nato. This took effect in May 1955, almost exactly ten years after the unconditional surrender of 1945.

It is possible to document the course of British official discussions about the German question during the wartime period and the first ten postwar years in detail, thanks to the 'Thirty-Year Rule', by which official archives are open for research thirty years after the date they are written – that means, at the time of writing, up to the year of the Federal Republic's accession to Nato, 1955. What is striking, for a present-day reader of these documents, is to note how often the British diplomats of 1945, or 1948, or 1952, use arguments which have remained part of the public discussion down to the present day. Would it be safe for Germany to be reunified as a neutral state between the Soviet Union and the West? Is real stability in Europe possible as long as Germany is divided? If Germany's Eastern frontier lies any further East than the Oder–Neisse Line, is reconciliation possible between Germany and Poland? If the military strength of West Germany is increased, will this not endanger the general relationship between East and West? These and many other familiar questions relating to Germany's place in a divided Europe, as we have known it since 1945, are all discussed in the record of British diplomacy before 1955: despite the changes which have occurred since then – not least through the building of the Berlin Wall of 1961 and the Ostpolitik of the Federal Republic (especially the Brandt–Scheel coalition of 1969–74) – many of the questions of earlier years are still valid today, and many of the answers are still instructive as an indication of the basic lines of British thinking.

When we consider the comments written by British diplomats forty years ago – many of which contain harsh judgements on Germany, as well as on the Soviet Union – we should remember the historical context. British 'liberal' opinion, in its great majority, had welcomed Bismarck's victory over the Second Empire of France in 1870, and felt considerable affinity with the socially and scientifically progressive German Empire of the years before 1914 (despite some concern about naval competition). The Treaty of Versailles (1919) had been strongly condemned by the majority of thinking people in Britain for its harsh treatment of Germany, and Britain exerted continuous pressure on France to relax the terms of the treaty in favour of the Weimar Republic (Locarno 1925, evacuation of the Rhineland 1930) and even of the Third Reich (Anglo-German Naval Treaty 1935, Munich Agreement 1938). The failure of these British attempts to 'appease' Germany's grievances by a policy of concessions led to a particular sense of betrayal and anger in Britain when the war broke out in 1939.

It can even be argued that the continuing strength of these feelings in Britain for some years after 1945, particularly after the realities of Britain's weak international position were made dramatically clear by the Suez crisis of 1956, helped to delay any widespread sense of reconciliation between the British and German people. Such a reconciliation, in contrast, *has* occurred between the Germans and French since the 1950s (a marked difference from the years after 1919, when British sympathy for Weimar Germany was strong, and France remained deeply mistrustful).

It is in this context – of past memories interacting with assessments of the future, and of scepticism about Germany combining with the mistrust of Soviet Russia, which the enforced alliance since 1941 had done only a little to reduce – that we must evaluate the evidence of the official British documents.

At the moment when the British member of the inter-allied European Advisory Commission, Sir William Strang, first proposed the division of defeated Germany into occupation zones, in January 1944, one of his junior officials, Gladwyn Jebb, commented prophetically: 'This card, played at this moment, will perhaps turn out to be especially significant for the whole future of Europe.' Another Foreign Office official, Frank Roberts, reflected the general British view that the partition of Germany would be only temporary, when he wrote that the splitting up of a great country, 'which is racially, economically, geographically and within certain limits historically a unit, is a step which goes fully contrary to the development of history'.[2]

This theme, that the division of Germany was unnatural and could not be of long duration, continued to be present in British minds as the actual process of Germany's division went ahead, and as the division became ever sharper in the years of the Cold War. For instance, a Foreign Office memorandum on 'Future Policy towards Germany', written by Oliver Harvey in May 1946, argued:

In any case, it is most improbable that the Germans will ever accept anything more than a provisional division of their country. It is utopian to think of a West Germany which is not in the long term united again with East Germany.

The point is, therefore, to see to it that this reunited Germany represents no danger for Europe. This can best be achieved by ensuring that: (a) Germany is constructed on a federal basis; (b) a special regime is set up for the Ruhrgebiet; (c) the whole of Germany, at the end of the occupation period, is subjected to a system of supervision . . .

This concept of the collective 'supervision' of Germany by the wartime allies continued to play a part in British thinking as in American thinking, but the development of the Cold War obviously made it completely unrealistic. From the late 1940s, for more than twenty years, Britain's Deutschlandpolitik concentrated on consolidating the links of the Federal Republic with the West. The speed of the Brandt government's Ostpolitik from 1969 onwards may have briefly surprised the British, but it never gave rise to serious British fears of a West German drift into neutralism or into a 'new Rapallo' position.

Detente and after?

Once the first phase of East–West rapprochement had been completed (with the normalization of Bonn's relationship to Moscow, Warsaw and even East Berlin, and the establishment of what President Nixon called 'the era of negotiations' between the two superpowers), Britain and Germany, together with the other members of Nato, settled down to the long negotiations in Geneva and Helsinki on the 'multilateral' stages of the Conference on Security and Cooperation in Europe.

One of the most interesting aspects of the 'Helsinki process' is the question of how far it brought to light concern or hesitations on the British side about the possible risks, if the two German states became closer to each other, of Germany coming to dominate Europe. In fact, there is little evidence of such fears in Britain. As London saw it, the process of inner-German 'normalization' proceeded as an integral part of the general attempt to overcome the divisions between the two parts of Europe. As this European detente process was itself undertaken in the framework of parallel attempts at detente between the two superpowers (the SALT agreements in particular), the overall environment of German–German relations was in conformity with the underlying principles of British policy towards East–West relations and the German question: namely, when relations between East and West as a whole are positive, the movement towards a reunification of Germany does not have the same threatening connotations which it holds during periods of East–West tension (i.e., at the end of the road, the Rapallo syndrome and the threat of another German–Russian reconciliation at the expense of the West).

In any case, the gradual development of inter-German relations during the 1970s, although it held out the promise of substantial change in the long run, could not realistically be seen in Britain, or anywhere else, as a process with any hope of leading to an early reunification. At the same time, the general relationship between London and Bonn was becoming much closer in the 1970s, partly as a result of British membership of the European Community, and partly owing to a convergence of British and West German views on the issues of defence and East–West relations.

At a Königswinter conference in the early 1970s, when the battle over Brandt's Ostpolitik in the Bundestag was at its height, there was an interesting example of the interaction between British and German politics. A Conservative backbench Member of Parliament, representing the views of the Heath government, delivered a powerful speech in favour of Brandt's treaties with Moscow and Warsaw, appealing in particular to the CDU/CSU politicians present to abandon their opposition to these treaties. It is possible that this intervention had an effect on certain politicians of the Union. It certainly represented the views of the British Foreign Office: when the Conservative Member of Parliament had finished his oration, he turned to a senior British diplomat beside him and whispered, 'Was that all right?' to which the mandarin responded with an approving nod.

Britain, it is true, had specific reasons for showing support for Bonn's policy during this time. After entering the Economic Community in 1973, thanks in part to the active support of Bonn, the Heath government hoped for West German agreement to the creation of a large European Community Regional Development Fund, to which Germany would be the main contributor. At a later stage (1974–6) the Wilson government hoped for – and in considerable measure was granted – the support of Helmut Schmidt in its attempts to 'renegotiate' the financial terms of Britain's European Community membership. Helmut Schmidt's powerful plea for Britain to remain in the Community, at the Labour Party's special party conference on the subject ('Comrades, stay with us: your continental comrades need you'), certainly played a part in the British electorate's vote of 'Yes' (by a 2:1 majority) in the referendum of June 1975.

The Federal Republic under Brandt and Schmidt, as the British saw it, was an economically strong and politically reliable partner. Although British television, films and popular reading-matter continued to find a very large market for material about World War II, in which the Germans naturally appeared as Nazi 'baddies', the opinion polls were beginning to show that a majority of British people regarded the Federal Republic as 'our best friend on the continent'. Perhaps the apparent British obsession with memories of World War II had more to do with pleasure in recalling a glorious moment of British history (a good moment both collectively and, for many, personally) than with anything specifically connected with Germany.

At the same time, those responsible for British foreign policy were reassessing the nature of British interests in Europe, of which Britain's membership of the European Community represented only one dimension. By the 1970s, the recurrent temptation for British political leaders to play the role of East–West mediators between the superpowers was much weaker (this particular form of demonstrative diplomacy had been taken over by Paris in the 1960s and by Bonn in the 1970s). There were no prime ministerial visits to Moscow between Harold Wilson's first and second visits (respectively in 1966 and 1975), and the second of these visits fell clearly into the 'Helsinki' framework of coordinated West European relations with the Soviet bloc, rather than any sort of British *Alleingang*.

The care which London took to coordinate its Ostpolitik with that of Bonn was indicated by the way in which Britain's establishment of diplomatic relations with East Germany was carried out.[3] Although there had been for some years a fairly active 'lobby' in London for diplomatic recognition of East Germany, it was clear to the Foreign Office that such a step, if undertaken before Bonn itself established formal relations with East Germany, would be totally incompatible with Britain's commitments under the *Deutschlandvertrag* of 1954, and could have a catastrophic effect on Britain's credibility and political standing in Germany. It was therefore out of the question for Britain to recognize East Germany until the Basic Treaty (*Grundvertrag*) between the two German states had been signed on 21 December 1972.

The very next day the British Foreign Secretary, Sir Alec Douglas-Home, sent a telegram to his East German counterpart Otto Winzer, proposing talks on the establishment of diplomatic relations; this telegram amounted in practice to British recognition of East Germany. However, in deference to the wish of the Federal Republic that no British Ambassador should go to East Berlin until the legality of the Basic Treaty has been confirmed by the West German constitutional court (which occurred only on 31 July 1973), it was not until January 1974 that the British Ambassador took up his post.

It was, moreover, strongly stressed from the British side that East Berlin (where the Embassy was located, above a shop in Unter den Linden) was regarded, not as the capital of East Germany, but as its 'seat of government'. The British, together with the other Western powers, made a formal declaration that the four-power rights and responsibilities in Berlin, and their joint responsibility for 'matters affecting Germany as a whole' would not be affected by the new developments. In practice, British relations with East Germany have been kept at a distinctly low level of activity, concentrating mainly on economic and cultural issues, and avoiding any active discussion of political or strategic matters which might create problems in London's relations with Bonn.

As the détente mood of the 1970s gave way to the 1980s and the 'new Cold War', with the crises in Afghanistan, Poland and elsewhere, and the new hostility between Washington and Moscow, the discussion inside Germany on the German question rose sharply in intensity. To understand the reactions of the Western allies of the Federal Republic, including Britain, we have to recall that this discussion of the German question (including its 'openness' and the possibilities of self-determination and reunification) occurred precisely at a moment when East–West relations in general were going through a bad phase. The situation of 1982 had something in common with that of 1952: much discussion of German reunification, at a time when the general East–West context meant that this reunification could come only through Germany's neutralization and its possible slipping towards the East.

A leading article in *The Times* on 12 August 1981, the twentieth anniversary of the Berlin Wall, summarized British feelings quite well in arguing that the division of Germany, 'looked at against the broad sweep of European history . . . cannot look like anything but a temporary aberration', and that the question of reunification 'lurks there awaiting more propitious times'. This realization that any prospect of reunification could only be for 'more propitious times' led to a generally sympathetic response in Britain to the attempts of first Schmidt and then Kohl to maintain contact between the two Germanies, even in a period when East–West relations in general were bad.

An interesting summary of British views of German Ostpolitik was given by Lord Carrington, then Foreign Secretary, in a speech in Stuttgart in April 1981:

Your reconciliation with your Eastern neighbours gave great satisfaction to your fellow Europeans. It gave us all a greater sense of security too. The resulting increase in your contacts with Eastern Europe and the Soviet Union enriched the lives of millions and did much to erode the mistrust which divides this continent of Europe . . . you have been an ally for a quarter of a century . . . Yet we appreciate that your history, your geography, your status as a divided nation, have given you a perspective on East–West relations that is not the same as ours.

As for the Deutschlandpolitik of the Kohl government, Britain gave support to Bonn's attempt to pursue a dialogue with East Germany (and other Eastern interlocutors) without loosening the Federal Republic's ties with the West. Reunification, in the British view, could come only when the overall relationship between the two blocs was a great deal more relaxed, and Bonn's Ost- and Deutschlandpolitik should be seen as a contribution to this goal.

In the meantime, until the two parts of Europe in fact come closer together, British policy holds firmly to the legal rights and responsibilities of the allies (in legal theory, all four of them) in Berlin. As we have seen, there are several reasons why this issue is important, including in particular the fact that the allies' position in Berlin would allow them to exercise some control over the development of the situation in Germany in general, in the unlikely event of developments there which might represent a risk to Europe's peace and stability.

The British standpoint on the division of Germany was recently summarized by the Prime Minister, Mrs Thatcher, who pointed out that 'real and permanent stability in Europe will be difficult to achieve as long as the German nation is divided against its will'. The British commitment to Germany's right of self-determination was also confirmed in the Prime Minister's support for the 'Political Declaration on the 40th Anniversary of the End of the Second World War', issued at the Bonn Economic Summit in May 1985: 'Considering the climate of peace and friendship which we have achieved among ourselves forty years after the end of the war, we look forward to a state of peace in Europe in which the German people will retain its unity through free self-determination.'

This commitment to self-determination for the German people has been a permanent element in British policy since the *Deutschlandvertrag* of 1954, which expressed close agreement between the Federal government and the Western allies, including the United Kingdom. In terms of the practical politics of this issue, all British governments since that date have held the same view as successive governments in Bonn on the essential point: if the price to be paid for the exercise of self-determination by the Germans (i.e. for reunification) were to be the shift by the Federal Republic from the Western alliance to a neutral or non-aligned position, that price would be too high. As long as this is the price demanded by the Soviet Union, therefore, British and German governments are likely to continue to hold the same view in future.

This means that, as the British see it, the only practical hope of allowing the Germans' undoubted right of self-determination to be put into practice lies in a general improvement of East–West relations in Europe. In this sense, British policy is fully based on the concept that the German question can be resolved only by 'Europeanization' or by a 'European solution'.

As this record of the forty years since 1945 has shown, British attitudes to the German question have shown some elements of continuity (the facts of geography for Germany as 'das Land in der Mitte', have after all not changed), but also considerable elements of change. The intimate relations between the political (and administrative) elites of the two countries, which have developed in many years of alliance partnership, mean that British politicians, of all parties, feel considerable confidence that the Federal Republic is unlikely to undertake any rash or dangerous steps.

It is true that British observers of the German scene remain somewhat puzzled by the ambiguous dichotomy between, on the one hand, the grandiose debate on Germany which preoccupies wide circles in that country, and, on the other, the modest nature of the 'small steps' of which Deutschlandpolitik in practice consists. As the experienced German journalist Robert Held expressed it, in reporting on an Anglo-German meeting of political scientists and other observers (*FAZ*, 5 July 1985):

The fact that Deutschlandpolitik is never absolutely clear to the British, as to other Western neighbours, was underlined by the remark that Deutschlandpolitik is on the one hand severely limited in its possibilities, but on the other hand has in a sense enormous dimensions in all directions: for the Federal Republic's partners, 'a dimension that stands out'.

On balance, however, the dominant British view is that the active foreign policy of any likely West German government – even one led by the SPD, whose views in opposition have led to some anxiety in Britain – would be unlikely to give any cause for alarm. West German policy, despite frequently heated debate over theoretical alternatives, is seen in practice as likely to be marked by continuity and moderation.

Notes

1 Eberhard Schulz and Peter Danilow, *Bewegung in der deutschen Frage? Die auslandische Besorgnisse über die Entwicklung in den beiden deutschen Staaten* (Bonn: Forschungsinstitut der Deutschen Gesellschaft für Auswärtige Politik, 1985).

2 This and other quotations from British documents of the period are taken from Rolf Steininger, *Deutsche Geschichte 1945–1951* (Frankfurt: Fischer, 1983).

3 See Marianne Bell, 'Britain and East Germany: the Politics of Non-Recognition', M.Phil. dissertation, University of Nottingham, 1977.

III CHANGING PATTERNS IN GERMANY

7 West German foreign and security interests

ROGER MORGAN[*]

One of the paradoxes of the Federal Republic's international situation is that it is at the same time the West European state with the most acute need for security and stability (it is one of Nato's few member-states to possess an extensive land frontier with the Warsaw Pact) and also the only West European state with a direct and explicit interest in changing the territorial status quo – by extending self-determination to the whole of the German nation. In theory, the apparent contradiction between the Federal Republic's wish to be secure (against change imposed from the East), and also to revise the European map, can be reconciled by the thought that peaceful change of an unstable status quo, in the name of an overriding principle such as national self-determination, may be the only way to achieve true peace and security: but, again, it may not. In practice, since the division of Germany has proved to be an unshakable feature of the European system for nearly forty years, the Federal Republic's diplomatic efforts have concentrated on ensuring security through a close alliance with the West. The 'revisionist' strand in West Germany's objectives has been represented by a series of declarations – in favour of reunification, self-determination, the softening of the effects of the division, or a 'security community' based on cooperation between the two German states.

Even though the international influence of the Federal Republic has increased steadily through the years (as a function of the country's growing economic weight, and the passage of time since 1945, to mention two of the major factors), the fundamental fact of national division has remained unchanged. It is more than twenty years since widespread talk of 'German Gaullism' began: the concept of a more assertive national policy associated with Franz-Josef Strauss and others. It is also twenty years since Willy Brandt, then leader of the opposition, accused the Christian Democratic

* Parts of this paper are based on my chapter 'Dimensions of West German Foreign Policy', published in W. E. Paterson and Gordon Smith, eds., *The West German Model* (Frank Cass: London, 1981). They are reproduced, in shortened and updated form, by permission of Frank Cass and Company.

Chancellors Adenauer and Erhard of leaving the Federal Republic 'an economic giant, but a political dwarf'. The Federal Republic has since then become in many respects a political giant too, with the ability to resist unwelcome pressure from others and the ability to influence world affairs in many ways. But the fundamental obstacle to real power status – the division of the country – still persists.

A further paradox of West Germany's situation, indeed, is that it is difficult to make much progress in improving the situation of the citizens of East Germany – 'safeguarding the substance of the German nation' – without giving increased recognition to East Germany as a regime, and thus deepening rather than overcoming the gap which divides the nation. After abandoning the imperatives of the Adenauer era, when Bonn's foreign policy gave the highest priority to weakening the international standing of the GDR through the 'Hallstein Doctrine' and other measures, the new Deutschlandpolitik of the 1970s and 1980s ran the risk of consolidating East Germany as a system through the official recognition that was necessary to develop contact with its citizens. To be sure, the standard answer to this problem, given by those responsible for the Ost- and Deutschlandpolitik of the Brandt and Schmidt years, was that the de facto recognition of the second German state was a necessary price to pay for the chance of maintaining the unity of the nation, and that, in the very long term, such a recognition would perhaps be seen as a necessary step towards reunification. It was, however, legitimate for the supporters of Chancellor Kohl to ask, when the Christian Democrats returned to power in 1982–3, for a balance-sheet showing exactly what thirteen years of Ostpolitik had actually contributed towards solving the German question.

Priorities in Bonn's foreign policy

The Federal Republic of the late 1980s is thus without any doubt one of the giants of the world economy, and exercises a giant's influence on the affairs of Nato and the European Community. At the same time, Bonn experiences the fundamental constraint of the division of Germany in essentially the same way as the truncated and still occupied Western protectorate of 1949: a state which came into existence to further Western interests in the Cold War, rather than a state with its own autonomous external policy.

Even though the past twenty years have seen the active involvement of West Germany in 'North-South' relations – e.g. through heavy economic interdependence and a high profile as a member of the UN – the facts of history and geography dictate an overwhelming priority for the East–West dimension. Lying as it does on the East–West divide, which passes through the centre of Germany, West Germany is acutely sensitive to the slightest change in East–West relations, whether it be the success or failure of superpower arms control negotiations, developments in economic relations between Western Europe and the Comecon area, or the repercussions of the political situation in Poland.

Underlying this sensitivity to all East–West developments is concern for the security of the Federal Republic and for the future of Germany as a whole: Bonn's foreign policy is heavily marked by a specific priority, that of Deutschlandpolitik. The history of Bonn's successive responses to this predicament is well known. In the first fifteen years or so after the Federal Republic's founding in 1949, Adenauer and his successors gave unquestioning priority to building up West Germany's ties with the West. The Federal Republic was firmly integrated into the structures of Western cooperation – economic, political and military – and sceptics, such as the SPD opposition, who asked how these Western commitments would solve the 'German problem' were told that reunification could come only after a long period, through a policy of 'negotiation from strength'.

This one-sided policy of tying the Federal Republic to the West, with its concomitant ban on links with the Soviet bloc (and even on diplomatic relations with states that recognized the 'so-called GDR'), failed to bring a solution to the 'German problem' any nearer. In fact, the building of the Berlin Wall in 1961 made reunification seem, if anything, further away than ever. Thus, as the SPD opposition abandoned its earlier resistance to the Federal Republic's essentially Westward orientation, the CDU-led governments began the process of 'small steps' towards a normalization of relations with the neighbours to the East. This process, when pushed harder by Brandt's Social Democrats in 1969, led to the establishment of official relations with East Germany and Poland by the early 1970s. It meant that the Federal Republic had, by adopting detente-oriented policies similar to those of Washington, Paris and Bonn, 'joined the crowd', in a period which President Nixon called the 'Era of Negotiations'.

There were plentiful East–West negotiations during the 1970s, and West Germany was at the heart of many of them: in particular the CSCE process leading to the Helsinki agreement, and the MBFR talks leading – as yet – to no agreement. How far, however, did this new period in East–West relations meet the security and political needs of the Federal Republic?

In terms of security, the stabilization of East-West relations which was achieved in the early 1970s, specifically through the Four Power Agreement on Berlin but also more generally, made Germans feel safer. The detente process also allowed Bonn to achieve an important part of its political aim in Deutschlandpolitik: greatly increased contacts between the two parts of Germany, and thus a contribution to 'maintaining the substance of the German nation'. At the same time, East German insistence on *Abgrenzung* (demarcation) and on its own status as a permanent and fully sovereign state, pointed to the depressing conclusion that political self-determination for all Germans would not be achieved any more easily by Brandt's policies than by Adenauer's.

The wave of violent debate about the 'German question', the 'German identity' and Germany's future which swept through the country in the early 1980s was partly a reaction to this disappointment with the fruits of Ostpolitik. The form and content of the debate were shaped by the external context of the breakdown of East–West detente, and the internal controversies over the change from Schmidt to Kohl, with the Greens, the anti-missile demonstrators and the Silesian refugee organizations all contributing to a confused controversy about the future of Germany and the threat to peace. However, the underlying issue was the paradox of West Germany's combination of economic strength, political maturity, high international prestige, and total inability to make real progress in solving the fundamental problem of national division.

Had Brandt's Ostpolitik, by recognizing the existence of the second German state, and the passage of time, by allowing greater German self-confidence, made the Federal Republic a more 'normal' state? And 'normal' by what standards? If self-assertiveness was a sign of normality, West Germany under Helmut Schmidt was certainly a 'normal' state. The Federal Republic, which constantly told the world, through the mouths of Chancellor Kohl and his ministers, that Germany's right to self-determination must never be forgotten, was behaving 'normally' too, by international standards – even though it was drawing attention to a basic abnormality of its situation.

But how far can self-assertiveness go, and what can it achieve? The catch-phrase 'German Gaullism', first used in the distant days of the 1960s, when Adenauer, Strauss and others accused Chancellor Erhard of neglecting Paris in favour of Washington, has been used again in the 1980s. The SPD in opposition has taken a strongly anti-American line, for instance on some of the strategic and scientific implications of SDI; the Kohl government has sometimes thundered in patriotic tones against the iniquities of East Germany and the Soviet Union; and spokesmen of West Germany have insisted that West Germany should give more weight to 'the German interest'. However, none of this can really be compared to full-blooded Gaullism; and in any case Gaullism has been abandoned even in its country of origin.

If France's freedom of action is limited, that of the Federal Republic is even more limited. This is in fact one reason for the striking proliferation of alternative scenarios for Germany's international role, on the part of commentators, intellectuals and opposition politicians. It is inevitable that Germany's situation will go on producing demands for change, from the right-wing patriotic demonstrations of the student corporations (demanding that reunification should even include Austria!) to the Greens' visions of a Germany neutralized and reunified.

Demand for change, however, is a minority interest. The political parties which promise great changes while in opposition adapt more or less to the previous foreign policy once they are in power (even Brandt's Ostpolitik, like Kohl's, was a continuation of existing trends), and the element of consensus among the parties which can seriously expect to hold office in Bonn (this does not include the Greens) is very substantial. There are of course conflicts in party-political rhetoric, and underlying tensions which have to be resolved by bargaining and compromise, but the actual policy 'mix' emerging from Bonn shows a high degree of continuity. Even the breakdown of the traditional consensus over defence policy, when the SPD set its face against the deployment of new Nato missiles in 1982, looks like proving less cataclysmic in practice than it seemed to observers at the time.

West Germany in four complex relationships

The Federal Republic is in fact a stable and in many ways a predictable state, which is still preoccupied – quite understandably – by the highly unsatisfactory relationship between state and nation (or 'states and nation') in Germany. The paradoxical nature of this position – in which strength coexists with vulnerability, influence with interdependence, and active involvement in some international issues with reticence towards others – can only be explained by considering how the international system has changed at the same time as Germany's potential influence has risen.

It can be said that the foreign policy of the Federal Republic has developed on the basis of steadily growing economic strength, combined with originally non-existent diplomatic and military resources, with the aim of inserting the embryonic West German state into a succession of international relationships, each of them designed to shape part of the external environment in accordance with Germany's as well as its partners' interests. The principal relationships which may be identified have been (not necessarily chronologically, since they have in fact coexisted over time): first, the integration of the Federal Republic into a West European entity expressed essentially by the Coal and Steel Community and by the Common Market (as well as the Council of Europe, etc.);

101

second, the binding of Germany into the Atlantic Alliance through Nato, WEU, and the most intimate relationship possible with the United States; third – much delayed in time, and much more diluted in character – a relationship with the Soviet bloc which began with Adenauer's very limited agreement with Moscow, blossomed via the 'small steps' of the 1960s into the Ostpolitik of Brandt, and has been maintained sceptically but determinedly by Schmidt and, after initial hesitation, by Kohl; and, fourth, the even more diffuse set of relationships involving the Federal Republic in world economic management and specifically the 'North–South dialogue', including the UN agencies, the Conference on International Economic Cooperation and its aftermath, and most especially the industrial world's relations with OPEC.

Despite all their manifest differences, these four sets of relationships have in common, from the West German point of view, that they were designed to provide a framework – a dependable and, as far as possible, predictable set of mutual obligations – within which certain of West Germany's major needs, and those of its partners in each case, could be met. Such a structure, although obviously important for any state in the modern international system, was particularly desirable for a country in the position of the Federal Republic, which had to make its way in the postwar world from a position of economic near-bankruptcy and political isolation. At the time, West Germany in any case purported to regard itself as no more than a provisional entity, destined to disappear when the goal of national reunification was achieved. Pending this obviously long-term prospect, the Federal Republic expected to find status, stability and solutions to its economic and security needs in its membership of a succession of overlapping but widely different international structures: West European, Atlantic, East–West and North–South.

An accumulation of unrelated developments has in the event made the Federal Republic a leading partner (though by no means the dominant one) in each of these relationships. Even without national reunification, which has receded to an infinitely remote horizon, the economic weight of the Federal Republic has made it by far the most influential member of the European Community, a power in Atlantic relations which has been nominated by some of its American admirers as worthy to run the alliance in 'bigemony' with the United States; in the East-West context, a power which the Russians, and to some extent the Chinese, treat with great respect and attention; and, in global terms, a power with a substantial voice in North–South and other economic debates.

The stature of the Federal Republic in each of its international roles is due, of course, not only to its intrinsic strength, but also to the fact that each one of these international frameworks has failed, in different ways, to develop the cohesion which some of its architects anticipated: a cohesion in which the element of interdependence would be so strong that the power of individual states, even the largest ones, would be constrained and even progressively diminished. This proposition must be examined in relation to each of the four principal partnerships in which the Federal Republic has been engaged.

The European connection

In the first of these partnerships, the West European one, both the preponderant weight of the German economy and the scope for German influence in an essentially intergovernmental rather than supranational negotiating framework have become very obvious during the 1970s and 1980s. In terms of size, a West German economy which represents one-third of the resources of the entire Community puts Bonn in a strong bargaining position. The fact that this has not been used to press for specific lines of Community policy results mainly from the fact that the present balance of Community policies and spending programmes is broadly acceptable to the Federal Republic.

West German policy in the Community has concentrated in the main on promoting economic integration by the removal of obstacles to the free movement of goods, capital and labour, by the development of a strict competition policy and by related measures of 'negative' integration. The Common Agricultural Policy had also, by the 1970s, proved to be advantageous to the Federal Republic – as was dramatically shown by the German veto on the limitation of support for grain prices in 1985. On the other hand, any further measures of interventionist, or 'positive', integration, such as large-scale industrial, regional or social policies, have proved less welcome to West Germany on grounds either of economic doctrine or of financial cost, and West Germany's influence, in the economic recession from 1973 onwards, has been used to check the development of policies of this kind.

In any case, the reluctance of West Germany's Community partners to pursue integration beyond the scope of the policy area under Community control at the start of the 1970s – essentially agriculture and trade – ensured that steps towards supranational integration would be much less likely than the growth of intergovernmental cooperation. In this intergovernmental framework, the Federal Republic has made important contributions, for instance by actively promoting the system of European Political Cooperation between the foreign ministries of the Nine, by making effective use of the European Council meetings of the heads of government, and by pressing in the 1980s for institutional reforms in the direction of 'European Union'. However, the net effect of all these

103

developments, in the mid-1980s, has been that the Federal Republic stands in a class of its own as an economic power in a Community whose supranational authority is unlikely to grow, and which is likely to prove only a limited framework for containing German national power and a limited vehicle for the promotion of German national interests in the years ahead. West Germany, like the other European members of Nato, will continue to try to establish a 'European identity' in defence and security matters, but only within the limits set by the primacy of the Atlantic Alliance.

The American relationship

Some of this analysis also applies to the second of Germany's main international partnerships, the Atlantic Alliance and especially the relationship with the United States. It was never expected, of course, that this relationship would develop into an institutionalized Community of the kind envisaged by the pioneers of the Common Market – except, perhaps, for specific occasions, as for instance when the Multilateral Force (MLF) of the mid-1960s was seen by its begetters as the nucleus of an Atlantic Defence Community. However, Bonn's relationship with Washington was and still is seen as the most important single element in the Federal Republic's foreign policy: a close understanding with Washington has been of vital importance in some of the most critical phases of Bonn's foreign policy, including the worst years of the Cold War when Dulles (with reservations) supported Adenauer, and also the years of active Ostpolitik when Kissinger (again with reservations) supported Brandt.

As is well known, there was an unhappy history of bad communications and outright conflict between the Schmidt and Carter administrations. Quite apart from the temperamental and other personal barriers between the two leaders, German–American relations were marked in the late 1970s by a number of real conflicts of interest, including many which reflected Germany's growing status and the declining authority of the United States as the leader of the West. The conflicts covered such diverse issues as German sales of nuclear technology to Brazil, American development of the so-called 'neutron bomb', disputes about how to handle the question of human rights in relations with the Soviet bloc, the appropriate Western response to the Iranian seizure of hostages and the Soviet invasion of Afghanistan, and, finally, the whole future of East–West detente in the aftermath of this invasion.

Washington's concern that Bonn's wish to maintain detente might crucially weaken the Western alliance, expressed in a tactlessly worded letter from Carter to Schmidt on the eve of the latter's visit to Moscow in

June 1980, inevitably recurred with increasing force under the Reagan administration. Even though the Kohl government has worked hard to remain on good terms with Washington, despite such difficult issues as SDI, there are enough serious conflicts of perspective and of real interest to ensure that the 1980s cannot be an easy time for an increasingly fissiparous Atlantic Alliance containing an increasingly powerful Germany.

The Ostpolitik

The third of Germany's substantial relationships – that with the Soviet bloc, which has developed essentially from Brandt's Ostpolitik of the early 1970s – has always had a much less intimate character than either of the two Western partnerships. Despite some Western fears that a 'new Rapallo' was in the making, and despite Strauss's allusions to the sinister machinations of the SPD's 'Moscow faction', the Ostpolitik has been firmly rooted in Westpolitik; neither Brandt nor Schmidt allowed the Federal Republic's involvement with the Soviet bloc to grow to a point at which it threatened their country's fundamental commitment to Nato.

Despite this, the importance to West Germany of continued detente has become very clear in the period since the Afghanistan crisis. Despite its strongly pro-American stand on strategic issues and its solidarity with the Olympic boycott, the Federal Republic has continued to insist that detente in Central Europe should not be jeopardized by a crisis in Central Asia. The importance of detente for West Germany lies not only in the economic significance of Soviet orders from the West German engineering industry, especially in a period of recession, or in the value to West Germany of Soviet natural gas supplies which will soon provide 3–4 per cent of Germany's energy requirements. There is also the vital human dimension represented by the fact that detente does something to soften the harsh division of the German nation. As a West German foreign policy expert argued in 1980 to a congressional committee in Washington, the West should not forget 'those 8 million West Germans that can now annually go to East Germany, those 1.5 million East Germans annually visiting the West, or the 60,000 German emigrants we extract every year out of East Europe'.

Even though the GDR's position on detente in general remains tough and uncompromising, the Federal Republic is likely to persist in its efforts. The main point to note, in the context of the present argument, is that in East–West relations, as elsewhere (and quite notably in inner-German relations), the Federal Republic is beginning to emerge as an autonomous international actor, negotiating its way through a confused and partially disintegrating environment, rather than functioning as a wholly integral part of a cohesive East–West structure of the kind envisaged when President Nixon proclaimed the 'Era of Negotiations' at the start of the 1970s.

North-South relations

In the fourth and last of Germany's international partnerships, the North–South dimension, the underlying pattern is even harder to perceive, partly because the original design was a more multifarious and in some ways less ambitious one than in the other three contexts. However, the same basic theme of a comprehensive design becoming fragmented, and Germany emerging as a more autonomous and more influential actor, can be discerned in the process by which the original picture of Europe–Third World relations (German and other European aid being distributed partly bilaterally, and partly through the EEC's Yaounde and Lomé Conventions, the quid pro quo for which being raw materials and markets) has given way to a much more differentiated world. This world has involved West Germany in relations with oil-rich and newly industrializing, as well as underdeveloped, countries, and has brought to light increasing divergences of view between the industrialized countries themselves on the proper approach to North–South relations.

These divergences are partly a reflection of more general disagreements about the philosophy of political intervention in economic policy, whether international or domestic: for instance, disagreements between West Germany and some of its partners in the Conference on International Economic Cooperation had their roots in the West German principle of non-intervention in market forces.

Currently, West German approaches to the problems of North–South relations appear to be marked by pessimism about the chances of any foreseeable economic aid from the industrial countries being adequate to cope with the problems. German thinking heavily stresses the degree to which existing Western aid programmes have been eroded in real terms by the population explosion and by the soaring cost of energy in the Third World. The lesson appears to be drawn that future Western aid – to the extent that it can be afforded – should be concentrated on certain developing countries where some positive effects can be anticipated, and perhaps also on specific sectors of development, such as energy resources. Such an approach implies a more nationally oriented West German development policy than hitherto, and the same phenomenon of a more independent German stance in relation to world economic issues, can also be detected in such different fields as economic cooperation agreements with oil-producing countries and others, or possible sales of West German military

106

equipment to countries as far apart (politically, as well as geographically) as Chile and India.

Conclusion

In all the main areas of Germany's international involvement – Western Europe, the Atlantic Alliance, the East-West relationship and the North-South complex – we can thus detect signs of the same underlying pattern: an increasingly authoritative Federal Republic emerging into a position of growing influence over an unstructured and less predictable environment. Many West Germans regret that the structures within which the Federal Republic sought to integrate itself into the international system have failed to develop in the way in which they were expected to do. However, the fact that they have failed – at least relatively – by no means signifies a return to the worst features of the international anarchy of the 1930s. The West Germans and their neighbours have learned to practise many of the habits of cooperation during the years when interdependence appeared to be the dominant rule of their lives, and there are few, if any, forces within the West German political system that would dispute the need for foreign policy to be conducted as if structures of interdependence were still being strengthened instead of weakened: such conduct can, of course, limit or reverse this weakening.

This analysis of how the Federal Republic's international situation has evolved has, inevitably, faced the fact that forty years of separate history have consolidated the separate positions of the two German states. In practical terms, as far as answers to the immediate questions of West German foreign policy are concerned, we are likely to see much more continuity than change, even if the present CDU/CSU/FDP government is replaced by one led by the SPD. In opposition, particularly during the dramatic period of the missile debate, the SPD has taken up policy positions far removed from those of the government. However, the history of Bonn's foreign policy has essentially been one of continuity, in which those who disagreed with the established majority consensus have come in practice to accept it. Thus the SPD, by 1960, had abandoned its resistance to the main lines of the Westpolitik laid down by Adenauer in the 1950s; the CDU and most of the CSU, by 1980, had in practice accepted the Ostpolitik pursued by Brandt and Schmidt in the 1970s; and there are strong indications that the SPD, if it returns to office in the late 1980s or early 1990s, will by then have adopted a policy on East–West relations not dissimilar to that of the Kohl government of today.

8 East German foreign and security interests

FRED S. OLDENBURG

Like any other state, the German Democratic Republic's foreign and security policy is determined by its basic characteristics and position in world politics. In the GDR's case, however, the combination of being a communist-ruled state, a front-line state within the socialist camp and a part of a divided nation, makes its web of interests particularly complex.

Dominated by the Socialist Unity Party (SED), the East German political system fits the general pattern of late totalitarian rule typical of Eastern Europe. As an outpost of the Soviet Union's European empire, it is situated at the juncture of two incompatible value systems, two hostile military blocs and two competing economic communities. Following the Polish crisis, which began in 1980, the GDR became Moscow's most important ally in Eastern Europe. But the most important influence on the GDR's foreign and security policy is its existence as a separate German state, created by Stalin during the Cold War, out of the defeated Third Reich.

The GDR's ruling class is the only one in Europe without either full political or national legitimation. Nevertheless, one has to bear in mind that the GDR is an extremely stable political system in the centre of Europe and it is very effectively ruled – the result of an elitist ideology (Marxist-Leninism), the stationing of 380,000 Soviet soldiers, and an elaborate system of repression combined with a successful welfare authoritarianism. Yet despite this history, during the past three years the GDR's political reputation has greatly improved in the East as well as in the West. In the overall context of world politics, the GDR has assumed a more significant role as a German, and as a socialist, state.[1]

This has not been an easy transition to make. For years East Germany was isolated diplomatically by West Germany and most of the non-socialist world as 'illegitimate' – its very existence as a state called into question. In the early 1970s, as West Germany improved its relations with the Soviet Union and the rest of Eastern Europe, the GDR was still obliged to settle for less than full recognition as a sovereign state by West Germany. The Basic Treaty between the two Germanies in 1972 was based on Willy Brandt's formula of two German states, but one German nation. This was felt, by both the Ulbricht regime and by the Honecker regime that succeeded it in 1971, to be an unflattering blemish on the GDR's statehood.

Thus, for the first half of the 1970s at least, the members of the SED Politburo thought they could best serve the basic interests of the GDR elite by a new ideological subordination to Moscow, by more offensively stressing their integration with the Soviet camp, by subordinating their inter-German, and especially their Berlin, policy to that of the Soviet Union,[2] by sharply 'delimiting' socialist GDR from capitalist West Germany, and finally by supporting the Soviet Union politically as well as militarily in its efforts to extend its influence in the Third World, above all in Africa.[3] In short, the new East-West detente of the 1970s was initially felt to be a risky and uncertain business for the GDR regime.

Yet, by the early 1980s, just a decade after the Basic Treaty was signed, the GDR presented a much more confident face to the outside world. The timid and defensive GDR of the early 1970s has developed a new interest of its own in maintaining German-German relations and preserving them to some degree from the deterioration in superpower relations. In 1984, the GDR joined some of its allies in the Warsaw Pact, including Hungary and Romania, in arguing for a special role for the smaller European states in East-West relations. Although a visit planned by Honecker to West Germany in 1984 was cancelled at Soviet insistence, the idea has not been dropped, and political and economic ties between the two Germanies appear to have flourished. This contrast between the GDR of the 1970s and the 1980s can best be explained by examining the different elements that have formed the framework of GDR foreign and security policy and how these have changed. Chief among these is the relationship with the Soviet Union.

The German Democratic Republic and Soviet bloc

The most important interest of the GDR's ruling class lies in securing its power and the system's stability, or, as they call it, in building socialism and communism. Even today this is possible only on the condition that the Soviet army remains stationed in Eastern Europe and in the GDR, that the Soviet bloc maintains a high degree of coherence and that, at the same time, the SED regime is offered increasing leeway to undertake whatever it thinks necessary for its own security.[4]

On the other hand, the SED leaders have gone through a quite singular historical experience: until 1954–5, their rule over one part of the divided German state was in no way secure. Only in 1954 did the Soviet government grant the GDR limited sovereignty. The Soviet Union's rights over the whole of Germany and Berlin are still in force. Only as late as 1964, and at the end of a long and hard argument with Khrushchev, did Ulbricht finally manage to get a treaty on mutual assistance with the Soviet Union. The fear that the East Europeans might offer concessions to Bonn after 1967 led to the 'Ulbricht doctrine' that effectively introduced an East German veto over contacts with Bonn and, in the end, to an interventionist attitude on the part of the Ulbricht group towards events in Czechoslovakia in 1968. After 1968 Ulbricht seemed to be at the peak of his influence with the Brezhnev leadership, but in reality the power of the old master of German communism was already on the decline.

In July 1969, when Kosygin and Brezhnev were aiming at a general detente, which included the Federal Republic, and at playing down the Berlin problem, Ulbricht still wanted full diplomatic recognition from West Germany before the process of detente could get under way. But by this time Soviet interest in better relations with West Germany outweighed East Germany's principles and led to Ulbricht's political demise. In his own interest and that of the regime, both of which he understood perfectly well, Honecker subordinated himself to the Soviet Union and took over completely the Soviet concept of integration and of the drawing-together of the bloc's member countries.[5] At the time, Honecker felt compelled 'irrevocably' to bind the GDR to the Soviet Union because of the danger of losing too much of his influence over Moscow's policy towards the West by compromising with Bonn. He appeared to have little choice: even the 1964 treaty between the Soviet Union and the GDR, which after all obliged the Soviet Union to 'consultations', did not alter the minor role assigned to the GDR within the Warsaw Pact. The treaty concerning the stationing of troops, agreed upon in 1957 and still in force, already provided the Soviet army, in cases of emergency, full freedom of movement and all emergency laws.[6] Even the friendship treaty of 1975 did not change anything in the Soviet Union's obligations concerning Germany 'as a whole'. The Soviet army, with twenty of its divisions stationed in East Germany, makes no secret of its responsibility to intervene in both Germanies (according to the enemy states formula, UN Charter, art. no. 53,2 and 107). It calls itself 'Group of Soviet Forces in *Germany*' (GSSD). Between 3 and 16 April 1985 (and previously in December 1972 and June 1974 during the preliminaries for the renewal of the Warsaw Pact), when the GDR repeatedly mentioned only the group of Soviet forces in the GDR, the then Soviet commander, M. M. Zaitsev, voiced vigorous objection.

This aspect of the GDR's subordination to the Soviet Union has always been a dent in East Germany's sovereign pride. It is also a means for both countries to signal their displeasure with each other's policies from time to time. The independent manoeuvring of different parts of the troops under the supreme command of the late Soviet Defence Minister, Marshal D. F. Ustinov, in June–July 1984, at a time when ill-feelings between East Berlin and Moscow were at their height, must have left the GDR authorities pondering. Similarly, when the GDR authorities ordered the closure of the Glienicker Bridge, reserved as a border crossing-point to Berlin (West) for the military personnel residing in Potsdam, they were ordered by the Russians to cancel the action within a few hours.

Such frictions have long been a part of GDR–Soviet relations, since the GDR chafes at the restrictions on its sovereignty that the 'open' German question places on it. The fact that not just West Germany, but also the Soviet Union, has an interest in keeping things that way has been one of the persistent handicaps on the devleopment of a more independent East German foreign and security policy. However, even here, developments outside the strictly bilateral GDR–Soviet relationship have pushd the Honecker regime over the years into a more public defence of what it ees to be East Germany's own better interests.

In some areas, such as East Germany's involvement in Soviet and Cuban foreign-policy adventures in Africa, the tasks assigned to the GDR coincided more or less happily with the GDR's own interest in forging a wider role for itself in the world, and the costs entailed were tolerable ones. However, as the detente of the 1970s began to disintegrate, East Germany's calculation of its own best interests also appeared to change. In the second half of President Carter's administration, when the East–West relationship seemed near to a complete breakdown, East Berlin distanced itself to a certain degree from Moscow. The real shock, however, came when the Soviet leadership, completely absorbed by the Afghanistan problem and paralyzed by possible consequences to be feared from Carter's definition of interests in the Gulf region, was unable to stabilize the situation in Poland in 1980.

The Polish crisis, particularly the years 1980–2, proved the Soviet empire to be quite fragile and the SED's rule to be on shaky ground, facing on the one side the Federal Republic governed by the Social Democrats and, on the other, a rebellious Polish labour movement.[7] The Soviet Union's excessive arms build-up, its armed intervention in Afghanistan and the resulting reactions in the West put detente at risk, a detente which in the end had proved more favourable to the SED leadership than it had at first anticipated. The growing rivalry between the two superpowers and a war hysteria in the Soviet Union after Nato's double-track decision of 1979 affected the role of the smaller European countries and apparently caused a crisis of confidence, in which East European party leaders became doubtful about the Soviet ability to conduct a creative Westpolitik.[8]

To complicate matters further, a worldwide economic crisis began to affect the socialist countries, while the Soviet Union postponed basic political and economic decisions concerning Comecon, the bloc's economic alliance, of which East Germany is a leading member. The whole of this picture of disintegration has to be seen against the background of the Kremlin's succession crisis, starting in the early 1980s, which considerably drained the Soviet leadership's power and caused a certain confusion, with contradictory signals being sent out from different authorities and even from within each individual apparatus of the Moscow power centre.

None of this altered the GDR's ultimate dependence on the Soviet Union, but it did make the GDR leadership think hard about what its own foreign and security goals should be. Not for the first time, the interests of a leading power (in this case, the Soviet Union) conflicted with those of a minor one, although both were ruled by communists. The question now facing the Honecker leadership was whether to continue the dialogue between East and West, or cooperate with the Soviet Union in restricting it, at the risk of further damage to East German interests.

The special relationship with the Federal Republic

The GDR's foreign policy has two fixed points: on the one side, there are relations with the Soviet Union and, on the other, a special relationship with the Federal Republic of Germany, a relationship which combines antagonism with cooperation. Both elements have to be kept in balance in order to look after the state's best interests.[9]

Although it rejects the political reasoning behind it, in practice the GDR accepts a special relationship between the two German states, in part because inter-German trade offers great economic advantages to the GDR, and also because the majority of the GDR's population refuses to be distanced from the other Germany. Good-neighbourly relations therefore help to keep the GDR citizens quiet. What is more, special German-German relations give the GDR a special political role to play, both in Europe and in Germany, at times of political change in superpower relations. The Soviet Union benefits because it hopes to influence West Germany by controlling German–German relations. Furthermore, the import of technology positively affects GDR exports. By far the biggest customer for East German exports is the Soviet Union.

Legally, however, East Berlin's basic point of view has remained unchanged. According to the SED, there is no longer a unified or single German nation. Instead, an independent socialist nation is developing within the German Democratic Republic. The two Germanies are, therefore, foreign states when dealing with each other and must base their relationship on international law. At the beginning of the Polish crisis, the GDR hardened its position by issuing the so-called Gera demands in 1980. These are: (a) the recognition of the GDR citizenship; (b) the removal of the central registration office (which registers crimes of GDR authorities committed against its citizens); (c) the upgrading of existing 'permanent representations' into full-scale embassies; and (d) the settlement of the Elbe frontier dispute between the two German states in favour of the GDR. The extent to which the Honecker leadership presses these various demands in public, however, seems to vary according to the state of the wider German–German relationship – and the pressures the GDR itself is under to heighten the points of difference, as opposed to cooperation, with West Germany.

In practice, however, the SED leadership apparently has no intention of questioning German–German ties. As a result, the GDR's German policy is caught in a series of tensions and conflicts. On the one hand, the Gera demands are upheld and, on the other, the practical and future interests of both leadership and population in East Germany lead the GDR to keep German–German ties intact and even to improve them. Furthermore, there is the obvious contrast between the 3 million or so GDR citizens who, for supposed 'security reasons', are allowed neither personal nor postal contact with West Germany, and the millions of West German visitors to the GDR. An average of 6.5 million West Germans and West Berliners travel to the GDR each year. Before the currency exchange requirements were doubled in the autumn of 1980, the figure was 8 million. Since 1964 pensioners have been allowed to travel from East to West; in 1980 roughly 1.5 million pensioners visited their relatives in West Germany. Each year there are more than 50,000 GDR citizens who are allowed to go to the West because of family emergencies. Even at the height of the missile crisis, 40,000 GDR citizens were allowed to emigrate from the GDR to West Germany; in 1985, the figure was 25,000.

Such contradictions aside, by almost any measure the German–German relationship looks in better shape in the mid 1980s than one would expect from the GDR's official policy of delimitation. The reasons form part of the explanation for both the apparent change in Honecker's attitude to East–West relations and his conflict with Moscow over his German policy.

One essential motive for keeping the special German–German relationship going is the invaluable economic and financial advantage that it gives the GDR, estimated at between \$0.5 and \$1.5 billion a year.[10] This amount includes the special 'swing' credit that helps finance any deficit in East Germany's trade with West Germany, transit and highway fees, compulsory exchange requirements for visitors, visa fees, payments by the West German government to enable East Germans to emigrate, payments for the release of political prisoners, hard currency shops and other service fees.

West Germany is also an important trade and financial partner (see Chapter 9). The GDR is able to buy high-quality goods without foreign currency, since all trade is calculated and managed in special units of account. In the aftermath of the Polish crisis, when many Eastern European countries were having difficulty borrowing in the West, West German banks granted two credits amounting to about DM 2 billion. This enabled the GDR to reduce short-term liabilities and to obtain further credits in Western Europe and the United States. In some ways, this special relationship with West Germany helps the GDR to be less dependent economically on the Soviet Union even though it is in the GDR's interest to be in close contact with both economies.

Nor, apparently, has it proved so disadvantageous politically in the GDR to appeal to a certain 'Germanness', despite the continued need ideologically to separate the GDR from West Germany as representatives of two different social systems. Despite the fact that in 1971, the SED leadership renounced the West German thesis of 'the unity of the German nation', and declared that the GDR was developing into an independent socialist nation on a socio-economic basis,[11] it proved harder to 'de-Germanize' than had first been thought. Then, on 12 December 1974, Honecker declared the citizenship of East Germany to be 'GDR', the nationality to be 'German'. Already at the 8th Party Congress in 1971, he had promised to restrict the policy of delimitation to a certain period of time, that is 'as long as the FRG is an imperialist state'.[12] And, in an interview on 6 July 1978, he hinted for the first time at the prospect of a united nation in the event of a socialist revolution in the Federal Republic.[13] When Honecker sent a letter to Chancellor Kohl at the height of the anti-INF campaign, he concluded it with the words 'in the name of the German people'.

This new-found confidence – no longer to feel directly threatened by the notion of a continued German nationhood – probably owes something to the fact that the GDR's chief ally, the Soviet Union, while it insists on keeping open its own rights in Germany, has not put the GDR under any great pressure to make concessions to West Germany that would threaten the stability of the GDR and its leadership. Similarly, the disadvantage of having to do business (however lucrative) with an ideologically and politically challenging West German state has since been more than outweighed by the legitimacy such contacts confer on the GDR leadership in the eyes of other states less directly involved in the German issue. Now widely recognized as a member of the world community, the GDR has less to fear from West Germany than when West Germany was the very state blocking international recognition of the GDR regime in the 1950s and 1960s. Even the Honecker visit to West Germany, when it takes place, will underline the formal state-to-state relationship that now exists between the two German states, whatever the finer legal points of West Germany's contention that their relations cannot be considered fully 'normal'.

A changing profile of interests

Relations between East Germany and the Soviet Union used to be correctly characterized as a state of unhappy subservience on the part of East Germany. This relationship has since undergone a number of gradual, but important, shifts. Despite this, elements determining East Germany's perceptions of its own foreign and security interests remained unchanged. Most important among these elements are: the SED regime's dependence on the presence of 380,000 Soviet soldiers on East German territory; the economy's dependence on reliable Soviet deliveries of raw materials and energy; and the regime's continuing concern about national and political legitimacy.

In the past, before it enjoyed widespread international recognition East Germany depended exclusively on the Soviet Union for its ability to defend its own interests. This was one of the reasons why East Germans quite enthusiastically assumed a number of cumbersome Third World commitments in support of Soviet foreign policy. Nowadays, and in particular since 1983–4, the GDR sees itself as being well established and even has direct relations with the other superpower, the United States. As a consequence, the GDR leaders' dependence on Soviet help on the international stage has much diminished.

This, combined with differences between East Berlin and Moscow over the Polish crisis, which the SED leaders believed directly threatened the economic and political stability of East Germany, and a difference of opinion over the best response to Nato's decision to begin deployment of new medium-range missiles to counterbalance Soviet SS–20s, led to a sharper profiling of East German foreign policy in the 1980s.

INF and Germany

At first the GDR's front organizations, in close cooperation with CPSU secretary B. N. Ponomarev, did everything they could to lend support to the West German 'peace movement'. At the same time, the GDR propoganda media addressed West Germany's leading circles with heavy broadsides faithfully echoing Moscow's threats of an approaching 'ice-age' in East–West relations and also of a freeze of inter-German relations, unless the envisaged deployment of American medium-range missiles was cancelled. East Germany may have genuinely feared the consequences for its improved international standing and for its profitable relations with West Germany if the INF decision went ahead.

Yet the East German attitude changed as soon as the West German parliament had decided, in November 1983, that the American missiles should be deployed as scheduled. The SED leadership began quickly to back-track in order to preserve its ties with West Germany. In the process it even permitted itself conspicuous deviations from the general foreign policy line of the Soviet Union, namely by seeking to downplay the significance of the deployment. And it strove to keep inter-German relations out of the fray instead of penalizing West Germany as the Soviet Union tried to do. The Soviet Union had at first been happy to try to use East Germany to persuade West Germany not to agree to INF deployment. But after the Soviet strategy had failed, the SED leaders suddenly became afraid that the threatened freezing of East–West relations might entail more than just economic disadvantages for the GDR. Honecker had to take into account strong tendencies towards restiveness on the part of the GDR population, which was already apprehensive of a dangerous escalation of the East–West conflict due to the war-scare propaganda promoted by the official Soviet media. Possibly, the SED leaders themselves were scared by the prospect that the GDR could become a target for Soviet and American medium-range missiles.

Therefore, the GDR leadership made it plain that it had by no means greeted 'with joy' Soviet 'countermeasures' announced on 25 October 1983. Simultaneously it openly embraced a policy of 'damage limitation'. In his efforts for continuation of the East–West dialogue, Honecker was actively supported by Hungary, as well as indirectly by Romania, Bulgaria and Poland. Thus, the profile of the GDR's foreign and security interests appeared to have changed as a result of a new-found confidence in dealing with West Germany, and the general crisis which at the turn of the 1980s once again threatened Soviet domination over Eastern Europe.[14] Whether the GDR is able to look after its own interests depends not only on Honecker's assertiveness, but also on how strong and united the Soviet Union's decision-makers are, on their concept of world and bloc politics, on the general condition of world politics and, last but not least, on economic pressures within the Soviet bloc. Following the appointment of Mikhail Gorbachev as Soviet leader in 1985, and starting with the Gorbachev–Honecker meeting in May 1985, Moscow and East Berlin have begun once again to coordinate more closely their foreign trade. However, a united concept regarding foreign policy will be harder to reach. Gorbachev gave little indication in his first year of just how the new Kremlin leadership would handle its allies in Eastern Europe, except to call for greater economic coordination.

The GDR, for its part, has made itself the advocate of a policy aiming at securing world peace and realistic coexistence. The introduction of this revised philosophy points to the possibility that the GDR, following influential Soviet authors, has begun to discard the distinction between 'just and unjust wars',[15] at least in case of a nuclear war – a distinction originating with Lenin.[16] Moreover, to secure peace is more important than to bring down the capitalist social order. Honecker himself, both in East German and in other Soviet bloc media, indirectly opposed those discussing a preventive war against West Germany.[17] On 4 July 1984, he said to the Greek Prime Minister, Andreas Papandreou: 'It would be a tragic mistake to try to solve the current problems of the world, including those between capitalism and socialism, by military means. It would lead to catastrophe.'[18] Addressing West Germany, Honecker used the expression 'common security', a phrase quite effective in terms of propaganda and going further than the Soviet position of 'equal security'. Perhaps this explains the somewhat reserved Soviet reaction in 1985 to an outline agreement between the SED and West Germany's main opposition party, the SPD, for a chemical-weapon-free zone, starting with the two Germanies. Although the proposal fitted neatly into Honecker's notion of 'common security', it may have gone too far for the Soviet Union.[19]

Conflict and coincidence: the Soviet Union

Of course, part of the apparent divergence at times between Soviet and GDR foreign and security interests can be explained by the confusion of the succession crisis in Moscow between 1982 and 1985, which occurred just at the time that East–West relations deteriorated sharply over the INF crisis and the Soviet Union walked out of the arms-control negotiations in Geneva. Like its neighbours in Eastern Europe, the GDR had difficulties reading the signals coming from Moscow. Between spring and autumn 1984, Moscow's attitude towards the West indicated refusal and confrontation, but other factors show that there existed differing opinions within the Soviet Communist Party. On many occasions, Honecker spoke up for reopening negotiations, including negotiations about medium-range missiles.[20] He expressed the opinion that more arms did not produce more security, without, however, criticizing the Soviet lead in SS–20s. It became more and more clear that the GDR felt Moscow's confrontational policy to be a political and commercial burden which put its internal and external security at risk. Above all, it threatened again the international acceptance of the GDR that Honecker had worked so hard to achieve.

As always, there are two sides to this issue. While East Germany's distinctive foreign policy in the early 1980s owes something to the development of the regime's interests in a new international climate of detente in the 1970s, and while there were times of obvious friction in GDR–Soviet relations in the early 1980s as East–West relations deteriorated, there was little that the GDR was doing that in the medium to long term threatened to harm Soviet interests. On the contrary, by trying to preserve a bridge to Western Europe, through West Germany, the GDR fitted neatly into a long-term trend in Soviet foreign policy that had been only temporarily set aside during the row over INF.

Although the GDR's offer of a 'coalition of reason' was originally directed towards the FRG, and was designed to preserve the benefits of German–German relations, starting in autumn 1984, it turned more and more towards socialist governments and parties in Western Europe and aimed at 'conceiving a socialist Europe policy'.[21] The Eastern bloc's summit meeting in Sofia in October 1985, and the following summit in Geneva between Gorbachev and Reagan in November 1985, can be interpreted as a confirmation of all those in Eastern Europe who had opted for damage limitation and continued dialogue despite follow-up armament and countermeasures. And although Gorbachev devoted much attention to this aspect of superpower relations, it was clear too that Western Europe was to be a separate target of his diplomacy. To exaggerate a bit, one could say that Honecker and Kádár were principally right. Inevitably, the concept of a 'socialist Europe policy' implies a certain degree of anti-Americanism. This fitted happily with Honecker's view of the 'Europeanization' of the GDR in a way that would enable it to deal more with Bonn.

Bloc politics

At the same time, however, the once ultra-loyal GDR began somewhat to change its attitude to loyalty and discipline within its own alliance. For example, having usually in the past been prepared to take its lead from Moscow when it came to ideological and other disputes within the socialist camp, the SED leadership is now apparently pushing strongly for a far-reaching normalization with Peking. During a visit to Peking in December 1985 by a delegation headed by Horst Sindermann, the president of the Volkskammer and a member of the Politburo preparations were begun for a meeting between Honecker and Peking leaders that, as things stand, have taken relations farther and faster than Sino-Soviet relations have yet gone. But of potentially greater significance in this respect was East Germany's support for the role of the smaller socialist states in East–West relations. It was at the end of March 1984 that Prague first directed its propaganda against smaller Eastern European countries who followed more closely their own interests than those of the bloc as a whole when defining their policies.[22] The Czechs won some support from Moscow, but not East Germany. Small wonder, since the accusations were clearly directed both at Hungary and also at the Honecker regime. Both were accused of 'capitulation' and of developing a 'theory of national communism'.[23]

At first the GDR kept its head down, since it was at the time apparently in some dispute with the Soviet Union over Honecker's plans to visit West Germany later that year. It ignored the Soviet and Czechoslovak attacks, since its own interests tallied best with those of Hungary. Hungarian rejoinders appeared selectively in the GDR press,[24] and included those which advocated a policy promoting peace[25] and the GDR–West German dialogue.

The policy of dialogue with the West practised by the SED has helped to create a new constellation in Eastern Europe. Because this time it joined forces with the less conformist countries – Hungary, Romania and probably also to a limited extent this time Bulgaria – it succeeded in defending itself against the more orthodox policy pursued by Prague and some of the more conservative elements in Moscow. Yet this new departure was possible only because the SED expected the Kremlin to change its own course in the long run.

One has to be careful not to overstate the GDR's boldness. The GDR leadership still relies for its own security on a high degree of political and ideological coherence within the Soviet bloc. As yet, the GDR has not developed a fully independent national identity. Therefore, there is no other basis for the legitimation of the East German ruling class than Marxism–Leninism and economic performance. One has to keep in mind, too, that the GDR is still economically dependent on the Soviet Union. As of 1984, 38.6 per cent of its foreign trade was done with the Soviet Union; in 1980, its debt amounted to 2.5 billion roubles. At the end of the last Five-Year Plan, this had risen to 3.7 billion. The trade turnover between Moscow and East Berlin is supposed to be increased by 28 per cent in 1986–90, compared with 1981–5.[26] Attempts which started in 1983 to reduce this mountain of debt have until now only managed to reduce the rate of growth of the deficit. Since 1982, the Soviet Union has cut its supply of raw materials to the GDR, but increasingly demands better-quality products from all its Comecon allies. In this way, foreign trade with the West has been curtailed.

All the same, the GDR has become less of a satellite than it was up to the early 1980s. The patron–client relationship needs redefinition.[27] The new, more consolidated Soviet leadership may try to pull the reins in Eastern Europe more tightly under its own control, and East Germany may find its freedom of manoeuvre more carefully watched. The fact remains, however, that one can no longer speak about identical interests between the two capitals. A better term would be 'parallel interests'. The Soviet Union certainly wanted to push the GDR to loosen its ties with Bonn and Washington. The same is happening again in an attempt to disrupt closer ties between West Germany and the United States concerning SDI. The Soviet Union would like to use the GDR to gain leverage over Western security policy in general. But the pressure today seems less direct than it was during 1982–4.

To sum up, in 1984 and 1985 the GDR tried, in foreign policy, to win full acceptance as a normal participant in the international system. It therefore attempted to secure greater leeway for itself in its relations both with Moscow and with Bonn – a development which would, the SED hoped, have the side-effect of helping to legitimize the regime in the eyes of the GDR's population. Beyond that, on a number of occasions the East German leadership sought to promote its own particular foreign-policy and security interests whenever the Soviet leadership appeared to be pre-occupied with other problems or with its own succession crises. But nevertheless two points must be made: by none of its more self-interested initiatives did the GDR actually jeopardize the basic ideological and military–strategic positions of the Soviet Union's hegemonic power. And, finally, whenever the Society leadership convincingly demonstrated its disapproval, the SED leadership never risked a real showdown, preferring eventually to give in. The reason is that, even more than any other East European state, East Germany's very legitimacy and survival depends on the existence of the Warsaw Pact and alliance with Moscow. Gorbachev is likely to reconsolidate control and discipline in the bloc, while recognizing the differences between parties. He will probably give the East Europeans more of a voice in bloc affairs. And because of his greater emphasis on dialogue with Western Europe, he will need both the discipline and the support of the GDR in his dealings with both West and East.

Notes

1 Cf. W. Hänisch (ed.), *Geschichte der Aussenpolitik der DDR*. Abriss (Berlin (East): Staatsverlag der DDR. 1984). S. Doerberg (ed.), *Aussenpolitik der DDR. Sozialistische deutsche Friedenspolitik* (Berlin (East), Staatsverlag der DDR, 1982). S. Quillitzsch (ed.), *Die DDR in der Welt des Sozialismus* (Berlin: Staatsverlag der DDR, 1985). W. Bruns, *Die Aussenpolitik der DDR* (Berlin (West), 1985). D. Childs, *The GDR: Moscow's German Ally* (London: Allen and Unwin,

1983). Hans-Adolf Jacobsen *et al.* (eds.), *Drei Jahrzehnte Aussenpolitik der DDR. Bestimmungsfaktoren, Instrumente, Aktionsfelder* (Munich–Vienna: Oldenbourg Verlag, 1979). J. Kupe, 'Aussenpolitik', in: *DDR-Handbuch*. Wissenschaftliche Leitung H. Zimmermann, vol 1, 3rd edn. (Cologne: Wissenschaft und Politik, 1984), pp. 104–22.

2 Cf. F. Oldenburg, *Die personalpolitischen Entscheidungen des VIII. Parteitages der SED*. Berichte des BIOst 22 (1972). N. E. Moreton, *East Germany and the Warsaw Alliance: The Politics of Detente* (Boulder, Co: Westview Press, 1978). See G. Wettig, *Community and Conflict in the Socialist Camp 1965–1972* (New York: St Martin's Press, 1975); G. Wettig, *Die Sowjetunion, die DDR und die deutsche Frage 1965–1976*. 3rd edn. (Stuttgart: 1977).

3 M. Croan, A New African Corps, *The Washington Quarterly*. 3, No 1 (Winter 1980) pp 21–37. H. von Loewis, 'Das politische und militärische Engagement der DDR in Schwarzafrika', *Beiträge zur Konfliktforschung* 1 (1978) pp. 5–54. M. J. Sodaro, 'The GDR and the Third World: Supplicant and Surrogate', in *Eastern Europe and the Third World, East vs. South* ed. by M. Radu, (New York: Praeger 1981).

4 Cf. F. Oldenburg, 'Die Autonomie des Musterknaben. Zum politischen Verhältnis DDR–UdSSR'. In R. Löwenthal und B. Meissner (eds.), *Der Sowjetblock zwischen Vormacht-Kontrolle und Autonomie* (Cologne: Markus-Verlag 1984), pp. 153–97.

5 Cf. H. Kirsch, Soviet–GDR Relations in the Honecker Era. *East Central Europe* 2 (1979) pp. 152–72. M. Croan, *East Germany. The Soviet connection* (Beverly Hills, Cal.: Sage Publications, 1976).

6 *Neues Deutschland*, 14 Mar., 1957. See B. Meissner, 'Die DDR im sowjetischen Bündissystem', *Aussenpolitik* 4 (1984) pp. 373–93.

7 Cf. D. Bingen, 'Die DDR und Polen: Ein Verhältnis wird bereinigt'. *DDR-Report*, 8 (1983) p. 430. F. Oldenburg, 'Die SED und die Klassenkämpfe in Polen', *Deutschland-Archiv*, 10 (1981) pp. 1048–58. F. Oldenburg, 'Das Verhältnis SED-PVAP wahrend der Krise in Polen 1980–82', *Polen 1982*. Sonderveröffentlichung des BIOst (July 1982) pp. 112–36.

8 H. Adomeit, *Widersprüche im Sozialismus, Sowjetpolitik in Osteuropa im Kontext der Ost–West-Beziehungen*. SWP-A2 I 1d, 85, Ebenhausen (February 1985). W. Berner, *Reformdruck, Machtfragen und Partikularismus im osteuropäischen Vorfeld der UdSSR 1980–1984*. Berichte des BIOst 20 (1984). G. Jozsa, *Ungarn im Kreuzfeuer der Kritik aus Moskau und Prag*. Berichte des BIOst 5 (1985). F. Oldenburg, 'Geht die SED eigene Wege im Sowjetimperium?' *Deutschland Archiv*, 5 (1984) pp. 491–96. W. Pfeiler, *Die Sowjetunion und ihr europäisches Bundnissystem* (St Augustin, July 1985). Ch. Gati, 'Soviet Empire, Alive But Not Well', *Problems of Communism*, March–April 1985, pp. 73–86.

9 See M. Croan, 'The Politics of Division and Detente in East Germany', *Current History*, 84 (Nov. 1985) p. 369–72 and 388–90. S. Kupper, 'Die DDR im sowjetischen System und ihr Sonderverhältnis zur Bundesrepublik Deutschland', in K. Kaiser and H.P. Schwarz, *Weltpolitik* (Stuttgart: Klett-Cotta, 1985), pp. 469 ff.

10 Cf. J. Garland, Paper for Third World Congress for Soviet and East European Studies Washington DC, 30 Oct. – 4 Nov. 1985, and J. Garland, *GDR–FRG Relations*, EUJ Collection Papers, Florence 1985.

11 For a description of this dilemma see W. Seiffert, 'SED und nationale Fragen', in W. Vernohr (ed.), *Die deutsche Einheit kommt bestimmt* (Bergisch Gladbach: Lübbe, 1982), pp. 161–79. See also: E. Schneider, *Der Nationsbegriff der DDR und seine deutschlandpolitische Bedeutung*, Berichte des BIOst, 33/1981, and R. W. Schweizer, 'Die DDR und die Nationale Frage'. *Aus Politik und Zeitgeschichte* 51–2, 21 Dec. 1985, pp. 37–54.

12 *Neues Deutschland*, 16 June, 1971.

13 Inteview with *Saarbrücker Zeitung*, 6 July, 1978.

14 As an example of hardliners against emancipation, see, O. Vladimirov, 'Veduschchiy Faktor mirovogo revolutsionnogo progressa', *Pravda*, 21 June, 1985: O. V. Borisov, 'Soyuz novogo tipa', *Voprosy istorij*, KPSS, 4 (1984) pp. 34–49. (Behind both pen names might be a group headed by O. Rakhmanin in the CC department which is concerned with 'relations with ruling Communist Parties'. Rakhamin's position was supported only by Prague, even in Moscow it is controversial). More prudent: N. Shislin, 'Pervaya Zapoved', *Novoe Vremy*, 35 (1985), 16. Equally reseved: O. Bogmolov, 'Soglasovanie ekonomischeskh interesov i politiki pri sotsializme', *Kommunist*, 10 (1985) pp. 83–93.

15 G. K. Shakhnazarov, 'Logika politischeskogo myshleniya v yaderuyu eru', *Voprosy filosofii*, 5 (1984) pp. 63–74. D. Proektor, *Ugroza evrope* (Moscow: 1981, revised edition 1983). The

Fred S. Oldenburg

Soviet discussion is to be found in P. H. Lange, 'Die sowjetische Militärdoktrin und der Westen', *Europa Archiv*, 6 (1984) pp. 179–86. See also P. Klein *et al.*, *Europa, Frieden oder Untergang* (Berlin (East): Staatsverlag der DDR, 1984), pp. 40, 51ff. More references in W. Rehm, 'Wandlungen der Kommunistischen Militärdoktrin', *Deutschland Archiv*, 11 (1985), pp. 11, 98, 1208. J. Kuppe, 'Aspekte in der kommunistischen Kriegstheorie', *Deutschland Archiv*, 1 (1985) pp. 34–39. More sceptical, having emigrated recently to the West: F. Loeser, Ehrlicher Sinneswandel oder pragmatisches Taktieren, *Deutschland Archiv*, 9 (1985) pp. 919–26. Negatively viewing the GDR's intention to disarm: P. R. Weilemann, 'Chemiewaffenfreie Zone'. Ein Danaer-Geschenk der SPD *Deutschland Archiv*, 9(1985), pp. 943–8.

16 See *Philosophie des Friedens im Kampf gegen die Ideologie des Krieges*, ed. Militärakademie F. Engels (Berlin (East): Militärverlag, 1984), pp. 52, 75. H. Bonk *et al.*, *Friedenssicherung und Abrüstung* (Berlin (Ost), p. 164. There it says: 'World peace is based on peaceful coexistence... It does not presuppose the overcoming of antagonistic class structures, meaning the overthrow of the capitalist states.'

17 See 'Raketen im Planquadrat X', *Volksarmee*, 11 April 1983. L. Bezymensky, 'Nado li stuchat kulakom po stolu', *Novoyevremya*, 17 (1984) p. 26. See also Honecker, 'Für Sicherheit, Zusammenarbeit und gutnachbarliche Beziehungen', *Probleme des Friedens und des Sozialismus* 4 (1984), preprint in *Neues Deutschland*, 24/5 March, 1984.

18 Honecker: 'Nothing is more important than to preserve peace' in *Neues Deutschland*, 5 July, 1984, p. 3.

19 So E. Schultz, *Deuschlandfunk*, 13 Jan., 1986, 21h55.

20 i.e.: Interview for the French newspaper *Revolution*, also in *Neues Deutschland*, 6 Jan. 1984. See also 'Zur Auswertung der 7. Tagung des ZK der SED'. *Neues Deutschland*, 5 Dec., 1983, p. 2.

21 This expression was introduced by Honecker beginning November, see *Neues Deutschland*, 2–3 Nov., 1985.

22 Cf. M. Stefanak and I. Hlivka, *Rudé právo*, 30 March, 1984, p. 4. *Novoe vremya* 16 (1984) pp. 12–14. O. V. Borisov, *Voprosy istorii* KPSS, 4 (1984) pp. 34–49.

23 Cf. G. Es'kov, *Pravda*, 18 Dec., 1985 and 21 June, 1985.

24 See R. Asmus, *East Berlin and Moscow: the Documentation of a Dispute* (RFE Munich 1985).

25 *Neues Deutschland*, 21 Feb., 12 Apr., 30 July, 21 Aug., 1984.

26 See C. Meier, *Die Wirtschaftsbeziehungen DDR–UdSSR am Ende der Fünfjahrplanperiode 1981–1985*. Berichte des BIOst no. 6, 1986.

27 W. Kuhns, The German Democratic Republic in the Soviet Foreign Policy Scheme, *Soviet Union/Union Sovietique*. 12, 1 (1985) pp. 77–102. See especially S. Kupper, 'Die DDR im sowjetischen System und ihr Sonderverhaltnis zur Bundesrepublik Deutschland' p.461.

9 The economic dimension

MICHAEL KASER

The two German states rank lower on the world scale than they did before World War II and their separation. In 1936 the territory of the Reich that now forms the Federal Republic of Germany and of the German Democratic Republic generated a GNP of $26.8 bn, which was 41 per cent of that generated in the United States ($64.7 bn).[1] In 1980 the GNPs of the two states, as measured in a recent study for the World Bank estimating domestic purchasing power, aggregated to $928 bn, or only 36 per cent of the $2,587 bn of the United States that year.[2] The reduction is, however, due entirely to the relative decline of the Eastern part of Germany, for the Western state ranks higher. As a percentage of the con temporary GNP of the United States, the territory of West Germany (excluding West Berlin) represented 29.7 per cent in 1936 but 32.0 per cent in 1980, while that of the GDR (including East Berlin) represented 11.7 per cent in 1936 but only 3.9 per cent in 1980.

In 1936 the GNP per capita of the Western part of Germany was on average the same as that of the Eastern part (only 7 per cent greater) but by 1980 it was, on the purchasing power calculations just cited, 2.3 times that of the Eastern state: for West Germany it was $13,590 per capita and for the GDR $5,910.

A narrower lead of West Germany over the GDR is shown by other methods of valuation for international comparison. The World Bank study done at the tourist exchange rate of the GDR mark and the unitary market exchange rate of the DM shows the GDR as $7,140 per capita: the $13,590 of West Germany was thus 1.9 times that of the GDR. A recalculation for the Deutsche Institut für Wirtschaftsforschung of GDR values into West German prices for 1976 puts the GNP per capita of West Germany at only 1.2 times that of the GDR.[3] A technique pioneered by the Hungarian statisticians F. Janossy and E. Ehrlich and developed by the UN Economic Commission for Europe yields for 1980 a West German per capita GNP 1.69 times that of the GDR:[4] this technique bypasses prices by employing physical indicators of output.

By whatever method of valuation, each German state is the richest member of its military alliance, but those alliances differ in their income dispersion, with the Warsaw Pact showing a narrower and Nato a wider spread. In 1980 per capita GNP on the World Bank study the GDR ranked 41 per cent above its alliance superpower, the Soviet Union, and 2.2 times above its alliance's poorest member, Romania. West Germany was 20 per cent above its alliance superpower, the United States, but 5.7 times above its Nato ally Portugal (and still more above its poorest ally, Turkey). The Warsaw Pact is economically more homogeneous than Nato, but East Germany ranks higher among its peers than West Germany does within its group. The same does not apply to their economic organizations. The GDR leads in per capita terms the Council for Mutual Economic Assistance (Comecon) and West Germany leads the Organization for Economic Cooperation and Development (OECD), but the GDR bears about the same ratio to Vietnam within Comecon as the FRG does to Turkey within the OECD. It is an incidental outcome of relative wealth and demography that there are Vietnamese workers employed in East Germany as there are Turkish workers in West Germany.

It is of further relevance to the military-economic relationship that both Germanies are important to their alliances for research and development of military technology. The GDR is engaged in laser technology and anti-satellite weaponry for the Soviet Union, just as the Federal Republic is pre-eminent in the optics and cryptoprocessing needed for the United States' Strategic Defence Initiative (SDI): the rail gun, essential for one such system, was invented in West Germany. There has been no public avowal on the Warsaw Pact side, but the Federal Republic agreed in March 1986 to collaborate on research for President Reagan's Strategic Defence Initiative.[5] For conventional military supplies Nato procurement is nevertheless greater in the Federal Republic than that of the Warsaw Pact is in the GDR, because the latter is heavily dependent on the Soviet Union for its *matériel*.

The Germanies in world trade

The maintenance of German dominance in world trade in manufactures can be attributed to the exports of both German states over the past fifty years. In 1937 Germany was neck-and-neck with the United Kingdom as the world's leading exporter of manufactures – $2,003 m from the Reich and $2,005 m from the United Kingdom – and well ahead of the United States at $1,750 m.[6] By 1983 West Germany was neck-and-neck with Japan ($146.6 bn against the Japanese $142.2 bn), but only a little ahead of the United States ($132.9 bn); in 1984 Japan overtook West Germany ($165.0 bn against $148.6 bn).[7] Exports of manufactures by the GDR were $17.6 bn in

1983 and $17.9 bn in 1984.[8] The combined exports of the two Germanies in 1984 were hence just $1.5 bn ahead of the biggest single exporter, Japan.

For trade as a whole, the two Germanies are much alike: the sum of imports and exports as a ratio to GNP was in 1980 0.41 in West Germany and 0.36 in East Germany and, as is suggested below, is likely to converge. Each ratio is over double the trade dependency of its alliance leader, for the United States is only a little less autarkic than the Soviet Union, as Table 1 shows. The slightly lower trade propensity of East over West Germany reflects the historical and systemic under-training of the Soviet-type command economy. No member of Comecon reaches the high pro-pensities of Benelux or Ireland and, generally, the ratio for a Comecon country is lower than for an OECD country with a similar natural resource endowment and development level: thus Czechoslovakia shows 0.41 and Austria 0.55. In 1983 West German exports were 9.4 per cent of world exports while GDR exports were 1.5 per cent.

Inter-German trade is more important to East Germany than to West Germany. Thus, aggregating turnover (the sum of imports and exports) the Federal Republic was the GDR's third largest trade partner in the first half of the 1980s (after the Soviet Union and Czechoslovakia – Poland ranked higher in the 1970s); its inner-German trade was 6.4 per cent of its total with all partners in 1983 and 6.0 per cent in 1984; the Federal Republic and the rest of Western Europe accounted for 98.4 per cent of imports in 1983 from Western industrial partners. The fact that East Germany undertakes only 1 per cent of its foreign trade with the United States and Japan (compared with 11 per cent with those two countries by West Germany) shows that the GDR is seriously under-trading with the two principal sources of advanced technology and consumer-goods innovation in the world. Western production technology and consump-tion innovation comes to the GDR largely through West Germany. The Federal Republic's turnover with the United States is surpassed (on 1984 returns) only by France and with Japan only by its neighbours and the United Kingdom, and its trade with the GDR ranks much lower than that flow represents for the GDR, a mere 1.5 per cent of turnover in 1984 (1.3 per cent of exports and 1.7 per cent of imports); the GDR is only the four-teenth largest partner for the Federal Republic's imports and the sixth for its exports. Even if the Federal Republic's EEC partners are omitted, the GDR ranks only ninth for imports and tenth for exports. Trade shares and ranks are a comparison of like with like: GDR figures are used for the GDR and West German returns for West Germany, but serious discrepancies are encountered if GDR data are set against those published by West Germany.

Criticism must be directed first to the respective governments on their

Table 1 *Per capita GNP and foreign-trade participation in Nato and Warsaw Pact countries in 1980*

	Per capita GNP		Imports and exports as ratio of GNP
	US$	US = 1	
Nato			
Belgium	12,180	1.07	1.13
Denmark	12,950	1.14	0.54
France	11,730	1.03	0.39
Germany, FR	13,590	1.20	0.41
Greece	4,380	0.39	0.37
Ireland	4,880	0.43	1.22
Italy	6,480	0.57	0.48
Netherlands	11,470	1.01	0.93
Norway	12,650	1.11	0.68
Portugal	2,370	0.21	0.60
Spain	5,400	0.48	0.27
United Kingdom	7,920	0.70	0.53
United States	11,360	1.00	0.18
Warsaw Pact			
Czechoslovakia	4,740	0.42	0.41
GDR	5,910	0.52	0.36
Hungary	4,390	0.39	0.38
Poland	3,730	0.33	0.27
Romania	2,680	0.24	0.43
Soviet Union	4,190	0.37	0.13

Source: Paul Marer, 'Alternative Estimates of the dollar GNP and Growth Rates of the CMEA Countries', Joint Economic Committee of the US Congress, *East European Economies: Slow Growth in the 1980s*, Washington DC, 1985, vol. 1, p. 174; he furnishes no comparable data for Turkey (Nato) and Bulgaria (Warsaw Pact).

presentation of trade returns. The GDR does not detail imports and exports by country, as are availabe for every country in Europe, save Albania, but publishes only turnover, which hence had to be used above for the partner rankings. Because West Germany does not regard the GDR as a foreign country its statistical yearbook under *Aussenhandel* omits the GDR, exchanges with which are to be found in the domestic commercial section *Handel, Gastgewerbe und Reiseverkehr*. Moreover, where the foreign trade section speaks of 'exports' (*Ausfuhr*) and 'imports' (*Einfuhr*), the GDR headings are 'deliveries of the Federal territory' (*Lieferungen des Bundesgebietes*) and 'acquisitions of the Federal territory' (*Bezüge des Bundesgebietes*). So determined are the West German authorities to isolate inter-German trade that they forbid international organizations to do what has just been done above, that is, to add the two sets of figures together. The OECD is thus compelled to put a dash for West German trade with the GDR and the UN Economic Commission for Europe (ECE) cannot put it in the same tables as the rest of West German trade. It is surely time for the Federal Republic to relegate the legal niceties to a footnote to the statistics. Needless to say, the Comecon Secretariat in its statistical yearbook adheres to the injunctions of its statistically-shy members, the GDR, Romania and Vietnam.

Secondly, inter-German trade is variously reflected in GDR and West German returns. Raimund Dietz, a citizen of the Federal Republic working in the Vienna Institute for Comparative Economics, has compiled and exhaustively analysed the two sets of figures reproduced in Table 2. Because, as already mentioned, the GDR obscures imports and exports by merging them, only turnover can be measured: inter-German turnover is systematically under-valued as reported by the GDR in comparison with that reported by West Germany. He finds the differential enlarging between 1970 and 1979 (the GDR figure being 0.80 of that reported by West Germany in the first of those years and 0.49 in the last) and then narrowing (to 0.71 in 1983). At least some of the divergence arises because GDR exporters or importers are required to invoice DM transactions as if the parity was 1:1 with the valuta mark (VM). The link of each with the inter-German accounting unit, *Verrechnungseinheit* (VE), is notional and was at its most extreme in 1979 when the dollar was 0.287 VM but 0.546 DM. Dietz also notes differences between the two reporting systems with respect to services associated with commodity trade and to re-exports and re-imports.

As Dietz's compilation in dollars shows in Table 3, inter-German turnover at current prices rose almost exactly four times between 1970 and 1983 on GDR figures and 4.5 times on West German figures. Without appropriate unit-value or price indexes to deflate these increases, a suitable comparison is with the aggregate East–West turnover of Western Europe (OECD members, excluding inter-German trade) in current dollars, the rise in which was just over six times, and with the East–West trade of Eastern Europe (Comecon members other than the Soviet Union, but including inter-German trade), also in current dollars, the rise in which was 3.9 times.[9] West German trade with Eastern Europe and the Soviet Union, but without the GDR, over the same period rose 6.5 times and East German trade with the OECD, including West Germany, rose 4.9 times. These flows include oil, the price of which rose rapidly in the 1970s and, if this is allowed for, it is possible to conclude that inter-German trade has risen somewhat more slowly than East–West trade in general, but that the difference is not such as to support a contention that political factors have either constrained or encouraged inter-German trade.

127

Table 2 *GDR and FRG statistics of inter-German trade turnover*

	GDR statistics		FRG statistics		Ratio
Year	Mn VM	Mn $	Mn DM	Mn $	(2):(4)
1970	4,050.0	964.3	4,411.2	1,205.2	0.800
1971	4,294.6	1,022.5	4,816.8	1,379.8	0.741
1972	4,827.7	1,247.4	5,308.8	1,664.9	0.749
1973	4,935.2	1,418.1	5,658.0	2,117.0	0.670
1974	5,997.3	1,723.3	6,922.8	2,675.1	0.644
1975	6,474.6	1,860.5	7,263.6	2,952.3	0.630
1976	7,360.0	2,114.9	8,145.6	3,234.9	0.654
1977	7,751.0	2,227.3	8,302.8	3,575.4	0.623
1978	7,972.7	2,291.0	8,424.0	4,193.9	0.546
1979	8,708.7	2,502.5	9,308.7	5,078.6	0.493
1980	10,077.3	3,053.7	10,871.4	5,980.8	0.511
1981	11,047.2	3,327.4	11,625.8	5,144.1	0.647
1982	12,527.4	3,620.6	13,021.5	5,366.1	0.675
1983	13,559.6	3,830.5	13,825.0	5,414.6	0.707

Source: Official statistics compiled by R. Dietz, 'Der Westhandel der DDR', *Deutschland Archiv*, no. 3, March 1985, p. 298.

Inter-German trade

In the light of the quantitative analysis, it is appropriate to consider the factors motivating inter-German trade.[10] On the side of the Federal Republic, three principal reasons may be put forward. First, its commercial relations constitute a commitment to those living in the other Germany; trade is 'representing' the flag rather than 'following' the flag of the adage. Secondly, the West German government perceives the non-commercial payments it makes to the GDR as a legitimation of that role. Thirdly, the normalization of inter-German economic relations helps to ensure the security of West Berlin. Political objectives also figure in GDR objectives in maintaining trade with the Federal Republic. First, the flow of goods gives GDR citizens a sense of contact with their Western co-nationals – the GDR government is concerned lest other channels, notably the peace movement and the Protestant Church, be more used. Secondly, trade with the GDR encourages a positive interest on the part of the Federal Government in relations with Eastern Europe generally, keeping West Germany somewhat more neutral with respect to the United States than might otherwise be the case. Without such economic attraction, the argument goes, West Germany would be more pliant towards the United States and, for example, accept more of the SDI budget. But the principal motivation is economic.

Technology transfer from the West is chiefly through the Federal

Table 3 *Estimates of GDR convertible-currency payments ($ mn)*

	1980	1981	1982	1983
Visible trade balance	−1,655	3	1,437	903
Services, remittances, and interest	−679	−1,128	−553	33
Current account balance	−2,334	−1,125	884	936
Net external assets	−12,264	−12,680	−11,054	−9,467

Source: Daniel Bond and Lawrence Klein, 'Impact of Changes in the Global Environment on the Soviet and East European Economies', Joint Economic Committee of the US Congress, *East European Economies: Slow Growth in the 1980s*, Washington DC, 1985, vol. 1, p. 28–9.

Republic. Not only does the common language facilitate this flow, but the two states share a technological culture. There was great controversy in the GDR in the 1960s before the technological reference standard was made the Soviet *Gosstandarty* (GOST) instead of the *Deutsche Industrie Normen* (DIN), but as Comecon's Standardization Institute is in East Berlin, incompatibilities between GOST and DIN have been minimized. The preference for technology embodied in West German equipment is reflected by the vastly higher purchases from that country than from the United States, but is also to be explained by the greater severity of controls on 'dual purpose technology' by the United States than by other Nato states even after the 1982 CoCom alignments. The transfer of technology from West to East Germany is greater than the reverse flow, but the latter has been increasing in equipment whereas investment goods sold by West Germany to the GDR was 1,271 m DM in 1983 and the reverse sales 755 m DM, the 1984 sales were 1,032 m DM and the return 878 m DM, reducing the net West German outflow from 516 m DM to 154 m DM in a single year. Several GDR consultancy firms sell their services in West Germany and at the 1985 Leipzig Fair there was a special display of 'immaterial exports'.

West German transactions constitute about 2.5 per cent of East German GNP, but their effect in opening bottlenecks and in providing supplies and services at very short notice renders them of much greater value. So necessary on occasion are West German spare parts or repairs that the courier or technician may be nodded through the frontier without formality or in extreme cases smuggled across. The reception of West German television programmes throughout East Germany and the inflow of DM remittances require some Western consumers' goods to be on sale in the GDR. Such sales, caustically termed *Jeanssozializmus* (on a par with 'gulash communism' in Hungary), usually reach the retail market at high

129

prices through the *Exquisit* or *Delikatesse* chain of shops but some are made available through the ordinary *Handelsorganization* (HO) as preferential supplies to local worker households. Because a lot of cheap consumer manufactures are sold by the GDR, the balance in this group is an Eastern export surplus.

Both the GDR and West Germany are short of energy and raw materials and mutual trade in that group is confined to a little coal eastward and some brown coal briquettes and oil products westward. The GDR takes a great deal of chemicals and chemical raw material from the Federal Republic: in 1984 materials for basic organic chemicals were valued at 0.6 bn valuta marks (VM) in the GDR import returns and all chemical materials were 1.3 bn DM in the West German export data. The GDR returns show deliveries as especially important for raw materials for plastics and furniture (together being 0.6 bn VM in 1984) and the Federal Republic lists raw materials and producer goods as aggregating 3.9 bn DM.

Inter-German tariff and credit relations

As an exporter to the Federal Republic, the GDR has two valuable advantages over other members of Comecon: a protocol to the Treaty of Rome grants it duty-free access to the Federal Republic, though not to the rest of the European Economic Community (EEC), and the two central banks provide each other with a swing credit, which is of major importance for GDR imports. Provided that a certificate of origin is furnished, no duty is levied on transactions either way, although West Germany imposes quantitative restrictions and price minima on specified commodities in the same way as it does with all other Comecon members. The quota list valid for 1 January 1986 to 31 March 1987 comprises 41 commodities limited by total value and 58 limited by total volume.[11] Some goods imported duty- and levy-free enter other EEC states without paying the required sums, and some from Comecon states other than the GDR have been falsely recorded as of GDR origin in order to enter the Federal Republic duty-free – a notable case, which reached the European Court of Justice, was of Polish geese passed off as of GDR origin. Some off-shore sales on GDR account are not settled in VE and can escape recording on GDR exports in the trade statistics, as in 1982–3 when 3 m tonnes of Soviet oil were resold in West Germany on GDR account.

Until 1982, a GDR bilateral deficit was characteristic not only on services (though in the balance of payments partly offset by West German transit dues and charges), but also of goods. While, as discussed below, recourse was had to normal bank finance and commercial credit, the GDR has regularly benefited from the annual swing credit. From 30 July 1982 the swing credit was decreased from its previous annual rate of 800 m DM in two steps to 600 m DM, the level at which it ran for the calendar year 1985. An agreement covering 1 January 1986 to 31 December 1990 (convenient for the GDR in embracing an entire five-year plan) raised the level to 850 m DM annually. At an anticipated turnover of 16 bn DM the liquidity ratio furnished by the credit will be of the order of 8 per cent. A concurrent agreement for the same five year period operates for non-commercial settlements (*nichtkommerzielle Zahlungsverkehr*): over the 1986–90 period the GDR undertakes annually to provide 70 m DM to create a fund from which the Federal Republic can convert transfers from inconvertible GDR mark (M) accounts held by residents of West Germany. The provision is almost exclusively for retired persons who have emigrated to West Germany (exit visas not normally being given to those of working age) and who wish to draw on bank accounts in the GDR (from lifetime savings, legacies or the proceeds of property sales); a pensioner cannot draw more than 200 DM per month from such accounts nor on any GDR pension (but a German is entitled to West German citizenship and hence to a West German pension). Remittances by West German residents to relatives in the GDR and their own travel in the GDR (including a visa fee of 15 DM per person and a compulsory exchange of 25 DM) and numerous government-to-government payments constitute a large counter-flow, which Oldenbourg (Chapter 8) sets at between 0.5 and 1.5 bn DM annually (see p.114).

The GDR government has outgrown its early fears that trade would render the country so dependent that the West German government could exert political leverage on it; the expectation was held in West Germany also. At that time the GDR evolved the economic policy of 'promoting disturbance-free development' (*Störungsfreimachung*) and political 'delimination' (*Abgrenzung*). So far has the attitude changed that East German officials have reportedly said that the Federal Republic is now the only partner on which they could rely. West German attitudes can still be expressed in Egon Bahr's formula of the early 1960s, *Wandel durch Annäherung* (change through rapprochement), but, as Löwenthal put it,

it would be entirely mistaken to see this move towards rapprochement in the context of past hopes for reunification in a national state, let alone of dreams of pan-Germanism. It is totally wrong to see it as mainly the fruit of West German economic bribes, as the Soviets pretend. Honecker is a Communist, and Communists are not inclined to make political concessions in return for economic favours, gladly though they may accept the latter.[12]

Until 1982, the partner on which the GDR could place maximum reliance was the Soviet Union: Soviet energy and raw materials underpinned the rapid increases in industrial output of the 1960s and 1970s (1980 net industrial output was 2.2 times that of 1965 on both the official and Alton's indexes).[13] The dependence was deliberately chosen – the chief planner, Apel, committed suicide in 1965, reportedly after failing to limit that reliance – and was common to most European members of Comecon. Assured of Soviet oil, and later gas, the share of coal in Eastern Europe's energy consumption dropped from nearly 85 per cent in 1960 to just 55 per cent in 1980. At Comecon's annual session in 1980 (Prague, 17–19 June), the Chairman of the Soviet Council of Ministers, Alexei Kosygin, had publicly declared that oil sales to other members would remain 'at the high level of 1980' and would aggregate 'almost 400 m tonnes' over 1981–5. For the GDR the 1980 level was 19,011,000 tonnes, and 19,036,000 tonnes were duly delivered in 1981; for 1982, however, a cut of 2 m tonnes was imposed without prior consultation. The suddenness of the reduction, which was aggravated in the ensuing year (17,709,000 tonnes in 1982, 17,051,000 tonnes in 1983 and 17,068,000 tonnes in 1984), was a political shock and a severe blow to the economy. Deliveries under the Comecon five-year agreements were (and in 1986 remain) priced at the world average of the preceding five years and hence were, at least until the sudden collapse in world oil prices in 1986, both much cheaper and payable in the Comecon clearing currency (the transferable rouble administered by the Bank for International Economic Cooperation). Imports of oil from other sources, nearly all payable in convertible currency, rose from 2,865,000 tonnes in 1980 and 2,709,000 tonnes in 1981 to 4,036,000 tonnes in 1982, 5,597,000 tonnes in 1983 and 6,168,000 tonnes in 1984. The bill for non-Soviet oil would have risen 2.15 times between 1980 and 1984 had not the OPEC price been cut in March 1983, but even so, with the price 88 per cent of 1980, it was 1.9 times larger.

The additional convertible-currency outlay coincided with East Germany's worst external financial crisis. At the end of 1981 GDR debt to Western lenders amounted to $14,860,000 gross and $12,680,000 net, following the borrowing for 'import-led growth' in the 1970s and heavy borrowing for current needs in 1980–1: estimates of the external balance are in Table 3. The suspension of debt service and the request for rescheduling by Poland and Romania and the sudden loss of convertible currency reserves by Hungary, all compressed into a few months of 1981–2, dried up Western sources of lending, not only for new money but to roll over maturing loans. The short maturities on East European credits had had the additional disadvantage of pushing up servicing costs because international interest rates were rising as loans were rolled over. ECE estimates show that the average interest rate (London interbank offer rate) on a basket of Eurocurrencies rose from 6.8 per cent in 1978 to 14.6 per cent in 1981;[14] the spread above that rate payable by East European borrowers rose sharply (from 0.7 per cent in 1979 to 1.3 per cent in 1982 according to the OECD).[15]

The GDR situation in early 1982 implied rescheduling, but this was avoided by prompt assistance from the West German Bundesbank, accompanied by a vigorous economy drive to import less and export more. Whereas in 1980 the visible balance with non-socialist countries had been in deficit by 5,454 m VM and by 197 m VM in 1981, it was in surplus at 5,219 m VM in 1982, at 4,690 m VM in 1983 and 3,846 m VM in 1984. In convertible-currency terms the estimates in Table 3 show a turnaround from a 1980 deficit of $1,655 m to a surplus of $903 m in 1983, accompanied by a similar swing on invisibles from a deficit of $679 m to a surplus of $33 m. The repayment of debts in the West was, however, accompanied by borrowing from the Soviet Union, not to finance an import deficit (which would have compensated the cut in domestic availabilities, especially severe in the retail market), but to offset a sharp decline in its terms of trade as Soviet energy and materials prices caught up on the Comecon moving-average formula with the world level. Oldenburg's chapter in this volume puts the GDR debt to the Soviet Union at $3.7 bn in 1985 (see p.119).

In the medium term therefore the GDR extracted itself from the 1981–2 financial crisis by the means that the IMF would have recommended: import substitution, export promotion, deflation (in the sense of maintaining the previous rigid suppression of prices rises in HO shops while absorbing purchasing power through the *Exquisit* and *Delikatesse* network) and a cutback of investment (the constant-price share of which in net material product dropped from 22.7 per cent in 1980 to 19.6 per cent in 1983).

In the shorter term the provision of additional Western lending was decisive in the avoidance of rescheduling. The exact degree of assistance by banks, encouraged by the West German government, cannot be identified (because their reports to the BIS exclude, on government instructions, assets and liabilities with the GDR) but Table 3 incorporates an estimate. By the end of 1984, when the GDR gross debt had been further reduced to $11.2 bn gross and $6.6 bn net, the latter comprised only $1.2 bn to banks in West Germany (the largest single creditor country being Austria). The two major governmental interventions were in June 1983 when the West German authorities announced a guarantee of 1 bn DM for financial credits to the GDR and in July 1984 when they provided guarantees to a West German bank consortium for 960 m DM. The quid pro quo in improving political relations was stressed in each instance.[16] Renewed bank borrowing took place in 1985 largely to establish reserves for the purchase of capital equipment under the 1986–90 Plan (approved by the Party Congress in April 1986). By late 1985 reserves were $4.8 bn, mostly deposited in Swiss, rather than West German, banks, while the offsetting debtor obligations will have been reduced during 1985 by the depreciation of the dollar against the West European currencies in which many outstanding loans were denominated (the GDR is one of the few countries, nevertheless, for which no breakdown of liabilities by currency is available).

Trade prospects

The greater liquidity in convertible currency now available for GDR trade with the West (though still lower than the norm for Western countries) might suggest an orientation for the 1986–90 Five-year Plan towards trade with the West. It has been reported that Konrad Naumann, who was relegated from the Party Politburo in 1985, had been opposed to the recommencement of borrowing in the West.[17] But that borrowing may be rather for security – to avoid a crisis like that of 1981–2 – rather than the basis for trade expansion. The undertakings at the Comecon Summit (Moscow, 12–14 June 1984) linked the supply of Soviet energy for 1986–90 to Eastern Europe's delivery of foodstuffs, consumer manufactures and special construction materials, all to world quality or performance standards. A bilateral programme of cooperation to the year 2000 specified the main lines of exchange for the GDR and the Soviet Union. The economic interest of the Federal Republic is unlikely to counter this trend, because if the GDR sells more to Comecon partners it will have relatively less with which to earn DM to buy in West Germany (subject to a certain overall likely rise in trade intensity). The size of the swing credit has been fixed through to the end of 1990 and, although the GDR again has a good bank ranking for credit-worthiness, there is little to attract the provision of more bank loans if GDR export industry is (as is patently the case) to be more specialized on sales to Comecon.

The trade dependencies of the two German states are likely to converge in the second half of the 1980s, the Eastern rising while the Western falls. Although no five-year target has been published for all trade, the directives of the Eleventh Party Congress forecast a 29 per cent rise by 1990 over 1985 in trade turnover with socialist partners against a range of 24 to 26 per cent for net material product.[18] The real rate of growth of West German trade is likely to be restrained by the slow growth of its market-economy partners, by the indebtedness of Third World countries and by the encroachment of protection (the heavy United States trade deficit is attributable particularly to the export surpluses of Japan and the Federal Republic). The differential in expected rates of GNP growth over the next five years – probably 4 to 4.5 per cent annually in East Germany and 3 to 3.5 per cent annually in West Germany, with higher population growth in the latter – yields a perspective of converging per capita GNP in the very long run.

But the increment in trade volume arising from the GDR's rising trade propensity and more rapid product growth will not generate much more exchange with the West because of the policy priority accorded trade within Comecon. The West German government's political interest in maintaining broad economic relations is not weakened by this prospect because a sufficiency of inter-German trade is assured by GDR import requirements in the new plan. The need for spare parts and replacement of capital installations is evident from the Polish example cited below and past purchases render West Germany the likely continuing supplier. Moreover, as a study by Höhmann has shown, East German imports of grain have remained consistently high – 3.4 m tonnes (excluding rice) in 1970 and 3.8 m in 1983, peaking at 5.1 m in 1976 and with a low of 2.5 m tonnes in 1982.[19] The GDR's sales prospects in the West generally should be enhanced by the better quality of export products. A member of the Institute of Economics of the GDR Academy of Sciences quoted (in a conference paper of December 1985) as highly applicable to export goods the call of Günter Mittag (Secretary of the Party CC): 'The creation of new use-value in conformity with demand . . . is the salient characteristic of the *Kombinat*.'[20] The GDR as an energy-deficit economy will benefit from the collapse of the world oil price – in April 1986 one-third of that in early 1983 – but the effect on its terms of trade with the Soviet Union (its main oil supplier as already noted) will be delayed by the operation of a five-year moving average (1986 prices in Comecon being the world prices of 1981–5).

A consideration that might weigh with the GDR party and government in promoting more, or at least maintaining constant, trade with the Federal Republic is the political attraction of stable economic ties when market partners remain relatively in recession and when United States measures to staunch its parallel budget and trade deficits are to be anticipated. They could argue that such a trend would promote a decoupling of West Germany from the United States. Advocates are to be found in West Germany of a policy Bender terms the 'Europeanization of Europe' (*Europäisierung Europas*),[21] and among its critics the American Ambassador to Bonn, Richard Burt, in a notable address on 18 November 1985 to the Hans Seidel Foundation in Munich.

Similar economic and political considerations apply to the Federal

Republic's trade with other members of Comecon and to the latter group's trade with the rest of the industrial West. It is, however, still more difficult to know what precisely has been happening quantitatively in these exchanges than in the inner-German trade: GDR returns are still further above those aggregated by OECD (from national statistics converted into dollar values) than they are with respect to West Germany alone. Dietz, to whom Table 4 is also due, suggests a number of factors in the astounding differential, for by 1983 the GDR claimed a turnover with OECD (excluding the Federal Republic) over double that recorded by the OECD. One minor differentiation, accounting for no more than 1 per cent of turnover, is the absence of GDR trade returns with Ireland and New Zealand, which are of course covered by the OECD data.[22] Dietz believes that the GDR does not rework its exchange rates sufficiently quickly while the OECD revalues flows as rates actually change: this must weigh more significantly in recent years when the DM/$ rate has fluctuated widely. Much transit trade must be missed by the OECD data: United States grain is reported shipped to West Germany but the latter omits it as an import and hence as an export to the GDR because it is only in transit. GDR sales to other EEC countries than West Germany are recorded as an export, do not figure in the West German data (being transit trade) and appear in the third EEC partner as an import from West Germany. The same transit problem arises for Third World shipments in either direction, which count as transit for West Germany but which the Third World country considers as trade with the GDR.

Judged against the aggregate turnover of OECD countries with Eastern Europe and the Soviet Union, the GDR seven-fold trade rise with that group over 1970 to 1983 on its data and 5.3 times rise on OECD data compares with a 6.1 times rise. The implication (since OECD data are best compared with OECD data) is that the GDR's turnover with OECD (excluding inter-German trade) has risen somewhat less fast than OECD trade with Eastern Europe and the Soviet Union, but the latter embraces some massive increases in which the GDR has not shared – American and Canadian grain sales to the Soviet Union, the latter's oil sales for convertible currency and Japan's trade expansion with Eastern Europe other than the GDR. If rough allowance is made for these trends extraneous to the GDR, it has probably participated in East–West trade on about the same trend as the OECD experienced generally; the Four-Power Berlin agreement and the inter-German accords of 1971–2 seem not to have released any previously frustrated trade flow.

Comecon states, although also signing up at the 1984 Summit for more mutual trade, have so diminished their imports from the West in their financial adjustment drives as to require some return to higher purchases.

136

Table 4 *GDR and OECD statistics of GDR turnover with OECD members other than FRG*

Year	GDR statistics Mn VM	GDR statistics Mn $	OECD statistics Mn $	Ratio (2):(3)
1970	5,606.0	1,344.8	835.2	1.598
1971	5,972.9	1,422.2	917.3	1.550
1972	7,221.0	1,865.9	1,442.1	1.634
1973	9,968.9	2,864.7	1,416.4	2.022
1974	13,793.4	3,963.7	1,954.8	2.028
1975	12,782.6	3,673.2	2,165.3	1.696
1976	16,850.0	4,842.0	2,383.7	2.031
1977	14,037.7	4,033.9	2,327.9	1.733
1978	14,031.0	4,032.0	2,902.9	1.389
1979	19,571.3	5,624.0	4,037.4	1.393
1980	22,882.7	6,934.1	4,579.0	1.514
1981	26,794.1	8,070.4	4,688.0	1.721
1982	28,317.5	8,184.3	4,073.0	2.009
1983	33,593.3	9,490.1	4,386.0	2.164

Source: As for Table 2.

Bond and Klein (to whom Table 3 is also due), taking a 'baseline scenario' that OECD real GDP, the main determinant of Comecon sales to that group, will by 1988 be 17 per cent higher than in 1982, forecast Eastern Europe's 1988 non-socialist trade as 12 per cent above 1982 for exports and 34 per cent above 1982 for imports (deflating their current price projections by their price index).[23] This takes no account of the improvement in the availability of convertible currency in the GDR which should arise from its savings on buying OPEC oil. It would be rational for Eastern Europe to direct such savings to renewed capital-goods imports. Indebtedness from 1981 brought severe cuts in buying equipment, to a point demonstrated by a staff member of the Institute of Economics of the Polish Academy of Sciences, Wojciechowski.[24] Allowing for depreciation and converting to constant prices, the 1985 stock of imported equipment would be 38 per cent of market-economy origin and 62 per cent of socialist country origin, compared with 55 and 45 per cent respectively in 1980. As he points out, further depreciation accompanied by exiguous new imports from the West would dangerously reduce the share of advanced technology in the Polish capital stock.

Political developments must affect the actual course of events. The Reagan–Gorbachev Summit of November 1985 and the promise of at least two further annual meetings may lead, through arms discussions, to a weakening of the strategic embargos which limit purchases by Comecon members of high technology in the West. The negotiations between the Comecon Secretariat and the EEC Commission have recommenced and, within an arrangement between the two sides, bilateral treaties with the EEC could promote more imports from Comecon signatories. Western business could be attracted into joint ventures and equity investment in East European enterprises: as these are already legally permitted in Bulgaria, Czechoslovakia, Hungary, Poland and Romania, it must be a matter of time before foreign equity is allowed some minority partici- pation in GDR enterprises.

Finally, third-country cooperation might generate more East–West trade. Because the GNP of the GDR is so much smaller than that of West Germany, it is possible that the share in it going as development aid may be about as much even as West Germany (which at 1.06 per cent is among the highest providers). GDR aid goes to fewer recipients: mostly as obliga- tions within Comecon to Cuba, Mongolia and Vietnam, buy-back invest- ments such as for coal with Mozambique and assistance to African and Asian states described as 'of socialist orientation'. Where trade and con- sultancy is associated with aid, viable links between West and East German enterprises could be established for operations in a Third World country. The Hallstein doctrine of acute rivalry between the two Germanies in this and other spheres is long buried and the Third World's need for trade has been increased by their immense indebtedness.

This last offers the possibility of ending an economic theme on a hope- ful if modest political note. There are only eighteen official crossing points for all modes of transport along the 1,378 km frontier between the two German states, an armed border of the 'First' and 'Second' Worlds: cooperation in the 'Third' World could open some new connections.

Notes

1   The FRG excludes West Berlin, but the GDR includes East Berlin. The 1936 GNPs are from United Nations, *Yearbook of National Accounts*, 1938–47, New York, 1950, pp 125 and 129, and the division of territorial GNP is from P. Studenski, *The Income of Nations* New York, 1958, p. 384, who cites German estimates for the GNP of the 1936 Reich as 81.4 bn RM, of which the territory which became the Federal Republic accounted for 47.6 bn RM; it is here assumed that West and East Berlin generated equal shares of this 7.5 bn RM for all Berlin. The United Nations, *Economic Survey of Europe Since the War* (Geneva, 1953, p. 26, Table 8), put the 1936 GNP of the territory that is now the GDR as 15.0 bn RM. The residual of 11.3 bn RM is that of the territory of the Reich incorporated into Poland and the Soviet Union. Conversion of the Reichsmark at the average for 1936 of $0.403 (M. Kaser and E. A. Radice (eds.), *The Economic History of Eastern Europe 1917–1975*, vol. 1, Oxford, 1984, Table 0.1, p. xii) of a territory now the FRG (but without West Berlin) of 47.6 bn RM gave $19.2 bn and of a territory now the GDR with East Berlin of 18.8 bn RM gave $7.6 bn. The very detailed comparison of the GDR and FRG between 1936 and 1955 in *Economic Bulletin for Europe*, vol. 8, no. 3, pp. 45–86 (drafted by R. Nötel) does not cite the money values of NDP in each territory (giving only indices and percentages).

2 P. Marer, 'Alternative Estimates of the Dollar GNP and Growth Rates of the CMEA
   Countries', in Joint Economic Committee of the Congress of the United States, *East European Economies: Slow Growth in the 1980s* (Washington, DC, vol. 1, 1985), p. 174. His new
   estimates, on a purchasing power parity basis, commissioned by the World Bank, are
   more fully set out in P. Marer, *Dollar GNPs of the USSR and Eastern Europe* (Baltimore,
   Md, 1985).

3 H. Wilkens, *The Two German Economies. A Comparison between the National Product of the German
   Democratic Republic and the Federal Republic of Germany* (Farnborough, 1981), p. 70 (trans-
   lation by L. Furtmüller of *Das Sozialprodukt der Deutschen Demokratischen Republik im Vergleich
   mit dem Bundesrepublik Deutschland*, West Berlin, 1976). The study was for the Deutsche
   Institut für Wirtschaftsforschung (DIW).

4 T. Alton, 'East European GNPs: Origins of Product, Final Uses, Rates of Growth and
   International Comparisons', in Joint Economic Committee of the Congress of the
   United States, *East European Economies*, vol. 1, p. 126. Alton projects the ECE estimates for
   1975 (*Economic Bulletin for Europe*, vol. 31, no. 2, p. 30) on his estimates of growth 1975 to
   1980; the ECE methodology was that of F. Janossy and E. Ehrlich, *A gazdasági fejlettség
   mérhetősége és uj mérési modszere*, Budapest, 1963, and was drafted for the *Bulletin* by
   Ehrlich.

5 *Express* (Cologne), 18 April 1986, published the secret text of the treaty of 27 March; it
   stipulates that the United States controls the fruits of any joint research and any dis-
   semination to third countries.

6 H. Tyszynski, 'World Trade in Manufactured Commodities 1899–1950', *The Manchester
   School*, September 1951, p. 280. His sterling values converted at the exchange rate in
   Kaser and Radice, *Economic History of Eastern Europe*.

7 GATT, *International Trade 1984/85*, Geneva, 1985, Appendix Table A8.

8 In 1983 74.4 per cent and in 1984 74.2 per cent of GDR exports were manufactures
   (*Statistisches Jahrbuch der DDR 1985*, p. 240), and total exports were 84,227 m and 90,402 m
   Valuta-Mark respectively (*ibid.*, p. 241). GATT, *International Trade 1984/85*, Appendix
   Table A7, gives GDR exports as $23.7 bn in 1983 and $24.1 bn in 1984, whence manufactures $17.6 bn and $17.9 bn respectively. Sales of manufactures to twenty-two Western
   market economies in 1981 were $1,783 mn (*Economic Bulletin for Europe*, vol. 35, no. 4,
   Appendix Table 3.3); this is a more accurate calculation to compare with Western data
   than that derived from the very broad categories in the GDR *Jahrbuch* but has not been
   made for all GDR trade.

9 *Economic Bulletin for Europe*, vol. 36, no. 4, Appendix Table 2.2.

10 For detailed analyses of FRG–GDR trade see J. Garland, 'FRG–GDR Economic Relations' in Joint Economic Committee of the Congress of the United States, *East European
   Economies*, vol. 3, pp. 169–206; and K.-H. Gross, 'Die inner-deutschen Wirtschaftsbeziehungen', *FS Analysen*, No. 5, 1985, part 2, pp. 27–48. See also R. Asmus 'East and
   West Germany; Continuity and Change', *The World Today*, April 1984, especially pp.
   149–50 and M. Haendcke-Hoppe, 'DDR Aussenhandel im Zeichen schrumpfender
   Westimport', *Deutschland Archiv*, vol. 16, October 1983, pp. 1066–71 and her 'German
   Democratic Repubic: Foreign Economic Relations', paper to Nato Colloquium April
   1986. A broad comparison including trade is K. C. Thalheim, *Die wirtschaftliche Entwicklung
   der beiden Staaten in Deutschland* (Berlin, 2nd ed, 1981), which also has an extensive
   bibliography. On the inner-German trade constituent of the change of Ostpolitik in the
   late 1960s, see A. J. McAdams, *East Germany and Detente* (Cambridge, 1985), esp. pp. 76
   and 209.

11 *Bundesanzeiger*, 6 November 1985.

12 R. Löwenthal, 'The German Question Transformed', *Foreign Affairs*, Winter 1984/5,
   p. 313.

13 T. Alton, 'East European GNPs', p. 111.

14 *Economic Bulletin for Europe*, vol. 31, no. 2, Table 2.17.

15 OECD, *Financial Market Trends*, June 1984, p. 45.

16 P. Danylow, 'Der aussenpolitische Spielraum der DDR', *Europa Archiv*, 25 July 1985,
   p. 435.

17 *The Economist*, 30 November 1985.

18 Report by Willi Stoph to the Eleventh Congress of the SED, *Neues Deutschland*, 20
   April 1986.

19 K. Hohmann, 'Bereitstellung und Verwendung von Getreide in der DDR nach 1970', *FS Analysen*, No. 2, 1985, p. 19.
20 G. Mittag, *Okonomische Strategie der Partei: klares Konzept für weiteres Wachstum* (East Berlin, 1983), p. 63.
21 P. Bender, *Das Ende des Ideologischen Zeitalters* (West Berlin, 1981).
22 R. Dietz, 'Der Westhandel der DDR', *Deutschland Archiv*, vol. 18, March 1985, pp. 284–304.
23 D. Bond and L. Klein, 'Impact of Changes in the Global Environment on the Soviet and East European Economies', Joint Economic Committee of the Congress of the United States, *East European Economies*, vol. 1, pp. 7–21.
24 B. Wojciechowski, 'Przemiany strukturalne a trudności importowe Polski', *Gospodarka planowa*, no. 9, 1984, p. 373.

10　The human dimension

HERMANN RUDOLPH

There are two German states. Are they, as the official version in the Federal Republic maintains, 'two states in Germany'? Or are there also 'two Germanies'? There is one indisputable fact: West Germany and East Germany are by now very different from each other. This can be seen already at first glance. For example, the common usage of language takes note of this difference by describing both states as 'the two Germanies', or the GDR as 'the other Germany'. But, on a more fundamental level, where Germany is defined not merely in the abstract terms of international law, but rather as an entity with a national, social and cultural identity of its own, these questions address a very sensitive point.

The official formulation describing two German states as 'two states in Germany' presupposes that there is such a thing as *one* Germany, which is prevented only by the existence of two states from manifesting itself as such. On the other hand, to speak of 'two Germanies' suggests that the existence of the two states now dominates the thoughts and feelings of people to such an extent that there is no room for the notion of *one* Germany. This formulation implies not just two states and two systems but also two societies, cultures and mentalities, which have no closer connection with each other than with the societies, cultures and mentalities of any of the states on this or the other side of Europe's dividing line.

It is against this background that the question of the cultural and human dimensions of the partition of Germany derives its vital political significance. The question is not only: how do people cope with such a process? It is also to what extent these two states constitute the solution of the German problem, in that they are accepted by the people as a satisfying, final form of their collective existence, and to what extent they remain uncertain in their identity. The GDR, for example, sees itself not merely as a state in the traditional sense; it also has as its central goal the political, economic, social and spiritual–cultural transformation of society. It therefore demands more from its citizens than the free democratic states, since the acceptance of the state also involves the acceptance and support of the transformation of society to a 'socialist' society. Only then can the state feel that its rule is secure.

But we can gain a full understanding of the present situation only if, to quote the German historian Johann Gustav Droysen, 'we understand and explain how it came about'. Only the historical perspective can help us to recognize the nature of the process that we are dealing with. One thing is certain: these questions did not exist forty years ago. The fathers and grandfathers of those Germans, citizens of the Federal Republic or the GDR, party members of western or eastern orientation, constituted one society, regardless of whether they lived in the western or eastern part of the country. This brings to the fore the deeper consequences of the German partition.

Politics has altered the fate of the people within two, or at the most three, generations. Depending on where somebody happened to be at a particular point in time, in the West or in the East, his future was a different life, different experience and even, to some degree, different convictions – providing he did not attempt to correct this accident of history by fleeing to the other part of Germany. It would be too much to suggest that one and the same person, if politically motivated, could just as easily become an SED party secretary if living in the East, as make his career in a bourgeois party if living in the West. Erich Honecker, for example, the SED General Secretary, who was born in the Saarland, which today is part of the Federal Republic, went to East Berlin after 1945, whereas Hans-Dietrich Genscher, now Foreign Minister in Bonn, a native of the area close to Halle in what today is East Germany, went to the West. But doctors and other professional people would have less trouble using their talents in whichever part of Germany they found themselves.

But is it really true to say that the Germans constituted a homogenous culture, before they were thrown into the centrifuge of the clash between East and West? Doubts about this have been used repeatedly to promote the thesis that the division of Germany into two states finds some basis in German history. In this sense, for example, de Gaulle referred to the GDR as the state of the Saxons and Prussians. Likewise, in discussion among Germans, the view has sometimes been expressed that there was a certain logic of German history leading to the division of Germany. The GDR was founded on the virtues – or even more on the failings – of Prussia, whereas it was in the Federal Republic that liberal, anti-Prussian forces gathered. And the Federal Republic does indeed consist of that part of Germany which is historically distinguished by the political and religious variety of the old Reich. The other part, by contrast, in which the GDR arose, has been formed from the great territorial states of Saxony and Brandenburg Prussia, which are uniformly Protestant.

But all this does not mean that the division of Germany into two states was in any sense predestined. The differences that exist within Germany have been an element in its history since the Middle Ages. The two German states are not a consequence of this history as such – except perhaps indirectly as a result of its failure manifested in National Socialism. Rather, these states are the result of historical events since 1945, more precisely the East–West conflict, and the fundamental political and ideological decisions that derive from them. True, Germany has been a divided country for most of its history. But nonetheless it is wrong to conclude that the present division constitutes a return to this condition, implying that the unitary state of 1871 was merely a transitory episode in German history. That unitary state was the result of a long evolution leading towards German unity. The German division of today is generically different from all other German divisions – in that it represents the contrast between East and West. While it is true that in the GDR, Saxon and Prussian traits are dominant, it is also tempting to imagine this regime in a Bavarian or Swabian context.

Things that separate and things that unite

How much influence has the existence of the two states had, beyond the strictly political? How far and in what direction has division changed the lives of German people – not so much *between* East and West as *in* East and West (with one third of the population living in the East)? These questions can be put another way: what separates the Germans in the Federal Republic from those in the GDR beyond the issue of the state boundaries, and what do they still have in common despite those boundaries? From the perspective of the Federal Republic, a West European industrial society, one could add: in what ways is the society in the GDR special? How deep is its foundation? What are the influences upon it?

There are no precise answers to these questions, because they relate to a process in which little can be measured; answers come only from careful observation and analysis. Certain elements can be identified, which reflect the thoughts and feeling of people or else influence those thoughts. One such element is the transformation of the social structure. That has by now gone so deep that it is by no means absurd to suggest that the political division has also become a social one. Indeed, in the GDR a society has emerged in which many of the structural elements of West German society are missing: it has no traditional upper class, social stratification has been blurred and social differences are comparatively small; some groups, such as the self-employed, have diminished; and, finally, there are few, if any, groups in society (with the exception of the churches) that have an independent existence. Instead, society is managed by means of plans and edicts emanating from the state, which restrict the freedom of the individual.

Not only the social structure, but also the range of choices open to an individual in life, is limited by the monopoly of power enjoyed by the state. This affects career and professional possibilities as well as income. It applies to consumer habits, and shows itself in the monumental uniformity of the apartment blocks from Dresden to Rostock. The monopoly position of the state is also responsible for the regimentation of intellectual life and the restrictions on personal experience through travel. No matter what area one considers, the rhythm of life is always strictly controlled. While at one time one could hope that this was a transitory phenomenon, it is clear that it has since become a permanent feature of the system.

To draw attention to the social features of the system in the GDR is not to ignore its political aspects or its potential for repression. The dominating role of the party and its ideology, as well as the whole apparatus of repression available to state and party, is the primary influence on both the individual and society. However, the more the potential for direct repression retreats into the background, as the power of the state becomes secure, the more significant are the 'civil' restrictions on the everyday life of this society and its people.

As a result, GDR society is not merely characterized by greater equality of life-style; it is also more modest, traditional and narrow in its expectations and judgements than the society of the Federal Republic. It has certainly not become the kind of socialist society envisaged by the GDR leadership. Nonetheless, by attempting to force this concept upon society – and by suppressing all other tendencies and developments – the GDR regime has succeeded in changing society. This change has now become without question the foundation of a considerable independence, and thus GDR society differs also from the society of the Federal Republic.

On the other hand, there are still many things which link the two societies. The Germans in the Federal Republic and the GDR alike are first and foremost *Germans*. In other words, they are characterized by that collection of behaviour patterns and values – ranging from their alleged industriousness to their joviality and tendency to break out into the singing of choruses when inebriated – which in the course of history have come to be regarded as typically German, both among Germans themselves and among their neighbours in East and West. They see themselves as members of industrial societies which in their religious and ethical foundations are German in character. They consider themselves part of the same high culture. They share a common past, which means that when they look at history, they necessarily come across the same events and heroes.

Finally – and this must not be underestimated – Germans in both states are still connected through millions of family ties and acquaintances. Their true number can only be guessed at. However, there are indications that their scale is still very considerable. For example, in 1984 about 5 million trips from the Federal Republic and West Berlin to the GDR were registered; in the reverse direction, where travel is possible only for those who have reached pensionable age, the figure was about 1.5 million; there were about another 60,000 visits connected with so-called urgent family matters.[1] Since 1945 about 4 million people have moved from East Germany to West Germany.[2] But family ties and acquaintances are not restricted to such *Übersiedler*; they also connect people who have not moved their place of residence.

The people in the two German states share more than a common nostalgia and sentimentality. There are real forces at work in the substructure of the two states: in the interpersonal relationships, in cultural interests and activities, in the feeling of personal involvement with events in the other state. Their effect inevitably counteracts tendencies towards separate development arising out of the existence of the two German states. At the same time, it would be illusory to assume that they can provide a secure guarantee of the continuation of *one* Germany. Even those things that Germans in both states have in common have not remained untouched by these developments.

Even the understanding simply of what is or should be German is not entirely the same in the two states. This is because since the end of the war the Federal Republic has experienced the strong influence of West European and American ways of life, whereas the GDR has been deliberately cut off from such influences. The traditional attitude to work is bound to develop along different lines, when confronted on the one hand by an economy geared towards competitive world markets and, on the other, with the problems of a centrally controlled economy. Common culture and history take on different perspectives in the light of differing experiences and impressions.

It is worth bearing in mind that the two states were founded in the postwar years on very different cultural and historical world views. In the GDR the leadership has always tried to employ culture and history in the attempt to transform politics and society. In a sharp, polemical departure from traditional viewpoints it has virtually rewritten German history. A great part of the events and personalities, which up to then had been considered highlights of national history, were condemned as reactionary.

145

Luther was branded as 'puppet of the princes', just as the role of Prussia was condemned, and Bismarck was seen primarily as the man who implemented the laws against Socialists. By contrast, the Peasants' War, the workers' movement or the Communist Party, which played a marginal part in the traditional picture of German history, were now allotted a central role. Literature, theatre and art were made to offer an ideologically and politically expurgated picture of the German classics. These were presented as historical stepping-stones to 'socialist realism', which was declared to be the official understanding of art. Thus not only were certain guidelines established, to which art and culture had to conform, but also important influences and developments were excluded. Perhaps this deliberate and conscious exclusion is of greater importance than the attempted indoctrination. It affected not merely the traditional picture of history, but also the liberal, critical viewpoint, which in the postwar years grew in significance in the Federal Republic. In literature and art it excluded Western modernism, from Kafka to Joyce, from abstract paintings to atonal music, which constituted the great experience of the postwar years in the Federal Repubic.

Such were the essential differences between the two states in the treatment of their common history and culture. The GDR has not managed to subordinate history and culture in its domain entirely to political doctrine. But the attempt to do so has had consequences even for people who are sceptical of the regime. This is all the more significant, since the Federal Republic for its part also departed from the traditional perspective of German culture and history. It became, in short, more 'Western' than Germany has ever been. This is particularly obvious in the realm of culture and art, where West Germany has long since become a part of the Western international world culture – at times to such an extent that it threatened to eliminate the traditional peculiarities of German educational history. This is also true of its history: West German society has become sceptical of traditional interpretations, to the point of losing the image of that history which would be accepted by the overwhelming majority of the public.

In recent years these developments have begun to lose significance. The GDR has shown itself to be increasingly open to modern culture and art; modern expressions are no longer condemned, and at least some modern authors can get in to print. Step by step it has rehabilitated those aspects of German history which were rejected in the 1950s and 1960s. Likewise in the Federal Republic there is a great interest in Germany's own history. Nonetheless the shift in cultural and historical perspectives which stemmed from the existence of two German states remains a factor in the inter-German relationship.

In the Federal Republic, when plans for a museum for German history are discussed, the debate soon gets lost in controversies about whether it is possible at all to represent German history, or whether indeed there is still such a thing as German history. All the self-doubts which Germans have with regard to their past are brought to the surface. In the GDR there is such a museum. It presents history in a simple way, comprehensible to the public, and unashamedly from a particular point of view. Federal President Richard von Weizsäcker, when he was still mayor of Berlin, commented that in the GDR there was the beginning of 'a more stable, serious and, despite all the attempts at ideological adaptation, perhaps partially even more truthful, consciousness of German history than can be seen in the Federal Republic, which is both free and sometimes rather unsure of itself and unstable.'[3] This statement expresses the sigh of a well-educated citizen, who has been so exhausted by the academic propensity to endless discussion and West German self-doubt that the simple representation of history favoured by the GDR regime appears to have some attraction. But Weizsäcker's remark proves how much the perspectives from which history is perceived have shifted in West Germany and East Germany. On the other hand, the Luther celebrations in 1983 were a quite different event in the Federal Republic than in the GDR, even though they were about the same man: what was in the Federal Republic a memorial celebration, in which the main participants were churches, educational institutes and interested citizens, became in the GDR a highly official event of political significance. This is because, for the leadership of the GDR, its participation in the celebrations implied a new view of history – and for GDR citizens this was a political signal, quite apart from any other meaning Luther might have had for them.

It is certainly undeniable that Germans in the two German states have moved apart from each other. But this alienation is still interwoven with many interconnections, so that while there is some distance there is also closeness. The two societies could not become totally estranged or lose sight of each other. In the 1960s, when the division was made complete by the building of the Berlin Wall, there seemed to be a growing difference between the two states and two societies. Since the 1970s their mutual attraction has begun to increase again.

However, this attraction is not an equal one. People in the GDR look with greater intensity to the Federal Republic than vice versa. In fact this is an understatement: there is a 'primary asymmetry' in the relationship.[4] The Federal Republic has become the standard for the GDR whereas the GDR is for the Federal Republic the object of a somewhat restrained, often slightly charitable, curiosity. One reason is, of course, that the Federal Republic is the larger and wealthier of the two states. But this is not the only reason, even though West Germany's standard of living holds some attraction for GDR citizens. The asymmetry in the relationship is of a more fundamental nature; it has to do with differences in the political culture of the two states.

A brief outline of the special features of the political culture in the GDR will make this clear. The domination of society by the regime means that there is no room for unguided discussions, for the free information of public opinion and will, for criticism of the nature of the state or for public disputes and controversies which are more than staged debates. Everything which cannot or will not be expressed in conformity with the regime's policies is suppressed or diverted into private channels. Political behaviour in the traditional sense therefore becomes impossible. It is replaced by adaptation or the retreat into the 'niches' (as Günter Gaus has put it) of that society. The more this happens, the greater significance the Federal Republic assumes, because it serves as a kind of substitute public for the GDR: subjects can be discussed in West Germany about which there is only silence in the GDR; questions can be raised about subjects which in the GDR are swept under the carpet. West Germany represents a reality from which the GDR is often completely cut off.

The listening and viewing habits – to radio and television – of the people in the GDR bear all this out. Opinion surveys conducted among people who came from the GDR to the Federal Republic in 1984 showed that in those parts of the GDR where Western television can be received, 80 per cent watched the first and 64 per cent the second channel (the latter being rather more difficult to receive), while only 6 or 7 per cent regularly watched both GDR channels. There were similar results for radio: only 2 per cent listened regularly to East German radio in those parts of the GDR where West German broadcasts can be received clearly, and even in the Dresden area, where the reception of West German radio is not so good, the figure was only 7 per cent.[5] Of course, people who have gone to great lengths to change their place of residence from East to West Germany might be expected to show a greater liking for Western broadcasts. But the poll results were so clear that some general conclusions can certainly be justified, especially since even GDR officials admit that many East Germans tune in to West German media.

Of course, one cannot say on the basis of these observations that the people in the GDR tune in to Western media out of determined opposition to their own state. Nor is watching West German television programmes every evening necessarily some sort of 'emigration' from the reality of the GDR. This society has adapted so strongly to the conditions in which it must exist that most East Germans probably cannot imagine West German reality as their own. Rather, the West German media satisfy more basic needs than do those of the GDR: namely unfiltered information and entertainment that is not interlaced with moralistic, political exhortations. Thus it is a window on a world of richer and wider dimensions. This is particularly the case with respect to television. It is able to provide for the society of the GDR, which lives under such severe restrictions, a daily therapeutic form of crossing the border, not merely the border between East and West, but most of all the limits drawn around the individual. In this way, the use of Western media in the GDR strengthens the connections between the citizens of both states, it allows GDR citizens indirect participation in the life of the Federal Republic; they can get to know its politicians, as well as the products advertised in the media. At the same time they are well aware that people in the Federal Republic live in a way which would be impossible for them to emulate. It thus confronts them with the question to what extent they are or have become different, and thereby emphatically underlines the differences which have grown up between the two states and their societies.

A process of detachment

It is not merely the simple existence of two German states, but also the relationship between them, that has led to the developments in the two Germanies that we have discussed. A difficult and painful process of detachment has taken place. As a result, the Federal Republic and the GDR have gained a degree of independence from each other. However, the foundation of both states and the development of their own identity did not take place exactly simultaneously. True, the two states were founded almost at the same point in time, and their incorporation into their respective alliances also ran a parallel course. But becoming involved in the Western alliance meant for West Germany an opening towards the West – its culture, its style of public life and its political philosophy. At no time was there a comparable opening on the part of the people in the GDR towards the East. This was never a serious possibility. One reason was the resentment towards the Soviet Union that had built up during the Third Reich. However, the biggest obstacle to a move towards the Soviet Union was the way the Soviet Union treated Germany after the war, and the nature of the regime imposed on the Germans. To put it crudely, while West German society enjoyed the new experience which flooded Europe from the United States and thus broke from the past, meaning the Third Reich, its collapse and the postwar misery, the GDR was left sitting on the ruins.

This is not just a metaphor, but an accurate description of reality. The immediate postwar period, with its destruction and shortages, lasted much longer in the GDR than in the Federal Republic. West German society had returned to a world of civilian normality and wealth by the mid-1950s. The GDR, by contrast, remained confined within the limits of the Soviet-dominated bloc, its remaining reserves being drained to meet Soviet demands. All in all, this was a traumatic experience from which GDR society has still not fully recovered. In the Federal Republic there was a much more rapid development of a sense of identity, while the question of Germany as a larger entity retreated into the background. From the beginning of the 1960s opinion polls have shown that a majority of citizens of the Federal Republic, when asked which political entity they identified themselves with, named the Federal Republic and not, as before, the Empire or the pre-war Third Reich. Konrad Adenauer, the first Chancellor of the Federal Republic, has long since replaced Bismarck as the West Germans' admired father figure.[6] The belief in reunification as a political possibility has also rapidly diminished, with only 2 per cent expressing such a belief in the late 1970s. In November 1981, in an opinion survey carried out by the Allensbach Institute, almost half (43 per cent) of those asked what constituted the German nation replied 'the Federal Republic' (as opposed to 32 per cent who replied 'Federal Republic and GDR' and 12 per cent who also included the former territories in the East).[7] This does not mean that there is no attachment to the whole of Germany, nor does it preclude support for a special relationship with the rest of Germany. In short, the GDR is viewed by the majority of West Germans as a neighbour state in which there is great interest, but by no means as 'flesh of one's own flesh'. Germany as a whole (in the words of the diplomatic formula which has preserved the sovereign Allied rights in Germany since 1945) is either far back in memory or else far off in a vague future.

By contrast, in the GDR the state retained its provisional character in the eyes of many of its citizens for some considerable time; only later, particularly after the building of the Berlin Wall, did the real process of identity with the state begin. This development of national identity is not merely the result of changes within the GDR; it is also a reaction to the political and economic development of the Federal Republic. Hurt feelings no doubt play a part. There was an impression of having been neglected by society in the Federal Republic, of the 'West Germans' having 'written off' the East Germans – an expression which was for a long time used to describe this feeling. For the most part it comes from the need to lead an existence other than one seemingly derived from the West, like the feelings of a little brother who has always been left out. The spiteful, self-conscious brandishing of this identity in the face of the West Germans is proof of this. After all, the West Germans, given their high standard of living and weight in the world, represent a continuous challenge and threat to the self-image of the Germans in the GDR. Thus it is maintained in the GDR that while the West is materially wealthy, its inner being is impoverished; while the GDR has to be satisfied with less materially, it is at the same time more familiar, more humane and warmer. Or it is argued that although there are fewer opportunities in the GDR than in the West, there is at least an established order and a certain security for everyone, while in the West people are forced to join in the dance around the Golden Calf. All this is not entirely false. Nonetheless it bears the undeniable marks of a fundamental lie.

In the search for a common denominator for the particular development of the societies in the two states, one might say that the chief difference is that society in the GDR is on the whole more narrow and traditional. West German observers often summarize this by saying that the GDR is more 'German' than the Federal Republic. There is much to support this view, and without doubt a part of the growing attention which has been paid to the GDR is due to its 'old-fashioned' life-style, as well as its cities, villages and countryside. However, the development of the Federal Republic itself influences these perceptions. The Federal Republic has for good reason moved significantly away from the background of German tradition, a move supported by the overwhelming majority of its citizens. This is in great measure a consequence of its decision to be part of the West, which led to a change in traditional political culture. The change was also in part the result of fundamental modernization that took place in West Germany.

Nevertheless, from this Western viewpoint, the GDR does appear more 'German' than the Federal Republic. Furthermore, disquiet about the evolution of the Western industrial society, which has taken root more successfully in the Federal Republic in the postwar years than in almost any other West European country, causes this aspect of the GDR to be emphasized. It brings to the surface the sort of nostalgia that often accompanies deep changes in a society. However, it is not accidental that this has surfaced at the same time as certain intellectual circles (including the Greens) are toying with the idea of a 'new' nationalism. The vision of reunification by way of German neutralism, combined with anti-American attitudes and a longing to escape the precarious military situation in Europe by moving forward (or, if you like, backwards) to an era preceding the formation of the Eastern and Western blocs, dovetails neatly with this nostalgic view of the division of Germany. However, nationalism of this sort is likely to remain a 'nationalism without a nation', because it ignores the real situation of Germans in both states, particularly the GDR. Things that to the Western observer make the GDR 'more

151

German' may to its inhabitants be an expression of the stagnation and narrowness of the circumstances in which they find themselves and with which they must cope day by day.

All this shows just how sensitive the German–German relationship still is. Each of the two societies reacts strongly to what happens in the other. This is particularly true of the GDR, which experiences at least passively a very great deal of the life in the Federal Republic – from politics and culture to sport. For example, first-division football in the Federal Republic has a faithful following in the GDR, and even a phenomenon like the unofficial peace movement in the GDR would not be possible without the inspiration from the Western peace movement. To a smaller degree West German society has also remained sensitive to the GDR. This can be illustrated by the fact that the literature from the GDR is not treated in the Federal Republic as literature from a foreign country, but as a proper contribution to local literary life, and that an event like the reopening of the Dresden Oper (a famous theatre in the GDR) in February 1985, forty years after its destruction, also evoked great emotion among West Germans.

Towards two nation-states?

Nonetheless it remains a fact that the two separate states have become increasingly the frame of reference for people's lives; shared experiences are practically impossible. The question therefore arises whether the different identity that has emerged in the two German states has developed into a national consciousness, and, if so, what its nature is. And is there any reason to suppose that this is leading to the formation of quasi-national identities, which sooner or later will replace the idea of a German nation and will allow the two German states to become proper nation-states? Or, to put it the other way round: can the two societies that have emerged under the influence of two states in Germany still be united under the idea of one nation?

As far as the Federal Republic is concerned, the answer is clear: the state is accepted and supported by its citizens and has long abandoned its provisional character. In the GDR the answer is less clear. Probably most GDR citizens have resigned themselves to its existence as a state and even accept it. But what exactly is it that they accept? It is not the image that the leadership promotes. This consciousness of statehood is a more restricted one based on different premises than those implied by the state's political and ideological claims.

The reason is that this consciousness in the GDR did not emerge simply from adaptation to the state, but also from confrontation with it. Many attitudes and positions that at first sight appear to demonstrate adaptation seem, upon closer scrutiny, to reflect self-preservation and independence on the part of the people who live there – live there because they have to, but also because they want to, since this is where they feel at home. This consciousness is rooted in a different shared experience than that of West Germans. It is rooted in a feeling of belonging together, derived from the shared experience of their postwar history, which is their experience alone, and not that of the West Germans. It is in part also a feeling of belonging together in the face of the claims of the state. In this respect the GDR state is not accepted as that which it would like to be – namely the socialist climax of German history. But neither is it merely the oppressive-militant Leviathan, the bureaucratic power structure, the regimentation and repression that it sometimes seems outside. It is also the preserver of people's livelihoods and public order, it defines the area for professional achievement, in short, it provides the framework in which success, satis-faction and personal acceptance can be sought and found.

The identity that can be derived from such a consciousness must necessarily remain fragmentary. It will be limited to the sphere of life that can be shaped by the individual and will only partially include the public arena, while maintaining a careful and wary distance from the political realm. It is thus unable to perform the function of a true national identity by providing an overall orientation that includes a certain view of history and culture. The leadership of the GDR has been unable to provide such an orientation, even though it has put forward a variety of ideas for a 'socialist' concept of nationhood specifically related to the GDR. No matter how the various proposals were constructed, they were unable to displace the national concepts which had grown up over the course of his-tory, or even adapt them for their own purposes. They had little appeal to society in the GDR. All in all, the arrangement by which the leadership of the GDR and its society live together – motivated in the end more by resig-nation than conviction – is too unstable, too dependent on the potential for internal repression and the unchangeability of the wider European framework, to be able to sustain a genuine national claim.

The new approach to German history, which has emerged since the second half of the 1970s, should therefore not be taken to signify such a claim (contrary to what has often been thought in the Federal Republic). It is rather the admission that the attempt to construct a view of history tailored to the regime's needs, in which anything that did not fit the desired pattern of tradition was omitted or adapted, has failed. The GDR has long tried this, but too often the result was a very obviously inadequate picture of history. The effect was not to erase the perception of the arbi-trary character of the GDR state, but rather to underline it.

The recent rehabilitation of so many central characters of German history, from Friedrich II to Bismarck, is designed to fit the GDR into the mainstream of history and culture. It could also be a tribute to the present rediscovery of historical and national aspects of life in East and West. But above all, by rooting the GDR more securely in German national history, the regime hopes to stabilize the still precarious relationship between society and the state. By recognizing history, the principal streams of which it until recently opposed, the GDR state hopes to achieve recognition in those parts of society which have denied it such recognition so far, particularly because of its attitude to history. It is quite probable that it may succeed in this and that the state will thereby become more stable. However, the GDR will have to pay a high price for this recognition. Because of this new relationship to the past it will now be seen more clearly against the backround of German history, which is and remains a history of all of Germany. Thus the rehabilitation of the past both strengthens and challenges the GDR.

How does this affect the Federal Republic? It, too, has problems with its national identity. This is shown not only by the interminable discussions on the subject, but also by such phenomena as the Greens and the Peace Movement, as well as the great interest that historical exhibitions have evoked in the past years. All this suggests that people in the Federal Republic are in search of something – but what? German unity, for example? All opinion surveys on the subject support the clear conclusion that emerges from the public debate in the Federal Republic, namely that this is not so. True, the Federal government continues to support the goal of reunification in accordance with the 1949 preamble in the constitution (the Basic Law). From time to time it is suggested that this clause be removed. This is not only resisted by the three established parties, the CDU/CSU, SPD and FDP, but, according to an opinion survey, also meets with the disapproval of the majority of citizens.[8] However, within leading political circles there is common agreement that this goal cannot be achieved in the immediate future; this means that the German question is considered to remain 'open'.

Government policy towards the GDR, known as Deutschlandpolitik, is thus not a policy of reunification, but rather aims to make the existence of the two states more bearable. A number of seemingly innocuous enterprises serve this goal – for example, the attempt to improve travel, the widening of sporting contacts, the regulation of legal problems and currency flows, and cooperation over the problems that having a border within Germany creates for the inhabitants of both sides. While there is little support in the population of the Federal Republic for reunification as a short-term goal, there is strong approval of a step-by-step normalization of the German situation. Possibly the support is so strong because

Germans in the Federal Republic do not want to face up to the ambiguity inherent in it, since it simultaneously underpins the existence of two separate states and emphasizes what both states have in common. This ambiguity is a reflection of the international situation, which in the foreseeable future will not permit a radical change in the German situation, and at the same time of a national context which neither state can, or wants to, deny. At this point it is impossible to foresee if, in time, one of these aspects will dominate over and displace the other. Not only the Germans, but also the international situation, helps keep the German question open.

As far as Germans in the Federal Republic are concerned, their search for an identity is directed in the first place at the question of their place and role in the world in the face of a situation which in the foreseeable future will most likely remain unchanged, in Germany as well as in Europe. In the course of Deutschlandpolitik and Ostpolitik in the 1960s and 1970s the Federal Republic has in some sense bestowed recognition upon itself by finally shedding the political elements of its provisional character. Thus it has legalized a situation that has long since formed the basis of the life of its society. But since then it has become clear that this does not sufficiently answer the question: what is the Federal Republic?

When, for example, the national team of the Federal Republic or other top sportsmen take part in an international competition, for most West Germans they represent simply Germany, even if the opponents are Germans from the GDR. But this is a transient phenomenon which does not carry beyond the enthusiasm about sport. Up to now the Federal Republic has not become, in the eyes of its citizens, a nation-state. This is due not so much to the existence of two German states as to a lack of commitment to community-formation and will – a lack that characterizes both state and society in the Federal Republic. This weakness has its origin partly in the circumstances of the creation of the Federal Republic, and thus the question of the two states does come into play. However, the main reason for the Federal Republic's sense of insecurity about itself is no doubt the catastrophe of the Third Reich. This is still a heavy burden on Germany's national consciousness.

On the other hand, one can ask with reference to both states: is it still possible to think in central Europe about the formation of a nation-state arising out of present conditions? Does national consciousness not live by the political, cultural and emotional heritage of the one or two centuries that are recognized as the era of national movements? If this is the case, then the Germans and their two states would have to rely on the traditional concept of the nation. This could not be replaced by any development inside the two states and their societies in the foreseeable future.

155

Notes

1   Annual Report of the Federal Minister for Inter-German Relations, 1984.
2   H. Reinhard Koch, 'Flucht und Ausreise aus der DDR', *Deutschland Archiv*, 1/1986, p. 47 ff.
3   Richard von Weizäcker, Referat beim 74. Bergdorfer Gesprächskreis, 'Die deutsche Frage – neu gestellt', *Protokoll*, 1983, p. 13.
4   M. Rainer Lepsius, Stellungname bei der Öffentlichen Anhörung des Ausschusses für innerdeutsche Beziehungen des Deutschen Bundestages 1977, *Zur Sache* 4/77, Presse- und Informationszentrum des Deutschen Bundestages, p. 233.
5   According to research conducted by Volker Ronge, Man.
6   Erwin K. Scheuch, 'Die deutsche Nation im Bewusstsein der Bevölkerung der Bundesrepublik', in Klaus Weigelt (ed.), *Heimat und Nation. Zur Geschichte und Identität der Deutschen* (1984), p. 163 f.
7   See Elisabeth Noelle-Neumann, *Eine demoskopische Deutschstunde* (1983), p.85.
8   See, for example, the Emnid results of June 1985 in *Emnid-Informationen*, 5, 1985, p. 12 f.

11 The future of Berlin

JONATHAN DEAN

There is no 'Berlin' in agreed East–West terminology. When discussing Berlin issues, American, French and British officials often refer to 'Berlin', Soviet officials refer to 'West–Berlin', and West German officials refer to 'Berlin (West)'. Western officials are referring to 'Greater Berlin', the capital city of the Reich, whose territory, established through municipal reform in 1920, was divided into four sectors of military occupation at the end of World War II. With their terms, Berlin (West) and West–Berlin, West German and Soviet officials are referring only to the three Western sectors of Berlin. For Soviet officials, there is only one Berlin – 'Berlin, capital of the German Democratic Republic' (or GDR) – an area known to Western officials as the 'Eastern Sector of Berlin'.

An important conflict in political and legal concepts underlies these differences in geographic description. The conflict is so fundamental that the negotiators of the Four-Power Agreement between France, the United Kingdom, the United States and the Soviet Union, signed on September 3, 1971, could agree only on the term 'relevant area' as the subject of the agreement on which they had been working for some sixteen months. Yet when officials of both East and West today refer to the 'status of Berlin', they are referring to the same thing: the ensemble of rules and procedures which have grown up around divided Berlin. These rules and procedures, which prescribe and circumscribe the actions and interactions of representatives of France, the United Kingdom, the United States, the Soviet Union, and of the Germans in both parts of divided Berlin and Germany, form the Berlin regime.[1]

During the forty years of its existence, the Berlin regime has changed in important respects. Its original form was a set of agreed rules by which the four victorious wartime allies governed the former German capital. This arrangement lasted until June 1948, when the Russians blockaded Berlin. By the time the blockade was over, the Berlin regime had fundamentally changed in nature. Instead of an arrangement for joint administration of a unified city, the regime had become a four-power *modus vivendi* for administering a divided city in a divided nation. In 1971, the Four-Power Agreement, together with the implementing agreement between the Federal Republic and the GDR and the Berlin Senate and the GDR, made a major change in the Berlin regime, a change which reduced both the risks of the existing regime and the hardships it caused for Berliners. It did so primarily by formally associating the two German states which had emerged on the territory of divided Germany with the operation of the Berlin regime. In essence, though there were differences in the legal status of participants, the 1971 agreements converted the Four-Power Berlin regime to a Six-Power regime.

Experience of the past fifteen years confirms that the participants in the 1971 agreements succeeded in insulating and stabilizing a dangerous point of East–West friction which has repeatedly threatened to ignite a broad conflict. It was an outcome which can serve as an example in any deliberate long-term policy of crisis prevention in an era of continuing East–West competition.

The first and second Berlin regimes

Under the original Berlin regime determined by the British–American–Soviet wartime European Advisory Commission and as set forth in its Protocol of September 12, 1944, Berlin was divided into American, British and Soviet sectors of military occupation, to be administered by the individual commanders, not separately, but under the direction of the joint Kommandatura. As later emerged, in the Soviet view, the Western sectors of Berlin were part of the Soviet zone of occupation over which the Russians had by special concession permitted a superimposed administration by the Western allies. In the Western view, the rights in Berlin of the three Western allies – and of the Soviet Union – were original rights directly derived from their joint participation in the victory over Nazi Germany. The three sectors into which the city was originally divided became four in July 1945, when France was associated with the administration of the city and given an occupation sector of its own.

There was no provision in the Protocol of September 12, 1944 for access to Berlin, either for movement of Western military forces in and out of the city from their own occupation zones to the West, or for similar movement of German civilians or civilian goods. After Western forces took over their sectors in Berlin in June 1945, access to Berlin for their forces was based on a combination of oral agreements on road access and written understandings on air and rail movements. There was never, and there is not to this day, an agreed written understanding covering movement of military personnel by road. Procedures governing access to the Western sectors of

German persons and goods were largely derived from Allied rights in the Western sectors and were not covered by explicit agreement.

The original Berlin regime lasted almost precisely three years from the June 1945 entry of Western forces into Berlin. On June 18, 1948, the Western allies carried out a currency reform for the Western zones of occupation, the physical demonstration of their separate administration of Western Germany. On June 19, the Russians stopped rail and road traffic from the West to the Western sectors of Berlin. On June 24–25, all incoming and outgoing truck traffic and postal services to Berlin were stopped, as well as food deliveries to Berlin from the Soviet zone. On July 1, the Soviet representative left the Berlin Kommandatura, stating that there was 'no longer an Allied Kommandatura'. The Western airlift began on June 26, 1948, and continued with a total of nearly 250,000 flights until May 12, 1949. In September, 1948, organized groups of communist demonstrators pushed the elected Berlin Mayor and City Council out of the City Hall in the Eastern sector and, in November, a meeting of communist party members appointed a separate administration for East Berlin.

In its note of July 14, 1948, replying to the protests of the Western allies over the imposition of the Berlin blockade, the Soviet Union argued that the Western powers had violated wartime and postwar agreements providing for unified allied administration of Germany as a whole through moving to set up a separate government for West Germany, and had thereby also undermined the legal basis of their right to participate in the administration of Berlin. The note stated, 'Berlin lies in the centre of the Soviet zone and is a part of that zone.'[2]

When the blockade was lifted in the spring of 1949, discussions among representatives of the four powers in Berlin restored access to Berlin. But they did not reestablish the Four Power Allied Control Council or the Allied Kommandatura for Berlin. Instead, they established a new Berlin regime, a regime for a divided city in a divided country. It was a regime in which both the Soviet Union and the Western allies relinquished, for a time at least, their own views as to a desirable solution to the Berlin problem, either in the sense of incorporating the Western sectors into the Soviet zone of occupation, or in the sense of reestablishing a unified Germany where Berlin would once again become the capital city.

The Western powers insisted on retaining those remnants of the earlier four-power system which had survived the blockade: the Berlin Air Safety Centre and the circulation of Western military patrols in the Soviet sector. The procedures for access to the Western sectors instituted after the blockade was raised resembled those agreed in 1945. But there were significant differences: instead of the earlier West German personnel and locomotives, the East German Reichsbahn railroad system operated the allied military trains to and from Berlin. No Germans were permitted to be transported on allied trains, either as employees or as passengers travelling on allied passes. The number of permitted trains was reduced. Lists of crews of West German barges had to be submitted for approval to East German officials operating under Soviet control. There was in fact tighter Soviet control over access to Berlin than before the blockade.

Even more significant for the further development of the Berlin regime was the establishment in 1949 of separate governments in West and East Germany. In each case, establishment of the government formally ended direct military rule by the four powers in the parts of Germany controlled by them. Constitutions for each of these German governments were approved in the same month, May 1949. Significantly, each constitution laid claim to Berlin, declared respectively to be a *Land* (state) of the Federal Republic of Germany and the capital city of the GDR. In approving the West German 'Basic Law' or constitution, France, the United Kingdom and the United States specifically suspended those of its articles which claimed authority over Berlin, reserving for themselves the final say in questions concerning Berlin and Germany as a whole – and they continue to do so today. Acting for the Soviet Union, General Chuikov took parallel action toward the GDR, reserving for the Soviet Union the obligations arising from joint decisions of the four powers.[3] The establishment of the Federal Republic and of the GDR formalized the division of Germany and of Berlin. But, despite the fact that all four wartime allies had reserved their rights with regard to Berlin, these events also began a process of progressive 'Germanization' of the Berlin regime on both sides.

In the East, this development took the form of progressive devolution to East German authorities by the Russians of Soviet responsibility for their occupation sector in Berlin and for control of civilian access to Berlin. In September, 1955, the Soviet Union and the GDR signed a treaty ending the residual occupation regime for the GDR. This action paralleled a similar move by the Western allies in the Paris Agreements, which had taken effect in May, 1955. The Soviet–GDR treaty was accompanied by an exchange of letters in which the Soviet Union formally conferred on the GDR responsibility for supervising the border of the GDR with the Federal Republic, the surroundings of Berlin, the sector crossing points in Berlin and communication routes between 'West-Berlin' and the Federal Republic. In other words, the GDR received full responsibility for regulating and controlling German civilian traffic to and from the Western sectors of Berlin. However, the Soviet letter explicitly reserved to the commander of the Group of Soviet Forces Germany control over movement of allied troops between West-Berlin and the Federal Republic 'for the time being, until a pertinent agreement is reached'.[3]

In their weaker situation in Berlin, surrounded by an area under the control of the GDR authorities backed by Soviet forces, and in order to avoid undermining their own rights in Berlin, which were contested by the Soviet Union, the Western allies were punctilious with regard to actions associating the Federal Republic with the operation of the Western sectors. As noted, they suspended application to Berlin of Article 23 of the Basic Law of the Federal Republic which declared *Gross Berlin* – all of metropolitan Berlin – a *Land* of the Federal Republic. The allies declared that Berlin was not a part of the Federal Republic and not governed by it. Yet the Western allies supported the establishment of close economic ties between the Federal Republic and the Western sectors. By January 1952, through Bundestag approval of the 'Third *Überleitungsgesetz*', the Western sectors were fully integrated in the economic, legal, financial and customs system of the Federal Republic. Nearly every law and ordnance adopted by the Federal Republic was applied in Berlin, although only after review by the three Western Allies, who reserved to themselves the final decision in all matters of status and security.

Crisis of 1958–62: The Berlin regime under pressure

To deal with European and American concerns caused in 1957 by the success of the Soviet Union in launching its Sputnik satellite and developing the first ICBM, the Eisenhower government proposed deployment of Thor and Jupiter intermediate-range ballistic missiles in Europe. In December 1957, the Nato Council decided to accept this proposal. In addition to the American bombers already stationed in Europe, the new missiles, once deployed, could strike Soviet territory more rapidly (and in far greater number) than the few Soviet ICBMs which could reach the United States. These American missiles were stationed in the United Kingdom, Italy and Greece. The possibility of deployment in the Federal Republic was discussed, but was declined by Chancellor Adenauer.

Then, as twenty years later in the INF dispute, the Soviet Union reacted with great concern to the prospect of the deployment in Europe of intermediate-range American missiles, especially in West Germany. The Soviet Union supported the Rapacki proposal for a nuclear-free zone in Central Europe and a plan for a confederation of the German states. It also took action on Berlin. The new Berlin crisis began on November 27, 1958 with Soviet notes to the three Western powers and the Federal Republic in which the Soviet Union complained that the Western powers were arming West Germany with atomic weapons and missiles. This time, the Soviet government explicitly declared the London Protocol of September 12, 1944 null and void and demanded the termination of the 'obsolete' occupation of Berlin, either by transferring the Western sectors to the sovereignty of the GDR in whose territory the Western sectors were located, or, as a compromise, by converting West-Berlin into a demilitarized free city. If this latter compromise solution were carried out during a six-month grace period, the Soviet Union would withdraw from its remaining occupation functions for Berlin and for Berlin access and transfer them to the GDR. The Western allies would then have to negotiate an agreement with the GDR providing for transport to the free demilitarized city.[4]

In 1958, as in the 1948–9 Berlin crisis, the Russians again seemed to be testing for two objectives. These were: first, to use a crisis around Berlin to bring the Western allies and the Federal Republic to relinquish actions which the Russians opposed – in this case, deployment of American IRBM's in Western Europe and especially the Federal Republic; second, to push the Western allies out of the Western sectors, an objective which was strongly supported by the GDR leadership. There is some evidence that East German party leader Walter Ulbricht considered this Soviet threat of a separate peace treaty a serious commitment and was much annoyed when Khrushchev subsequently backed off from implementing it. Whether the Russians had serious expectations at the time that the Western allies could be pushed out is unclear. But, as his later actions in bringing Soviet missiles to Cuba showed, Khrushchev believed that the Soviet system was increasingly powerful and successful, that the Western system was in decline, and that pressure could pay off.

In any event, the Soviet intention to challenge and also to change the Berlin regime was clear. The atmosphere of crisis over Berlin increased the flow of refugees from East Germany into Berlin and the Federal Republic, running at a rate of 2,000 per day in July and early August of 1961. In the face of this increasingly serious loss of educated, skilled manpower, Ulbricht repeatedly pressed for the establishment of physical barriers to end mass emigration. The Russians finally agreed. On August 13, 1961, the GDR cut off East Berlin from the Western sectors by means of barbed wire fences and began the construction of the Berlin Wall. Elevated railroad and subway connections between the Western sectors and East Berlin were cut off, residents of East Berlin were forbidden to visit the Western sectors and West Berliners to visit East Berlin or East Germany. Postal and telephone connections had already been cut in June and July.

On August 18, the United States sent a combat unit up the autobahn to Berlin. But the Western powers did not carry out proposals that they challenge the Wall by military measures. They protested at the construction of the Wall but accepted its existence, to the great disillusionment of

Berliners and Germans generally. As a result a turning point in German thinking was reached which ultimately had important consequences.

The final act of this Berlin crisis came after the Cuban missile crisis had reached its own denouement in October 1962. In a speech in December 1962, the GDR party leader, Walter Ulbricht, said that peaceful co-existence required compromises on both sides and suggested negotiations between the two German states. Khrushchev, in a January 1963 speech in East Berlin, said that the Soviet Union had already gained its main point through establishment of the Berlin Wall and through calling the Western powers to order by stepping on their 'pet corns'.[5] He intimated that, for the moment, he would not press his demands for a change in the status of Berlin.

The significance of the Khrushchev crisis over Berlin was that the legal basis of the Berlin regime was more heavily contested than ever before, while the Western sectors of Berlin were now completely isolated from the Eastern sector and from the surrounding GDR.

The second Berlin regime in decline

However, following the wind-down of Khrushchev's Berlin crisis and Khrushchev's own removal from office, the Soviet Union suspended its pressures on the Western allies in Berlin. Instead, the Soviet Union and GDR shifted to a different target: the West German presence in Berlin and West German ties with the Western sectors. They attacked the 'illegal' practices of the Federal Republic in the Western sectors. The GDR deliberately used its control over access routes to Berlin to register its objections: for example, on the occasion of the Bundestag plenary session on April 7 1965, when it prohibited Bundestag deputies from using the access routes to Berlin, held large-scale manoeuvres in the area between the Western sectors and the Federal Republic, cutting off access completely six times for several hours at a time, and slowed down the processing of documents for truck transport to Berlin. On the day of the Bundestag session, the Soviet and GDR air forces flew through the air corridors, causing repeated sonic booms over the city.

In January 1968, the Soviet Ambassador, Tsarapkin, presented the West German government with a paper summarizing Soviet objections to West German activities in Berlin. The memorandum listed as objectionable practices: parliamentary weeks of Bundestag committee meetings; sessions in Berlin of the federal cabinet; the establishment of federal agencies in Berlin; the execution of official functions by West German government leaders while in Berlin; the election of the Berlin Mayor as President of the West German Bundesrat; and meetings in Berlin of West German political parties and national associations. The Soviets did not urge a change in the status of Berlin to an independent entity. Instead, they demanded that the Federal Republic respect the existing status of the city.[6]

In the middle and late 1960s, the rigid confrontational stance of the Cold War began to erode in both East and West. The thaw stopped abruptly in August 1968, with the invasion of Czechoslovakia by 70,000 Soviet troops. But the momentum toward detente was strong. President Johnson continued to press for the opening of the Strategic Arms Limitation (SALT) negotiations. The Soviet Union had received a decisive blow to its international standing and to its authority in the international communist movement through its military repression of Czechoslovak moves toward pluralism. Yet it made energetic efforts to regain international status.

Although East and West appeared to be moving toward a somewhat improved relationship at the end of the 1960s, the Western position in Berlin continued to deteriorate. In March 1968, the GDR published an ordnance forbidding federal ministers and senior officials to enter the GDR and to use transit routes to Berlin. Three months later, in June 1968, the GDR introduced the requirement that all travellers from West Germany to the GDR and to the Western sectors of Berlin, other than members of the allied garrisons, must have a GDR visa. A special tax was levied on freight shipments to the Western sectors. After protests to the Soviet Union by the Western allies and the Federal Republic, the implementation of the new requirements was nonetheless accepted. In practice, all pretence of four-power responsibility for civilian land access to Berlin had been eliminated, although four-power responsibility for air access continued, as it does to this day.

Parallel with this development toward full exercise of GDR control over the access routes to Berlin, political and public opinion in the Federal Republic was moving very rapidly towards acceptance of the GDR as a separate independent country on German soil, instead of as 'the Soviet Zone of Occupation' or the 'so-called GDR', as it was still called at the time. This trend was reinforced after the September 1969 elections, and the establishment of the Social Democratic-Free Democratic coalition government of Willy Brandt and Walter Scheel. In his speech on 28 October, 1969, presenting the programme of the new government, Chancellor Willy Brandt spoke of 'two German states in one nation'. In the debate on the government programme, Chancellor Brandt and Foreign Minister Scheel abandoned the 'Hallstein doctrine' (under which the Federal Republic, as sole legitimate representative of Germany as a whole, regarded third-country recognition of the GDR as an unfriendly act and broke relations with the third country). At the same time, the GDR itself was moving toward wider international acceptance. Between May 1969

164

and May 1970, the GDR, previously recognized only by communist countries, was recognized by ten non-communist countries.[7]

The prospect was that the Western allies would, step-by-step, be obliged to deal on access to Berlin, ultimately including military access, with a German Democratic Republic which they did not recognize and in whose relationship with the West there would not necessarily be any of the restraints which affected the American–Soviet relationship through their role as nuclear powers. Instead, the GDR, which was suspected of having instigated on its own many of the recent disruptions of access to Berlin, could continue to do so, or else act as the surrogate of the Soviet Union, and the Allies might have no rejoinder but direct force. Behind the Western concern over the GDR was recognition of the growing strength of Soviet nuclear arms, and of the parallel unlikelihood that Soviet control over Eastern Europe could be seriously shaken or – after the evidence of the Soviet intervention in Czechoslovakia – would evolve in any far-reaching way.

Moreover, the morale of the Berlin population was not impervious to the continual difficulties in access of civilian persons and goods to Berlin and was nervous about growing GDR control over the access routes. Berlin production and trade suffered because of uncertainties over delivery. For years, the Soviet Union had refused even to discuss Berlin access with the Western powers. The Berlin regime appeared seriously threatened.

Emergence of the third Berlin regime

In the customary meetings of British, French, American and West German Foreign Ministers on the margins of Nato ministerial sessions at Reykjavik in June 1968 and at Brussels in December 1968, then Foreign Minister Brandt had urged his Western colleagues to sound out the Russians about improving the access to Berlin and about easing visit and travel restrictions for Berliners. The American Embassy in Bonn urged that the Western allies seek to gain some advantage from the efforts of the Soviet Union to reestablish itself internationally after the serious political damage it had received from its invasion of Czechoslovakia; the Russians should be obliged to give concrete evidence of their intentions by agreeing to improvements in Berlin.[8].

Yet the foreign ministries of the three Western powers were reluctant to open discussions with the Soviet Union on the complex Berlin regime. They feared that the Russians would make far-reaching proposals for change which would have to be rejected, leaving the Berlin situation worse than before. It took over a year from Western agreement at Reykjavik to look into the issue before the first allied working paper for possible sound-ings with the Russians was ready. President Nixon had visited the Western sectors in February 1969, amid the controversy over the holding of the Federal Assembly in Berlin. In a speech at the Siemens plant, he signalled his willingness to discuss the Berlin situation. Henry Kissinger reports that, following President Nixon's return to Washington, Ambassador Dobrynin indicated to him Soviet willingness to negotiate on the Berlin question, and that mutual readiness to negotiate was confirmed in an exchange of letters between President Nixon and Premier Kosygin.[9] After further exchanges, the four-power negotiations began on March 26, 1970, in the building of the Allied Control Authority in the American sector of Berlin.

Given the complexity of their subject matter, the Berlin negotiations were of short duration; they ended on September 3, 1971, after a period of some sixteen months. The ensuing inter-German negotiations lasted only three months, between September and December 1971. The preamble of the 1971 Four Power Agreement states that the four governments, acting on the basis of their four-power rights and responsibilities, agreed that there should be no unilateral change 'in the area'. The operative pro-visions are: (1) a declaration by the Soviet Union that transit traffic by road, rail and waterway of civilian personnel and goods between the Western sectors of Berlin and the Federal Republic would be unimpeded, and would receive preferential treatment. (2) The three Western powers state that ties with the Federal Republic will be maintained and developed, taking into account that the Western sectors are not a constituent part of the Federal Republic of Germany and not governed by it; the agreement states that the federal president, the federal government, the Bundes-versammlung, the Bundesrat and Bundestag would not perform con-stitutional acts of governing the Western sectors. (3) The Soviet Union pledges improved communications and travel for Berliners to the surrounding area.

Further operative provisions are: (4) The three Western powers declare they would represent the Western sectors abroad in all matters concerning security and status. Subject to this limitation the Federal Republic could represent the interests of Berlin abroad, Berliners could participate in West German delegations to international meetings, and international conferences could take place in the Western sectors, if jointly invited by the Senate and the federal German government. The Soviet Union accepts this statement. (5) The Western powers state that the Soviet Union could establish a Consulate General and trade office in the Western sectors. The agreement stipulates that these arrangements would go into effect after satisfactory ageements on access and visits to East Berlin and the GDR by residents of the Federal Republic and the Western sectors had been concluded between the Federal Republic and the GDR, and between the Senate and the GDR, and that the four signatory governments would consult in the event of difficulties in the application of the agreement.[10]

The Four-Power Agreement was a success in the sense of achieving specific Western negotiating objectives. Each of the immediate Western objectives was agreed to: improved access, guaranteed by the Russians; improvement for visits and communications by Berliners to East Berlin and the GDR; Soviet acceptance of West German ties with the Federal Republic and the Western sectors; a more assured role for West Berlin in international ife.

The West paid something for these gains, committing itself *vis-à-vis* the Soviet Union to maintain the prohibition that the Federal Republic did not govern the Western sectors, and permitting a Soviet Consulate General in the Western sectors. The West failed to gain explicit mention of 'Berlin' in the agreement and there was no improvement of the Western position regarding the Eastern sector of Berlin. The big price – Western acceptance of the GDR in the United Nations – was not specified, but was clearly implied by the context of the negotiations.

In addition to the specific objectives just described, the Western allies achieved broader aims: to reduce the risk of confrontation over Berlin and to avoid a situation where the Russians could withdraw from responsibility for Berlin, leaving the Western powers confronted by a GDR which they did not at the time recognize and over which they had no hold. The Western allies gained these benefits before it became too late to do so through progressive international acceptance of East Germany. In particular, after a lapse of twenty-five years, the Western allies made good the fateful omission in the first Berlin regime, namely the absence of contractual agreement assuring access to Berlin by civilian persons and goods. They brought the Russians to reaffirm the 'occupation status' of the Western sectors, to accept ultimate responsibility for land access to Berlin by civilians, to drop their efforts to push the Western allies and West Germany out of the Western sectors, and to accept explicitly a West German role in the Western sectors at a certain level.

These steps were at the cost of GDR pretentions that the Western sectors were on East German territory and that the GDR was exercising sovereign authority in controlling civilian access to Berlin through its territory. Walter Ulbricht had publicly proclaimed, at the beginning of 1970, that there was no four-power responsibility for Berlin. His resistance to making these concessions to the West in the Four-Power Agreement played a major role in his being pushed out of office in May 1971. Some friction between Soviet and GDR views on the status of Berlin has continued. In November 1984, the GDR closed the Glienicke bridge, a route to the Western sectors used by allied military missions attached to the Soviet command in Potsdam, in a dispute with the Berlin Senate over who should pay the costs of repair. A few hours after the Western allies complained to the Soviet authorities in East Berlin, the bridge was reopened.

However, from the 1971 agreement, the GDR got advancement in international status and the certain prospect of further advancement to UN membership. The GDR also gained a lump sum transit fee for use of the access routes to Berlin and other hard currency payments totalling about DM 1 billion, which West Germany makes annually in connection with Berlin. (Transit lump sum payment DM 500 million, plus an average of DM 400 million in recent years for road improvements, and DM 100 million in payment for GDR services to Berlin, including waste removal).

From the Four-Power Agreement, the Soviet Union gained the desired advance of the GDR toward international recognition and consolidation, a reduction in the West German presence in Berlin and limitations on that presence. It overcame much of the onus of its invasion of Czechoslovakia and reestablished its standing in the West. Of greatest significance for Soviet general policy, through conclusion of the Four-Power Agreement and the related German–German agreements, the way was opened to achieve a major Soviet aim: ratification of the West German treaties with the Soviet Union and Poland which accepted the postwar borders of Poland and the Soviet Union.

Significance of the 1971 Berlin regime in the East-West context

The Berlin issue, which had been both product and cause of the East–West confrontation, was now deliberately decoupled from the continuing world-wide American–Soviet political and military competition. Over the decades of the confrontation over Berlin, the potential costs of East–West war had grown so great that both sides were willing to insulate the Berlin issue with a new modus vivendi. For the West, the continued effort to block the GDR from international recognition was not worth the ultimate risk of conflict with the Soviet Union. For the Soviet Union, continued pressure on Berlin as a source of leverage on the West or as a long-term means of squeezing the allies out of Berlin had become too risky in terms of its potential benefits. And that pressure had become counterproductive to the Soviet Union's attempts to gain formal Western acceptance of the status quo in Europe and to seek a more advangageous political and economic relationship with the states of the Western alliance.

In concluding the Four-Power Agreement, both sides suspended their long-term objectives and ambitions for Berlin, accepting that they could not be implemented at the time. By accepting a Western commitment to the Russians that the Western sectors were not a constituent part of the Federal Republic, the Federal Republic accepted continued suspension of the provision of the Basic Law declaring Berlin to be a *Land* of the Federal Republic. Although with evident distaste, the GDR suspended active pursuit of its effort to establish sovereignty over Western sectors or to declare them an international city as a step on the way to eventual incorporation in the GDR. All six countries acknowledged that no final solution of the Berlin issue was possible at this time, only a modus vivendi to administer an unresolved problem.

The 1971 agreement expanded the Berlin regime to cover civilian access to Berlin and, largely for this purpose, was further modified through directly associating the two states which had emerged on German territory with its operation. That is, the Four-Power Agreement converted the Berlin regime from a four-power to a six-power regime and established a set of rules for the interaction of the six. In the legal sense, it is a two-tier regime, with the four powers continuing their responsibilities at one level and the Federal Republic and the GDR associated at a practical level. But the day-to-day significance of the German contribution is considerably greater than that of the original four powers – a circumstance which may point the way to further evolution of the Berlin regime in the future.

In this six-power sense, today's mixed regime in Berlin is very much a regime of shared functions. The traffic of Western allies to Berlin by road and rail is controlled by the Soviet Union. Air traffic, civilian and military, continues to operate under 1945 rules and through the mechanism of the Berlin Air Safety Centre established at that time. In accordance with the 1971 Agreement, civilian ground traffic to Berlin is handled by the GDR under ultimate Soviet responsibility and in cooperation with the Federal Republic, which pays large lump-sum transit fees and subsidies for improvement of the land and water routes to Berlin and adjudicates the rare cases of travellers stopped or detained by GDR authorities on the land routes. The Berlin Senate and the GDR operate the mechanism for enabling visits by West Berliners to East Berlin and the GDR. The West German role in the Western sectors has been formally accepted by the Soviet Union and the GDR. Under the two-tier system, the interests of Berlin abroad in status and security matters are represented by the Western allies (a function which might be exercised in the Security Council or in peace treaty negotiations, but which has remained theoretical and unpractised) and on the second tier, day-to-day level, by the Federal Republic (though, again, a more important function in practical terms).

169

Jonathan Dean

Future of the 1971 regime

The implementation of the Berlin Agreement has proved quite satisfactory. Ground traffic to and from Berlin has moved smoothly and has increased threefold from a total of 7 million trips in 1979, to over 22 million trips in 1984.[11] Visits by West Berliners to the GDR have been at a high rate – over 3 million annually in the late 1970s. They declined in the 1980s (1.8 million in 1984); the decline is ascribed by some to the continued effect of high GDR currency exchange requirements, and by others to increasing age and mortality among West Berliners who have relatives in the GDR or East Berlin.

It is logical, given the geographical position of Berlin, to think of making the Western sectors a leading centre for international conferences, especially those involving participation of both Western countries and those linked with the Soviet Union. But prospects for large-scale development in this direction are uncertain. In practice, acceptance by the Soviet Union and the East European states of the right of the West German government and the Senate together to invite international organizations to meet in the Western sectors has been uneven. In 1985, Warsaw Pact members refused to participate in an international gynecological conference in West Berlin but raised no objection to scheduling future meetings of the IMF and World Bank in Berlin. There will be some progress in coming years, but Soviet and GDR reluctance, plus the competition of other centres like Vienna and Geneva, will impose limitations. The underlying problem as far as the GDR is concerned, and to a lesser extent, the Soviet Union, is that every gain for West Berlin can be seen as casting a competitive shadow over East Berlin. If some way could be found of sharing the prestige and other gains of hosting international conferences between West and East Berlin, this barrier might fall.

One potentially important function for Berlin, clearly suggested by its location and circumstances, would be as a centre and base for East-West arms control and confidence-building activity. The West German president, Richard von Weizäcker, has suggested that the second phase of the Conference on Disarmament in Europe, now convening in Stockholm, might be held in Berlin perhaps alternating between the Western sectors and East Berlin. Berlin has also been suggested as the natural site of a Nato–Warsaw Pact risk reduction centre, coordinating the exchange of information on previously agreed confidence-building measures, rapidly clarifying minor border incidents before they lead to a chain of escalating reactions, and discussing new military technologies and strategies with a view to formal or informal understandings or even avoiding those developments viewed as most threatening by one side or the other. Such

170

efforts to give Berlin an expanding role as the centre of arms control or confidence-building are entirely logical. But the main obstacle to this development has already been mentioned: the Soviet–GDR tendency to seek to limit the international prestige and importance of the Western sectors in comparison with East Berlin. Consequently, such efforts are not likely to receive Eastern acceptance for some time. The apparent solution to this specific problem is some sort of cooperative arrangement between East and West Berlin, but that too must await further evolution of attitudes on both sides.

The population of Western Berlin has recovered well from the psychological side-effects of the Four-Power Agreement, which relegated the city from the drama and purposefulness of being a frontier post of East–West confrontation to the status of just another nearly normal German city. Morale in the city is high. Investment is increasing, and 6,000 new jobs were created in 1984. Tourism has increased by 10 per cent in each of the past two years. There is discussion of making Berlin a tax haven, like Liechtenstein, and of relaxing tight West German rules governing trading in stocks.

Many experts feel that focusing on the new technology of microchips and electronics will reduce or eliminate the problems caused by transporting heavy manufactured products to and from an isolated Berlin. They envisage West Berlin as hooked in to the West German computer network and playing the same role, or even a more active one, as Frankfurt or Düsseldorf. They also consider that migrant Turkish workers will be an unexpected source of small-business impetus for the Berlin economy. These experts tend to criticize continued attempts to define a new role for West Berlin as superfluous and as a potentially risky misdirection of attention and effort.

Yet for all the success of the four-power regime and the promise of a healthy economy, West Berlin remains an alien body, a foreign presence in a suspicious and mistrustful environment, isolated from its own economy and culture. It would not survive except for the large subsidies which the West German government pays directly to the Berlin budget, a subsidy which amounts to over half the budget of the city (DM11.6 billion of the 1986 budget of DM22.1 billion). To this should be added the subsidies which the Federal Republic pays to the GDR for transit fees to the Western sectors, road and rail repair and construction and waste removal.

Is it possible that these subsidies could be diminished or threatened by future political change in the Federal Republic? If this were to occur, the West Berlin economy might go into a long decline which could theoretically end with some kind of amalgamation with the GDR. The economic recession of recent years has had no important impact on West German subsidies to Berlin. Yet some West German experts argue that, with the change of generations, there will be decreased interest in the issue of German unity, in relations with the GDR and even in West Berlin.

This appears improbable. Over the past forty years, the hopes of the West German public for progress towards German unity have been subject to continual discouragement. Despite this, and despite consequent well-founded scepticism in the German public as to any short-term prospects for change which would not threaten its own personal well-being and personal freedoms – despite all this – the interesting phenomenon has been the continuation of sustained strong public interest in the German issue. Emerging national feeling in the Federal Republic is strongly linked with the concept of an active inter-German policy and of a special German contribution to peace through development of the inter-German relationship. This concept has had the effect of transmuting resentment over the predominant role of the two great powers in German affairs, resentment which is decidedly on the increase, into dynamic motivation for long-term inter-German activity. Berlin is a national symbol for most West Germans and there is no visible prospect that this will change. These tendencies argue for the continuation of West German subsidies for West Berlin. But they also argue for a continuing interest in developing a closer economic relationship between West Berlin and the GDR.

Possibilities for long-term change

The Four-Power Agreement on Berlin did not end East–West competition over Berlin. Both sides have accepted that they cannot now press for a definitive solution that would suit them. Yet the competition continues. None of the participants in the new Berlin regime has given up its views of the basic situation – the view of the three Western allies that Berlin consists of all four sectors, of the Federal Republic that all of Berlin is a *Land* of the Federal Republic, and of the Soviet Union and GDR that West Berlin is on the territory of the GDR. Both sides still hope for a resolution on their terms in the very long term.

As we have noted, in the West, the West German government, backed overwhelmingly by public opinion, is insistent that the German question must be kept open for ultimate self-determination by German residents of the GDR. This objective, if ever realized, would probably result in rapid or step-by-step amalgamation of the two German states and the restoration of a united Berlin as capital of a unified Germany. Yet this outcome appears wholly improbable. The GDR is the keystone of the Warsaw Pact system in Central and Eastern Europe. Its loss would bring collapse of the

Warsaw Pact and deal a shattering blow to the Soviet system itself. While that system continues unchanged in its major characteristics, it is highly improbable that the Soviet Union would contemplate such action and there is no indication of far-reaching change in the Soviet Union. It is far more probable that the Soviet Union will indefinitely retain its hold over East Germany and Eastern Europe, making only those gradual and partial adjustments which appear necessary for the viability of the Warsaw Pact states. As far as the possibility of negotiated solution is concerned, the division of Germany and of Berlin appears likely to continue indefinitely.

Political opinion in the Federal Republic and in Berlin takes a similar view that the status quo is likely to continue as far as German unity is concerned. Consequently, their growing interest, shared by the present mayor of Berlin, Herr Diepgen, and also by the Social Democratic opposition in Berlin, is to develop West Berlin into a centre of financial services, banking, insurance, conferences, and speciality manufacture for the GDR, with perhaps a group of combined capital ventures, hotels, recreation facilities and industries in the areas of the GDR around Berlin, as well as cooperation in the cultural field. There has been limited progress in the cultural field. After negotiations lengthened by GDR – and Soviet – unwillingness to accept West German responsibility for the Western sectors, the Federal Republic and GDR signed a cultural exchange agreement in late 1985, which does provide for a limited exchange of acting ensembles from West Berlin and the GDR. And there is some cooperation between West Berlin film makers and the GDR on cultural, historical and travel films.

However, it is easier to conceive of such an entrepôt function than to realize it. Resistance in the Federal Republic and West Berlin to this concept, which was pronounced a decade ago, has perceptibly declined. Yet the governments of the Western allies and those West German officials who have responsibility for maintaining the status of West Berlin are of mixed mind. They do not wish to contemplate the risks of future dependency on the GDR. Accordingly, the Western allies have not issued the Mayor of Berlin blanket authority to enter a dialogue with the GDR on issues of economic cooperation, preferring to be consulted in each individual instance.

For its part, the GDR government remains unenthusiastic and sceptical for a complex of reasons. The GDR leadership has a long memory of the role of the Western sectors as a centre of anti-communist sentiment and anti-GDR propaganda. It does not now want to change the status of the city, or to appear to, or to get hooked up in the international political complications of expanded dealings with West Berlin, or to take actions which would have the effect of increasing the standing of the Western sectors in relation to that of East Berlin. In its eyes, the two Berlins are in a competitive situation. Moreover, when it does deal with Berlin issues, the GDR wants to deal directly with the West Berlin Senate. But the Federal Republic, alert to its responsibilities to Berlin, to the maintenance of its ties with the city, as well as to its right to represent the Western sectors to the outside world, insists that the GDR authorities deal with it in many issues involving Berlin, such as environmental questions. Moved by considerations like these, the GDR has preferred to find its Western services elsewhere.

There are economic difficulties too. West Berlin banks would apparently be inhibited by the terms of Military Government law 43 of 1946, which continues the legal basis of inter-zonal and now inter-German trade, from providing services to the GDR. The Western sectors are good customers for some products supplied by the GDR: coal, heating oil, building materials, dairy products and vegetables. But there is a limit to direct imports of this kind – West Berlin runs a large import surplus in trade with the GDR – and the quality of GDR consumer goods is still not competitive with that of Western suppliers. Wholesalers in the Western sectors help overcome the frequent bottlenecks in the GDR's command economy. But there is also a limit to the capacity of West Berlin commerce or industry to supply the GDR. And up to now the GDR has not been inclined to go for joint enterprises – after all, the GDR has a rich source of hard currency through inter-German trade itself. The GDR sees no great benefit in contributing to the economic viability of West Berlin.

Yet the attractions of West Berlin's hard currency is considerable. With ingenuity and with skilful use of the leverage from West German trade and other payments to the GDR, it should in the long run be possible to increase the economic relationships of West Berlin with the GDR. Some far-sighted officials in the GDR may even come to consider that development of a certain degree of economic interdependence between West Berlin and the GDR could contribute to gradual development of West Berlin into an independent international city, in accordance with long-term GDR ambitions in this direction. Thus, there are long-term possibilities for some growth of West Berlin–GDR economic ties. But it is improbable that such growth will have enough substance to make the economic connection of West Berlin with the GDR the major factor in its economy or to make West Berlin self-sustaining.

Decline of West German interest in Berlin, or, at the other end of the spectrum, of moves toward German unity as the basis of change in the status of Berlin have already been discounted. And there are limits to the development of West Berlin into an entrepôt city, like Hong Kong. What are the prospects for other, more far-reaching developments in the situation of the city?

Gradual improvement in inter-German relations over a period of years might make it possible to envisage agreement between the Federal Republic and the GDR, whereby West Berlin becomes a *Land* of the Federal Republic and the Federal Republic accepts that East Berlin is a permanent part of the GDR. But such a deal would require a new Berlin accord, implying elimination of the four-power structure in Berlin and the insurance which that structure provides for continuation of the Berlin regime. It is difficult to see what the gains in such a change would be or what the motivation for it would be, if things were already going well in the inter-German relationship and in a developing relationship between West Berlin and the GDR. Berlin politicians might press for this change, but they do not need it to play a major role in Federal German politics. The Greens might advocate it as a means of writing off the German past and making a fresh beginning. But their views are likely to remain those of a minority.

Soviet and East German interference?

On the Eastern side, there are also long-term ideas of change. Valentin Falin, then Soviet Ambassador to the Federal Republic, told West German Bundestag members at the time of the Four-Power Agreement that, in the very long term, the Soviet Union continued to hope that the Western sectors of Berlin would become part of the GDR. Piotr Abrassimov, long-time Soviet Ambassador to the GDR and Soviet negotiator of the Four-Power Agreement, has stated in interviews that the agreement does not change the Soviet and GDR view that West Berlin is on the territory of the GDR and rightfully belongs to the GDR. In February 1981, Erich Honecker said that the fire and water of the opposing GDR and West German systems could not be mixed into a unified system, but that reunification of Germany under socialism might be possible some day. Since the 1971 Agreement was concluded, the Soviet Union and GDR, in pursuit of their views on East Berlin, have dismantled the few remaining indications of separate status of the Eastern sector: separate voting in the Volkskammer, the East German parliament, and control points on entrance to Berlin from the GDR. Now, they are revising the borders of 'Greater Berlin' as used in the original four-power agreements by establishing new districts in place of the old.

These developments indicate that, to the extent of their possibilities, the Soviet Union and the GDR will in the future work towards incorporation of West Berlin in the GDR – if it is necessary as a half-way station, through establishment of West Berlin as an independent city under a new international treaty. But the chances of achieving this objective are slim. Short

175

of war, its realization would require several preconditions: Soviet achievement of enduring military superiority over the United States; a decisive breach between the Federal Republic and the United States; and development of the GDR economy to a state of decisive, enduring superiority over that of the Federal Republic. These possibilities seem as remote as the fundamental internal changes in the Soviet Union which would have to precede German unity under conditions acceptable to the West German population.

Yet West Berlin remains surrounded by the GDR. A revival of the Cold War for whatever reason could lead to resumption of pressures on Berlin and interference with access to Berlin. In some cases, such as efforts by the Soviet Union or GDR authorities to suppress widespread public unrest in the GDR, pressures on West Berlin might be by-products of other activities.

Given the record of the past, no one can exclude such possibilities. The Four-Power Agreement, as a contractual guarantee of civilian access to Berlin, is an advance over the situation pertaining at the time of the Berlin blockade when there was no agreement on this traffic. In the event of East–West difficulties, the Four-Power Agreement will at least make more clear to Western publics the responsibility for these actions and the issues involved. Of itself, this would not prevent interference with access to Berlin, but deliberate interference would be the beginning of a chain of events which could lead to war on a worldwide scale.

However, aside from limited pinpricks designed as signals for limited adjustments, the Berlin regime as defined in the 1971 Four-Power Accord seems secure in the foreseeable future. The inner-German relationship, with West German credits and loans to the GDR, provides a supportive framework for operation of the Berlin regime and positive incentives for GDR support of the new Berlin regime – and for Soviet support as well, because the Soviet Union is keenly interested in the political and economic viability of the GDR. The Soviet policy of political, economic and military detente toward Western Europe plays a further role in maintaining Soviet support for the Berlin regime. It would be inconsistent with this policy, which appears likely to continue, for the Soviet Union to undercut the Berlin regime and to cause serious difficulties for the Western sectors.

These factors make it improbable that the Soviet Union and the GDR would see positive benefit in returning to a policy of deliberate pressure on Berlin. Theoretically, it is possible that the Russians or the GDR would seek to apply pressure on access to Berlin in reaction to some American–Soviet confrontation in the Third World. It appears unlikely, however, that the Soviet Union would consider that the costs of reestablishing Cold War cohesion and militancy in the Western alliance which could result from such action would be worth the possible gains.

There remains the possibility of interference with Berlin access as a by-product of Soviet or East German efforts to repress widespread public unrest in the GDR. Such developments are more likely elsewhere in the Warsaw Pact, such as Poland or Romania, than in the GDR. If they do occur elsewhere in the Warsaw Pact area, other than the GDR, they are likely to create a political freeze in East–West relations and a possible halt in the forward movement of inner-German relations, but are less likely to bring direct reprisals against Berlin. In all cases of repression in Eastern Europe, the Soviet Union has been at pains to limit the collateral political damage to itself.

The possibility of widespread unrest in the GDR itself seems limited. The most active outside contribution to political stability in the GDR thus far has been Bonn's policy of promoting inner-German relations. The visits and contacts it promotes provide a psychological safety valve for the East German population. East Germans also receive material benefits from this policy, both indirect benefits from the important West German contribution to the East German living standard, and directly, in the form of a large flow of hard currency remittances and shipments of food and hard-to-get items.

To conclude this examination of possible alternative future development of the Berlin regime, the more extreme possibilities described here cannot be totally ruled out, but by far the greater future probability for West Berlin is for continuation of its present status accompanied by a gradually increasing, but not decisive, involvement in the East German economy. But if this is the case, one problem area already evident in Berlin is likely to increase in importance. This is the question of the long-term role of the Western allies.

The allied relationship with the Western sectors

Starting as a four-power structure at the end of World War II, the Berlin regime has been progressively 'Germanized' through the ever closer association of the two German states with its operation. This is particularly the case since the Four-Power Agreement formally associated the two German states with the operation of the Berlin regime. Under the 1971 agreement, the real weight of operating the Berlin regime has moved to the officials of both German states who can deal with each other directly without the need of four-power intermediaries. The four-power structure in Berlin has become a four-power superstructure. And, as East–West confrontation over Berlin has receded, appreciation in the West German and West Berlin publics of the need for this expensive and onerous allied superstructure has become weaker. Instead of a shield against communist incursions whose continuation is deeply desired, the allied presence in Berlin has become an insurance policy for remote contingencies whose cost is increasingly questioned.

Reflecting this change in attitude regarding Berlin, there have been suggestions in the Federal Republic with regard to establishing *Länder* (state) liaison offices in East Berlin, an action which would further weaken any shred of four-power status of the Eastern sector as part of Berlin as a whole, and for exchange of Ambassadors with the GDR, which would directly imply the end of four-power status for Germany as a whole as well as for Berlin and which would reopen the issue of the status of Berlin. In Berlin itself, a rising younger generation of officials to whom the Berlin blockade is a legend of the past is experiencing growing annoyance at intervention by the three allied powers in their decisions. Many activities of the 10,000 man allied garrison rub on public nerves: use of scarce park space to construct dwelling units for the forces, manoeuvres in the Grünewald or use of occupation funds to construct new shooting ranges in Berlin. These frictions are symbolized by the widely cited account of the French commandant in Berlin, who in 1980 summoned the then mayor to his office to discuss the pending visit to Berlin of President Giscard d'Estaing and kept the mayor standing before his desk while he issued instructions to him. It is quite evident that frictions like these will mount in coming years as the need for these Western troops becomes less evident and the costs of having them more annoying.

And there is a parallel problem for officials in Paris, London and even more distant Washington as the problems of the Berlin blockade, of Khrushchev's Berlin ultimatum and of contingency planning for Berlin recede still further into the past. If something does happen in Berlin, how can they make the situation and Western obligations clear to new generations of political leaders and to their public opinion?

All this suggests the desirability of some redefinition of allied practices in Berlin, within the framework of the existing regime, to systematically reduce the areas of friction without relinquishing the ultimate responsibilities which are the glue of the whole structure. Many ideas are under discussion to cope with this set of problems: an ombudsman for Berlin Senate-allied relations to the day-to-day level; submitting allied military personnel accused of crimes against West Berliners to trial by West Berlin courts; or substituting for the absent West German constitutional court, suspended by the allies, some sort of appeals tribunal composed of the three allied ambassadors and the Berlin mayor. There has also been some suggestion of following up the Four-Power Agreement with some action

178

rationalizing air access to Berlin, both as regards the regime governing the corridors and the addition of other carriers.

In the long run, there can be considerable confidence that, with the skill and imagination of the allied and German officials whose dedication has made a working success of the forbiddingly complicated Berlin regime, these problems will be solved. As regards the broader question of a more ambitious role or function for West Berlin, the question is whether it is really necessary to conceive of one. If so, proposals to hold the second phase of the Conference on Disarmament in Europe in Berlin might be more likely to gain Soviet and Warsaw Pact support, if the existence of the six-power regime were fully acknowledged and if East Germany was included along with the Federal Republic in a way that enabled each German state to share the burdens – and the glory. Yet, even with the considerable progress of the past fifteen years as a standard, today such possibilities appear distant, even though not impossible. With all the respect due to creative imagination and innovation about Berlin's future, it may continue to be the rule that the situation of West Berlin is a reflection of the actual state of the East–West relationship at any given time, rather than a factor which can initiate change in that relationship.

Notes

1 Paul Viotti has described the present situation in Berlin in terms of a security regime in his 'Berlin and Conflict Management with the USSR', *Orbis*, 28:3, Fall, 1981.
2 Wolfgang Heidelmeyer and Guenter Hindricks (eds.), *Documents on Berlin* (Munich: R. Oldenbourg Verlag, 1963), pp. 72–3: the book is subsequently referred to here as *Documents on Berlin*.
3 *Ibid.*, p. 174.
4 *Ibid.*, pp. 180–96.
5 *Ibid.*, pp. 342, 351.
6 Gerhard Wettig, *Das Vier-Mächte-Abkommen in der Bewärungsprobe* (Berlin: Berlin-Verlag, 1981), pp. 78–9.
7 Hans-Adolf Jacobsen, Gert Leptin, Ulrich Scheuner, Eberhard Schulz, *Drei Jahrzehnte Aussenpolitik der DDR* (Munich: R. Oldenbourg Verlag, 1979), p. 857.
8 Author's own notes, 1969.
9 Henry Kissinger, *White House Years* (Boston: Little Brown, 1979), pp. 100, 407.
10 The text of the agreement with useful commentary can be found in Honore M. Catudal, *A Balance Sheet of the Quadripartite Agreement on Berlin* (Berlin, Berlin Verlag, 1978).
11 Figures supplied by the Federal Ministry for Inner German Relations. From 1977 on, these figures have included travel by foreigners. Total travel by Federal Germans and West Berliners has more than doubled to over 15 million in 1984.

Index